Donald F. Proctor

Breathing, Speech, and Song

Springer-Verlag Wien New York

Donald F. Proctor, M. D.

Professor Otolaryngology, Anesthesiology,
and Environmental Health Sciences,
The Johns Hopkins Schools of Medicine and
Hygiene and Public Health, Baltimore, Maryland, U.S.A.

With 70 Figures

The illustration on the cover was reproduced from Acta Otolaryngologica, Suppl. 261, with permission of Almqvist & Wiksell, Stockholm.

Library of Congress Cataloging in Publication Data. Proctor, Donald F. Breathing, speech, and song. Includes index. 1. Speech—Physiological aspects. 2. Respiration. 3. Voice—Care and hygiene. 4. Singing —Breathing exercises. I. Title. [DNLM: 1. Speech—Physiology. 2. Voice. 3. Respiration. WV501 P964b.] QP306.P69 . 617'.533. 80-15713.

ISBN 3-211-81580-5 Springer-Verlag Wien-New York
ISBN 0-387-81580-5 Springer-Verlag New York-Wien

*This book is dedicated to my wife Janice
whose patient forbearance has allowed me
to pursue a multifaceted life,
to my children Nan Breglio and Douglas Proctor,
and to my granddaughters Eliza Mason,
Carolyn Proctor, and Nola Breglio*

Preface

I have attempted to prepare this volume in such a way as to provide a source of information on the normal physiology of speech and song as well as on the disorders of those functions. To the extent that I have succeeded it should be of interest to physiologists, physicians, and teachers and students of the voice.

The book is by no means a text on laryngology, nor is it a treatise on the physiology of breathing mechanics, nor yet is it a manual telling how to teach or learn voice production. If none of these, what is it? It is a discussion of the application of breathing mechanics to phonation of interest to the respiratory physiologist, of certain aspects of physiology and medicine of interest to the teacher or student of voice, and of the problems of voice production and its maladies of interest to the laryngologist.

I have undergone a number of experiences during the past 50 years which I believe have qualified me to undertake this task with some special hope of success. In my youth I studied voice for twelve years with four outstanding teachers and performed publicly as a lieder singer, in oratorio, chorus, and opera. Later I trained for and entered the medical profession in the specialty of otolaryngology. Later still I engaged in research on the physiology of breathing mechanics and phonation, especially singing. At one time I was a stammerer, but for many years now I have engaged in public speaking both in the teaching of medical students and in presentation of papers at scientific meetings. Thus I write from the point of view of the investigator, physiologist, practicing laryngologist, singer, public speaker, and erstwhile stammerer.

Inevitably, during the course of the fifty years since I first studied voice I have developed many prejudiced opinions and they are unblushingly interlaced with facts throughout the book. I have tried to indicate which is fact and which opinion but personal bias sometimes confuse the two. I hasten to add that I make no pretense at being a teacher of speech or song. The practicing voice teacher has accumulated experience from hours and years of work with a variety of pupils and their problems and has learned that which can be learned in no other way than from such experience, what techniques are most effective in which pupils. Nothing can substitute for that.

But it is my opinion that even the most skilled teacher can benefit from clearly stated physiological facts. The best teachers know they can never afford to stop learning. In some instances I do not hesitate to criticize certain practices in common use which I believe can only harm the voice. In other instances I have attempted to provide physiological explanations of useful methods of teaching which can be of assistance to both the teacher and student in reaching a more full understanding of how certain teaching methods succeed.

In addressing a book to so diverse an audience it has been impossible to avoid introducing, on one hand, certain technical details of little interest to one segment of readers while, on the other hand, dealing with some topics in a manner which must appear relatively superficial and over-simplified to the more sophisticated scientific reader. If I have succeeded in holding the reader's interest and achieving his understanding I need make no apology for that. I do urge the reader whose main interest may appear to lie in the later chapters not to skip lightly over the earlier ones. Comprehension of one is essential to a full appreciation of the other.

Some of my opinions may be in conflict with those expressed by other authors. Where this is the case I can only say that there may be, to coin a phrase, more than one way to skin a cat. But, more important, the subject in many respects remains controversial and the reader should be aware of varying opinions and their basis. The management of a vocal nodule is a case in point.

I must express my gratitude to David S. Melamet, Pietro Minetti, Frazer Gange, and Ernest Lert (all of them now dead) without whose wise teaching this book would never have been conceived. I am also indebted to Drs. Jere Mead and Arend Bouhuys with whom I collaborated in the research reported herein. In addition my thanks go to the late Wallace O. Fenn and the living Hermann Rahn and Arthur Otis who launched me on a career of research in respiratory physiology; to the late Dr. Samuel Crowe who taught me all I know of otolaryngology; to my secretary Mrs. Nancy M. Rent who has labored so patiently and well in typing the manuscript; and finally to my wife Janice whose patient forbearance and continual encouragement have enabled me to devote the many hours necessary for writing.

Baltimore, Md., May 1980   **Donald F. Proctor**

Contents

1. **Historical Background** 1
   Modes of Communication 1
   Development in Man 2
   Opera and Singing 5
   Singing and Health 7
   Physiology of Breathing 11
   References 13

2. **Structure of Breathing and Phonatory Mechanisms** 16
   The Upper Airways 18
   The Lower Airways 23
   The Breathing Pump 23
   The Larynx 26
   References 32

3. **Breathing Mechanics** 34
   Lung Volume, Airflow, and Air Pressure 34
   Methods of Study of Breathing Mechanics 36
   Consideration of the Static Forces in Breathing 37
   The Dynamic Forces of Breathing 39
   Role of the Larynx 42
   References 42

4. **The Nose and Air Modification** 44
   Nasal Air Modification 45
   Mucociliary Function 46
   Airway Secretions 47
   Nasal vs Mouth Breathing 49
   References 50

5. **Sound Production** 52
   Nature of Sound 52

Musical Sound 53
The Human Voice 55
Pitch Control 57
Neural Feedback 60
Sound Intensity 61
Resonance 62
Speech 62
References 64

6. **Breathing Mechanics and Phonation** 67
Phonation and Respiration 67
Breathing Mechanics in Phonation 69
Lung Volumes 69
Muscle Control 72
Physiological Studies 76
Muscle Training 84
References 86

7. **The Speaking Voice** 88
Importance of Speech to Man 88
Respiratory Mechanisms in Speech 89
Lung Volumes for Speech 92
Subglottic Pressure 93
Phrasing and Emphasis 93
Teaching of Speech 95
Diction 95
Song and Speech 96
Speech Problems 98
Speech Impediments 100
References 101

8. **The Art of Singing** 103
Physiological Studies 104
Elastic Forces and Muscle Control 106
Vocal Exercises 108
The "Break" in the Voice 110
High Tones 111
The Fourth Formant 114
Resonance 115
Diction 117
Performance and Pitfalls 118
Song Singing 119
Acting 123
References 124

9. **Care of the Voice** 126
Early Development 126
Vocal Misuse 127
General Hygiene 130

The Mature Singer 132
The Older Singer 134
Other Problems, Acute Laryngitis 134
Mucous Membranes 136
Pulmonary Disease 137
References 140

10. Detection and Correction of Faults 142
To Whom to Turn 142
The Laryngologist's Role 144
Specific Problems 147
Chronic Laryngitis 147
Nasal Problems-Allergies 147
Cough-Dry Throat 148
Vocal Misuse-Granuloma-Nodule 148
The Speaking Voice 152
Examples from Patients 154
Medications 156
Conclusion 158
References 159

Index of Names 160

Subject Index 164

Historical Background   **1**

If we had to pick one characteristic which distinguishes most clearly between man and beast what else could it be but speech? Indeed in the evolution of man as the species known as homo sapiens the time at which that designation becomes first applicable probably coincides with the time when employment of some form of primitive speech developed. Although it has been argued that man's large brain and other physical characteristics made speech possible there is reason to believe that the beginnings of speech communication may have influenced the development of the brain. Thus we might say that speech is as old as man. But, in contrast to other physiological functions, for some reason scientific inquiries into its origins and nature are of relatively recent date (6, 29, 32, 40, 52, 53, 56).

Actually it is now well recognized that the principle organ involved in phonation, the larynx, developed phylogenetically as a simple valve to prevent contamination of the lungs during swallowing. Its use (in combination with the breathing mechanism) for the production of sound must be considered a remarkable evolutionary development, and refinement of that use into a spoken language the single most significant event in the emergence of man. This book is devoted to a discussion of the mechanisms we employ to produce speech and song; and, in this chapter, we will consider some highlights in the historical background of our present knowledge.

Modes of Communication

Methods of communication other than speech are employed by man but are more essential to the lower species. The sense of smell is a vital means of communication between animals and their environment, as well as with one another. Except for the chemotactic biochemical exchanges between single cells, olfaction probably can be considered the most primitive means of transmission of information. Indeed it may be an important neurophysiological refinement of intercellular chemotaxis. As man has developed more complex methods he has retained the more primitive senses although they have suffered somewhat in acuity in the interim. Man's olfactory sense is far less efficient than in most beasts but remains important to us. It is one of our most effective mnemonic devices.

Touch and gesture, posturing and motion are all also means of expression. Again, although they play a more elemental and vital role in many animals, in man still the caress or the blow, the posture of the body, and gestures of the hands continue to take their part in our relating to one another. Sign language has been employed between people speaking different languages and between the deaf. Facial expression seems to have been a somewhat later development in evolution. Darwin's treatise, "The Expression of the Emotions in Man and in Animals", is a delightful exposition on the importance of this in many of the higher animal species.

Animal sounds produced with the larynx (the syrinx in birds) undoubtedly provide some simple form of language. There is some reason to believe that in the dolphin (36) this development may have reached a refinement comparable to that in man. A number of explanations have been offered as to why the higher apes fall so far short of man in the use of the phonatory mechanism. The differences in their oral, pharyngeal, and laryngeal anatomy do not seem to me to be sufficient explanation. Intellectually the higher apes and other animals seem capable of language. Chimpanzees and gorillas have been taught a simple sign system of transmission of information and dogs as well as other pets can learn to respond to specific verbal commands. It is particularly interesting that certain birds can learn to imitate our speech with remarkable accuracy (34) but not to use it as a means of intelligible communication. Recent years have seen a flurry of research on animal sound production and communication (47). Even the mechanism by which cats purr has been studied (44). Animals can certainly be trained to respond to a wide variety of stimuli and perform complex tasks leading to such rewards as food. But evidence of their ability to use abstract thought based upon symbols is still open to question.

Development in Man

We do not know how many thousands of years ago man began the transition from phonation for simple immediate communication from person to person to the use of it for planning and carrying information from place to place and from one time to another. But there is evidence that the telling of tales dates well back before the development of a written language. The poetry of Homer seems surely to have played an important role in Greek civilization prior to its being recorded in writing.

It is interesting that a relatively early development in connection with the telling of stories was poetry. What an exciting time it must have been when man first began to sense and employ the beauty of words to enhance the interest

Fig. 1. Apollo, the God of music. From A. Kircher, Musurgia Conversalis, Rome, 1650 (This and Fig. 4, 5 and 6 provided by the National Library of Medicine, Bethesda, Maryland, Courtesy of Carole Clausen, Department of the History of Medicine)

of the story. Perhaps the use of rhyme and rhythm increased the ability of the listener to remember and be able, in turn, to pass on the tale. It seems probable that melody and song must have been introduced at the same time. It is hard to imagine man, possessed of the ability to speak, to tell stories and to put them into poetry, without indulging in song if only as a means of celebrating those capacities. It would be interesting to know more about the transition from speech among men gathered around a communal fire to the complex performances of sophisticated drama in well built amphitheaters in the Golden Age of Greece. One can imagine the particularly skilled speaker attracting larger and larger groups to listen and then the response of that audience inspiring him to a more dramatic presentation of what he has to say. In the book of Job appears the statement, "the morning stars sang together, and all the sons of God shouted for joy". Speech and song have long been considered attributes of man but worthy of the Gods.

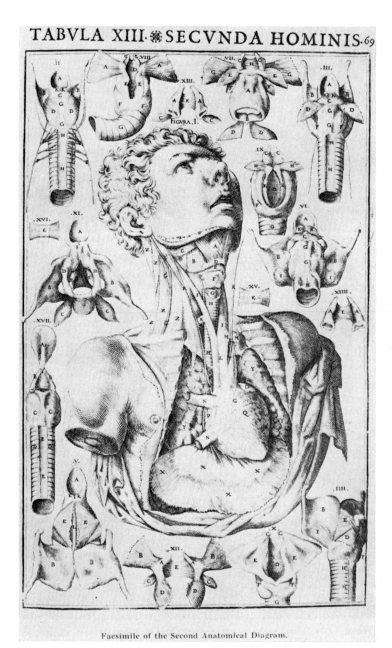

Fig. 2. Plate from Casserius (13) showing detailed anatomy of respiratory and laryngeal structures. (Used with the permission of M. H. Hast and the Editor, Acta Otolaryngologica)

Singing and dancing were an integral part of the great Greek dramas. One evidence of the early importance of the arts of speech and song is the character attributes of the nine Greek muses: Calliope (epic poetry and eloquence), Euterpe (music and lyric poetry), Erato (love poetry), Polyhymnia (oratory and sacred poetry), Clio (history), Melpomene (tragedy), Thalia (comedy), Terpsichore (choral song and dance), and Urania (astronomy). Apollo was considered the God of music (Fig. 1).

Whereas indulgence in speech and song span man's entire history and their refinement in oratory and theater cover at least several thousand years, appreciation and understanding of the physiology of phonation has come only in relatively recent times and has been dependent upon the acquisition of basic scientific knowledge. Developments during the past 400 years are especially pertinent to our point of view. Two milestones mark the beginning of that period. The history of opera begins in the year 1600 and in 1601 an early definitive scientific document on the voice was published.

The monograph of Casserius "The Larynx Organ of Voice" stands even today as an interesting analysis of the anatomy and physiology of phonation. In it is not only a thoughtful consideration of classical references to the use and importance of speech but also a remarkable description of the morphology of the organs of breathing and the larynx (Fig. 2). Thanks to Hast a good translation is now available to us (13).

Opera and Singing

Opera, more or less as we now know it, came on the scene in 1600 (8) and it seems clear that at about that time serious thought began, or at least began to flower, on the subject of training the singing voice. Jacopo Peri, with his colleague Caccini, are generally credited with the first opera "Euridice". Possibly even greater credit should go to Monteverdi's "Orfeo", also performed at about that time. Certainly Monteverdi (1567—1643) quickly assumed leadership in the field in Venice (where the first opera house was built in 1637). Opera's sister art oratorio came only a little later with the monumental work of Handel (1685—1759). In any event from the time of Peri, Monteverdi, and Handel there was a rapid increase in the interest in singing and the singer.

The advent of opera provided the major stimulus for the production of the fine singing voice. According to Brodnitz (8) this arousal should be dated 1597 when private performances of "dramma per musica" began. The practice of castrating boys to preserve their beautiful voices dates back to the middle ages (1, 8). Brodnitz attributes that development to the admonition appearing in Corinthians 13 : 34, "Let your women keep silence in the church; for it is not permitted for them to speak". Certainly the castrato, with the breathing capacity of the adult and the larynx of a child, possessed a unique vocal mechanism. Actually his breathing capacity may have exceeded that of the ordinary adult since they seem to have achieved unusual height. Remarkable performances resulted in part from the fact that, with the small larynx, singing was produced with very low airflows enabling them to sustain long passages on a single breath. Farinelli (the stage name of Carlo Broschi, 1705—1782) is said to have been capable of maintaining a high C for a full two minutes. Even with a vital capacity of six liters that would have required limiting airflow to 50 ml/sec. Moreschi, the last of the castrato singers, died in 1922. Evidently the castrato singer was not unattractive to women and their eligibility for marriage came in question. The book "Eunuchism Display'd" (1) seems to have been at least in part inspired by the plight of a young lady who fell in love with Nicolini a castrato who sang in the opera at the Hay-Market. Perhaps Nicolini was one of the eunuchs whose performance was described by Pepys.

In the diary of Samuel Pepys (42) are frequent references to the joys of attending operatic performances in London. In the year 1661 alone his diary records attendance at fourteen operas. During that year Pepys became an enthusiastic student of song and later on even turned to composition. One of his passages (30 June, 1661) goes, "Myself humming to myself (which now-a-days is my constant practice since I began to learn to sing) the trillo, and found by use that it do come upon me". During his visits to the opera Pepys comments on the eunuch singers and says he prefers the voices of "our women". Pepys' interest in that sex is notorious. Nevertheless some years later he acknowledged the performance of "the French eunuch", saying, "such action and singing I could never have imagined to have heard . . ."

A major development in our understanding of the vocal mechanism came in 1885. Until then no one had succeeded in actually visualizing the vocal cords in action in the living human being. Manuel Garcia, a singing teacher, was obsessed with the desire to view this source of the voice. One sunny day while walking in the park Garcia suddenly conceived of the idea of directing light into the throat with mirrors. He quickly had appropriate instruments made and succeeded to his overwhelming delight in viewing his own vocal cords (14, 27, 33). He reported his discovery to the Royal Society in London (Fig. 3) and this marked the beginning of the medical specialty of laryng-ology. From that day onward our knowledge of the larynx as the organ of voice slowly but steadily grew.

Numerous treatises on the voice appeared, a few of which are included in the list of references (4, 28, 35, 38, 41). Of special interest are those of Tosi (54) and Mackenzie (37). Two comments of the former show that problems with singers similar to those we have today existed in the Eighteenth Century. Tosi deplores the ". . . screaming like a hen when she is laying an egg" and describes the final cadences of some performances as appearing as though ". . . the throat is set a going, like a weather-cock in a whirlwind." Mackenzie's book is the classic description of the day of the laryngologist's views on the hygiene of the voice. A much more recent work on the important subject of control of the breath serves to show how little was really known on that subject as recently as four decades ago (16). Other writers described the then current views on laryngeal function (15), theories of the voice as a stringed instrument (10, 55), the role of the nasal cavities in resonance (48), and the question of whether or not women breathed differently from men (49, 51).

Opening of the Glottis.

At the moment when the person draws a deep breath, the epiglottis being raised, we are able to see the following series of movements :—the arytenoid cartilages become separated by a very free lateral movement ; the superior ligaments are placed against the ventricles ; the inferior ligaments are also drawn back, though in a less degree, into the same cavities ; and the glottis, large and wide open, is exhibited so as to show in part the rings of the trachea. But unfortunately, however dexterous we may be in disposing these organs, and even when we are most successful, at least the third part of the anterior of the glottis remains concealed by the epiglottis.

Movement of the Glottis.

As soon as we prepare to produce a sound, the arytenoid cartilages approach each other, and press together by their interior surfaces, and by the anterior apophyses, without leaving any space, or intercartilaginous glottis ; sometimes even they come in contact so closely as to cross each other by the tubercles of Santorini. To this movement of the anterior apophyses, that of the ligaments of the glottis corresponds, which detach themselves from the ventricles, come in contact with different degrees of energy, and show themselves at the bottom of the larynx under the form of an ellipse of a yellowish colour. The superior ligaments, together with the aryteno-epiglottidean folds, assist to form the tube which surmounts the glottis ; and being the lower and free extremity of that tube, enframe the ellipse, the surface of which they enlarge or diminish according as they enter more or less into the ventricles. These last scarcely retain a trace of their opening. By anticipation, we might say of these cavities, that, as will afterwards appear clearly enough in these pages, they only afford to the two pair of ligaments a space in which they may easily range themselves. When the aryteno-epiglottidean folds contract, they lower the epiglottis, and make the superior orifice of the larynx considerably narrower.

The meeting of the lips of the glottis, naturally proceeding from the front towards the back, if this movement is well managed, it

Fig. 3. Page from Garcia's original paper (27)

Singing and Health

An interesting aspect of the history of this subject relates to views on the relation between speaking, singing and health. Those interested should consult the three delightful papers of Finney (22, 23, 24). Through the whole course of ancient medical literature statements appear repetitively attributing health benefits to declamatory speaking and to singing. Galen (26) was a less enthusiastic supporter of these beliefs but even he stated: "Deep breathing is the specific exercise of the thorax and lungs; so is phonation and the use of the phonetic organs." Recommendations of vocal exercises for a wide variety of health problems persisted well into the Seventeenth Century. Its benefits to those whose voices were important to their careers were likewise recognized.

In 1560 the following appeared in the statutes of the Westminster School (23). "As the knowledge of singing is found to be of the greatest use for a clear and distinct elocution ... we will that all pupils in the Grammar school shall spend two hours each week ... in the art of music." In 1588 William Byrd stated in his "Psalmes, Sonets and Songs of Sadness and Pietie" (12) "... the exercise of singing ... is good to preserve the health of Man ... it doth strengthen all parts of the brest and doth open the pipes."

Fig. 4. Asthmatic taking a music lesson. (From Album Comique [2], National Library of Medicine)

Finney points out that toward the end of the Seventeenth Century a "fear of exercising the lungs" in singing and loud speech began to counteract this belief in its salubrious effects (24). Although it is by no means clear, it may be that some of this reaction was related to the prevalance of tuberculosis

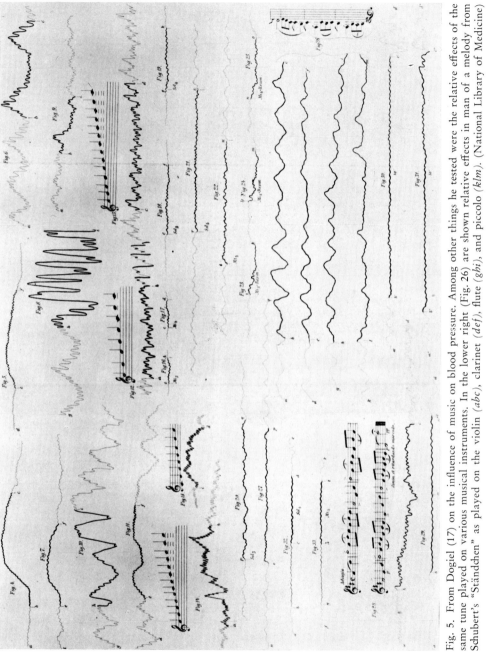

Fig. 5. From Dogiel (17) on the influence of music on blood pressure. Among other things he tested were the relative effects of the same tune played on various musical instruments. In the lower right (Fig. 26) are shown relative effects in man of a melody from Schubert's "Ständchen" as played on the violin (abc), clarinet (def), flute (ghi), and piccolo (klm). (National Library of Medicine)

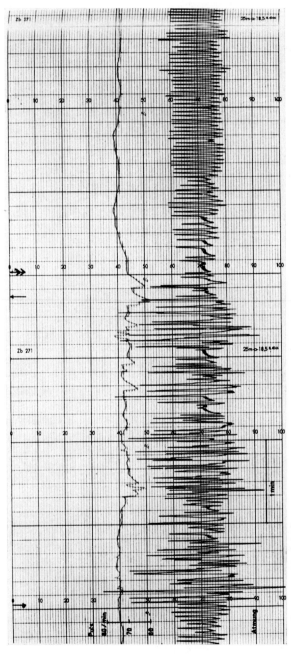

Fig. 6. From Harrer (30), used with the permission of the Editor, Med. Monatsspiegel. Shown here are records of pulse and respiration in a subject listening to dissonant atonal electronic music of Stockhausen (left), and melodic Chopin (right). (National Library of Medicine)

(phthisis). An interesting footnote to that trend appears in modern medical literature in the recognition that tuberculosis could be readily spread from an infected person to others singing in a group. We now know that a combination of the capacity of the larynx to produce a fine aerosol containing infectious organisms with the deep inspirations through the mouth which occur in singing can lead to the induction of infection in one singing with another who is infected.

As early as 1600 Fabricius (20) was seeking an explanation for health effects of singing. He noted that there was air in the "inner ear" (actually middle ear) and that, when sound reached this air, vibrations were set up and thence carried throughout the body. In 1624 Burton wrote in his "Anatomy of Melancholy" (11) that music is ". . . a soveraigne remedy against despaire and melancholy, and will drive away the Divell himself." While some writers advocated singing to strengthen the lungs and cure asthma others felt the reverse to be true. Another relationship with asthma was suggested when Aubry (2) postulated that musical syncopation had its origin in the symptoms of that disease (Fig. 4).

Dogiel (17), a pupil of Helmholtz, recorded the relative effects on blood pressure of listening to the same tune played on the violin, clarinet, flute, or piccolo (Fig. 5). Harrer (30, 31) recorded pulse rate and respiration in subjects exposed first to the dissonant, atonal, electronic music of Stockhausen and then to the presumably soothing effects of a melody of Chopin (Fig. 6). Ramazzini (43) and Singer (50) investigated the occupationally related hazards of singing and wind instrument playing (45).

In the latter part of the Nineteenth Century the use of photography came into play in the study of the larynx during phonation (9, 25). Improved techniques in recent years have made possible high speed cinematography of the larynx in action. Those films have led to a greatly improved appreciation of the nature of vibration of the vocal folds.

The subject of speech in the deaf deserves a treatise all its own. We need only mention here that, although teaching the deaf to talk with the hands in the belief that it was cruel to make them learn to talk persists in some quarters today, recognition that they could be taught to speak began two centuries ago. In 1760 Thomas Braidwood established a school in Edinburgh for teaching the deaf to speak, but, unfortunately, he kept his methods secret. In 1793 William Thornton was teaching speech to the deaf in the United States. Alexander Graham Bell took an interest in that problem and wrote a fascinating book in which he tried to develop a written language describing oral configurations in speech (3).

Physiology of Breathing

Now let us turn back to examine developments in the field of respiration physiology. Until the Seventeenth Century man's understanding of breathing was largely limited to the belief that it cooled the blood. In 1674 John Mayow beginning of a realization of the function of respiration and Mayow and other more or less contemporary investigators also began inquiring into the structures and forces involved in breathing, it was not until the Twentieth Century that the physiology of breathing mechanics flourished. But we can take 1674 as another dividing line, although its relation to our understanding of phonation was a long time coming.

In 1915 Fritz Rohrer began his publications on "Atembewegung" (breath movement) and this work culminated in his landmark publication on breathing mechanics in 1925 (46). Although this stimulated a number of investigators to apply themselves to this problem, it was not until the 1940s that Wallace Fenn with his colleagues at the University of Rochester (chiefly H. Rahn and A. Otis) brought the field of breathing mechanics into an orderly organized body of knowledge. Without this, and the work of investigators following in their paths, we might still be in the dark about the adaption of breathing to phonation.

Drawing together the knowledge of the larynx and the breathing published his experiments suggesting that breathing served to provide the blood with "nitro-aerial spirits" necessary to life (39). Although this marked the mechanism for our contemporary understanding of phonation has only occurred in the last 30 years. Perhaps the papers of Draper, Ladefoged and Whitteridge (18, 19) could be chosen to mark that transition. For the first time they brought to view the manner in which the breathing mechanism and its use are altered for the purposes of speech and song. Shortly after that Arend Bouhuys organized a symposium on Sound Production in Man, in New York City (6) under the auspices of the New York Academy of Sciences. That international meeting, along with the one organized in London by Barry Wyke and held in the Royal College of Surgeons in 1972 (Ventilatory and Phonatory Control Systems) (56), stand as expressions of our current knowledge in the field.

Finally, we should mention that along with current studies of the breathing mechanism in phonation have come numerous studies of the physiology of breathing in wind instrument players (5, 7, 21). Although here we have the source of the sound in the player's lips, or in the instrument's reed, or in the vibrating air column of a hollow tube, the use of the respiratory system and the lung volume, and even the pressures induced in the airway in the wind instrument player, are all quite similar to those in the singer.

Some authors have denigrated the importance of the scientific approach to the subject of speech and song, even stating that it does more harm than good to the field of voice training. It is perfectly true that even before 1600 teachers of voice were successful in training great singers and that many of our finest and most successful voice teachers today are apparently rather unaware of the true anatomical and physiological mechanisms involved. But in every field of human endeavor an increase in the base of fundamental knowledge is followed by advances. I am not proposing that a better scientific knowledge will result in greater singers than those of the past or present. We are not striving, as in athletics, to produce a new world record in this or that sport. I do hope that improved understanding will assist in overcoming some of the difficulties students have in learning to speak and sing, some of the difficulties teachers have in instructing them, and reducing the number of talented voices which are ruined by poor training. A motto inscribed on an early harpsichord "Sine scientia ars nihil est" (Fig. 7) expresses one side of this question. As a scientist I am equally in favor of saying "Sine ars scientia nihil est".

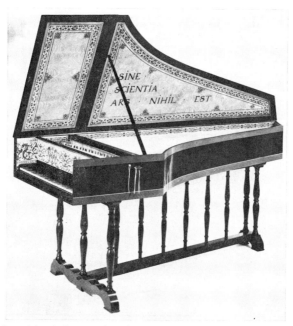

Fig. 7. Flemish harpsichord decorated with motto "Sine scientia ars nihil est" (Courtesy of Frank Hubbard, Harpsichord makers, Boston, Mass.)

References

1. Ancilla, C. (1718): Eunuchism Display'd. London: E. Curll. (Transl. R. Samber.)
2. Aubry, C. (1823): Album comique de pathologie pittoresque. Paris: Tardieu.
3. Bell, A. G. (1911): The Mechanism of Speech. New York: Funk & Wagnalls.
4. Berard, J. A. (1755): L'Art du Chant, dédié à Madame Pompadour. Paris: Dessaint & Saillant, Prault, Lambert.
5. Berger, K. W. (1965): Respiratory and articulatory factors in wind instrument performance. J. Appl. Physiol. 20, 1217—1221.
6. Bouhuys, A. (Ed.) (1968): Sound production in man. Ann. N.Y. Acad. Sci. 155, 1—381.
7. Bouhuys, A. (1969): Physiology and musical instruments. Nature 221, 1199—1204.
8. Brodnitz, F. S. (1975): The age of the castrato voice. J. Speech Hearing Dis. 40, 291—295.
9. Browne, L. (1883): On photography of the larynx and soft palate. Brit. Med. J. 2, 811—814.
10. Browne, L., Casson, H., Grant, J. D. (1886): The voice as a stringed instrument. Brit. Med. J. 1, 738—739.
11. Burton, R. (1624): The Anatomy of Melancholy. Oxford.

12. Byrd, W. (1588): Psalmes, Sonets and Songs of Sadness and Pietie. In: The Collected Works of William Byrd (1948), XII, XXXIV (Fellowes, E. H., ed.). London: Stainer & Bell.

13. Casserius, J. (1601): The larynx organ of voice (Transl. Hast, M. H., Holtsmark, E. B., 1969). Acta Otolaryngol. Suppl. *261*, 1—36.

14. Clerf, L. H. (1956): Manuel Garcia's contribution to laryngology. Bull. N.Y. Acad. Med. *32*, 603—619.

15. Desvernines, C. M. (1888): A critical and experimental essay on the tension of the vocal bands. J. Laryngol. *2*, 49—56.

16. Dodds, G., Lickley, J. D. (1935): The Control of the Breath. London: Oxford Univ. Press.

17. Dogiel, I. M. (1880): Über den Einfluß der Musik auf den Blutkreislauf. Arch. Anat. Physiol., 416—428.

18. Draper, M. H., Ladefoged, P., Whitteridge, D. (1959): Respiratory muscles in speech. J. Speech Hearing Res. *2*, 16—27.

19. Draper, M. H., Ladefoged, P., Whitteridge, D. (1960): Expiratory pressures and air flow during speech. Brit. Med. J. *1*, 1837—1843.

20. Fabricius, H. (1600): De Visione, Voce, Auditu. Venice.

21. Faulkner, M., Sharpey-Schafer, E. P. (1959): Circulatory effects of trumpet playing. Brit. Med. J. *1*, 685—686.

22. Finney, G. (1966): Medical theories of vocal exercise and health. Bull. Hist. Med. *40*, 395—406.

23. Finney, G. (1968): Vocal exercise in the Sixteenth Century related to theories of physiology and disease. Bull. Hist. Med. *42*, 422—449.

24. Finney, G. (1971): Fear of exercising the lungs related to iatro-mechanics (1675—1750). Bull. Hist. Med. *45*, 341—366.

25. French, T. R. (1889): A photographic study of the singing voice. N.Y. Med. J., 95—98.

26. Galen: De sanitate tuenda, Bk. I, Chap. XI, 87 (Transl. Greene, R. M.: Galen's Hygiene, 1951). Springfield: Charles C Thomas.

27. Garcia, M. (1854—1855): Observations on human voice. Proc. Roy. Soc. London *7*, 399—410.

28. Guttman, O. (1884): Gymnastics of the Voice. Albany: E. S. Werner.

29. Harnad, S. R., Steklis, H. D., Lancaster, J., eds. (1976): Origins and Evolution of Language and Speech. Ann. N.Y. Acad. Sci. *280*, 1—914.

30. Harrer, G. (1970): Somatische Aspekte des Musikerlebens. Med. Monatsspiegel *6*, 124 to 217.

31. Harrer, G., Harrer, H. (1977): Music, Emotion and Autonomic Function. In: Music and the Brain (Critchley, M., Henson, R. A., eds.), 202—216. Springfield: Charles C Thomas.

32. Huizinga, E. (1957): Larynx, voice, animals and man. Ann. Otol. *66*, 679—691.

33. Ingalls, T. H., Hemming, S. M. (1955): Laryngology's hundred-year-old debt to grand opera. New England J. Med. *253*, 468—469.

34. Klatt, D. H., Stefanski, R. A. (1974): How does a Mynah bird imitate speech? J. Acoust. Soc. Amer. *55*, 822—832.

35. Lamperti, F. (1587): The Art of Singing (Transl. Griffith, J. C., 1877). New York: G. Schirmer.

36. Lilly, J. C., Miller, A. M. (1961): Vocal exchanges between dolphins. Science *134*, 1837 to 1876.

37. Mackenzie, M. (1886): The Hygiene of the Vocal Organs. London: Macmillan & Co.

38. Mancini, G. (1977): Practical Reflections on the Figurative Art of Singing (Transl. Buzzi, B., 1912). Boston: Gorham Press.

39. Mayow, J. (1674): Tractatus quinque medico-physici, Quorum primus egit de sal-nitro, et spirita nitro aerae. Medico-physical works (1907). Edinburgh: Alembic Club, Reprint 17.

40. Montagu, A. (1963): A new theory concerning the origin of speech. J.A.M.A. *185*, 1017—1018.

41. Pandolfini, F., Labarraque, L. (1931): Principales directives théoriques et pratiques de l'éducation de la voix chantée. Paris: Vigot Frères.

42. Pepys, S. (1660—1669): The Diary of, H. B. Wheatley (1942). New York: Limited Editions Club, 10 vol.
43. Ramazzini, B. (1705): A Treatise of the Diseases of Tradesmen. London.
44. Remmers, J. E., Gautier, H. (1972): Neural and mechanical mechanisms of feline purring. Respir. Physiol. *16*, 351—361.
45. Roger, J.-L. (1803): Traité des effets de la musique sur le corps humain. Paris: Brunet.
46. Rohrer, F. (1925): Physiologie der Atembewegung. Handbuch der Normalen and Pathologischen Physiologie, Vol. 2, 70—127. Berlin: Springer.
47. Schön, M. A. (1970): On the mechanism of modulating the volume of the voice in howling monkeys. Acta Otolaryngol. *70*, 443—447.
48. Seiler, C. (1881): The effect of the conditions of the nasal cavities upon articulate speech. Trans. Amer. Laryngol. Assoc. *3*, 123—129.
49. Sewall, H. (1890): On the relations of diaphragmatic and costal respiration, with particular reference to phonation. J. Physiol. *11*, 159—178.
50. Singer, K. (1932): Diseases of the Musical Profession. New York: Greenberg.
51. Smith, W. (1890): On the alleged difference between male and female respiratory movements. Brit. Med. J. *2*, 843—844.
52. Stevenson, R. S., Guthrie, D. (1949): A History of Otolaryngology. Edinburgh: E. & S. Livingstone.
53. Tait, J. (1934): Evolution of vertebrate voice. Acta Otolaryngol. *20*, 46—59.
54. Tosi, P. F. (1723): Observations on the Florid Song, or Sentiments on the Ancient and Modern Singers (Transl. Mr. Galliard, London, 1743), 129, 166. First publ., Bologna.
55. Woods, R. H. (1893): Law of transverse vibrations of strings applied to the human larynx. J. Anat. Physiol. *27*, 431—435.
56. Wyke, B., ed. (1974): Ventilatory and Phonatory Control Systems. London: Oxford Univ. Press.

2 Structure of Breathing and Phonatory Mechanisms

In order to sustain life the adult human must breathe in and out of his lungs about 10,000 liters of air a day. The pump which accomplishes this never has a chance to rest, and during exercise that figure must be increased many fold. The work of breathing accounts for some 2 % (at a minimum) of the total energy consumed by the body. In view of these facts it is of interest that there are two circumstances which involve a deliberate increase in the work involved in lung ventilation, one is the choice of nasal breathing over breathing through the mouth, and the other is phonation. The choice of nasal breathing is related to the capacity of the nose to condition inspired air, an important physiological defense of the lungs (see Chap. 4). But we frequently elect to speak or sing purely for pleasure with no direct physiological gain. It is my objective in this monograph to examine the use of breathing for the purposes of phonation and to relate our knowledge of breathing mechanics to the most effective and euphonious production of speech and song.

This chapter is not intended to provide classically detailed anatomy of all the parts. Instead, we will consider them as an integrated whole to provide a suitable setting for the description of function to follow (Fig. 8). The respiratory tract is a system for pulmonary ventilation with the larynx a unit within that system, on one hand providing a valve closing off the lungs and lower airways, and, on the other hand allowing for a partial closure for sound production with airflow (4).

The respiratory system as a whole consists of the alveolar surfaces (approximately 70 m²) across which occurs the vital gas exchange with the capillary blood, the conducting airways of the tracheobronchial tree, the upper airways (of the pharynx, nose, and mouth), the larynx interposed between upper and lower airways as a valve, and the thoracic cage with its attached muscles serving as the pump to move air in and out of the system. Interspersed in this structure are the nerves, blood vessels, the lymphatic system, and connective and epithelial tissues. The portions especially relevant to our subject are all of the conducting airways, the pump, and the laryngeal valve.

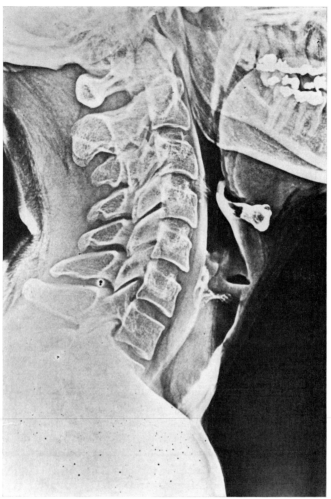

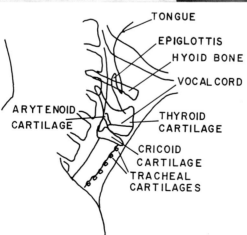

TONGUE
EPIGLOTTIS
HYOID BONE
VOCAL CORD
ARYTENOID CARTILAGE
THYROID CARTILAGE
CRICOID CARTILAGE
TRACHEAL CARTILAGES

Fig. 8. Above—xeroradiograph of the larynx with supraglottic structures above and trachea below. Below—diagram identifying some of the key structures. (Used with permission Editor, Amer. Rev. Respir. Dis., from Proctor, D. F. [1977]: The Upper Airways II, *115*, 315—342)

At least a rudimentary knowledge of respiratory tract anatomy is essential to an understanding of the processes involved in human phonation. Some teachers and students of voice are either ignorant of or misunderstand the breathing mechanism; and, whereas we breathe with ease in spite of such ignorance, effective employment of the breathing apparatus in speech and song may be better achieved if we understand its morphology and function. Many physiologists and laryngologists are not fully aware of the exact ways in which these structures come to bear on the process of phonation. Indeed, although a great deal has been written on the subject of breathing and the voice, only in the past few decades has appropriate research led to a more adequate, although still imperfect, body of facts. I intend to present the current state of our knowledge in terms plain enough to be comprehended by the non-scientific reader, while at least touching upon some of the more complex features of interest to the physiologist, phoniatrist, and laryngologist. Here, and in subsequent chapters, the reader is referred to the list of references for more detailed information.

The primary role of the airways is to provide a series of conduits for the exchange of gases between the atmosphere around us and the blood circulating through the alveoli. Optimum accomplishment of that purpose might seem to require the most immediate exposure possible of the blood stream to the atmosphere; but a moment's thought should show that to be both impractical and undesirable. We could hardly carry about with us a great sheet approximately the area of a tennis court. In addition the ambient atmosphere is generally characterized by physical conditions inimical to the body's internal environment and continually changing from hour to hour, month to month, and place to place with weather and climate, not to mention the ambient changes imposed by artificial heating and cooling. A further problem arises from the fact that our atmosphere is frequently polluted by noxious materials and particles carrying infectious microorganisms.

It is fortunate that we have evolved in such a manner as to keep the delicate gas exchange membranes of the lungs finely packaged and closeted within the chest, and to provide a system of conducting tubes communicating between them and the ambient air. This system of conducting airways permits the movement of air to and from the lungs' depths with minimal resistance to airflow and, at the same time, allows for adjustment of the physical character of inspired air to conditions compatible with those of the body interior. Now we shall examine the structures involved to see how these things are accomplished.

The Upper Airways

Since we normally breathe through the nose it makes a logical starting point (Fig. 9). Ordinarily the word "nose" is used in speaking of that external structure in the midline of the face. Although it is of considerable aesthetic value its role in function is a relatively minor one. For our purposes the significant region is the nasal passage which extends from the nostrils nearly halfway through the head to the pharynx. From the point of view of pulmonary ventilation the nasal passage is a nuisance since it is a high resistance airway accounting for nearly half the work of breathing. To appreciate the significance of its structure we must view it both as an airway and as an air conditioning system, and incidentally the seat of our organ of olfaction.

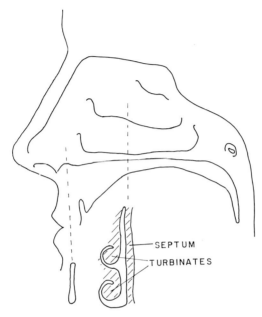

Fig. 9. Diagram of nasal anatomy. Above—the nasal passage as viewed from the midline of the head. Note the turbinates extending the full length of the main nasal airway. Eustachian tube orifice indicated in the nasopharynx. Below—sections through the nasal airway (right side) at locations indicated by dashed lines. Anteriorly the airway is simple and narrow: in mid passage it is still narrow but convoluted and extensive. Hatched areas are bone and cartilage of septum and turbinates

The chief characteristics of the nasal passage are:
1. Its division into two parts by the nasal septum;
2. A narrow constriction just beyond the nostrils;
3. A main passage with a large surface area and cross section but a narrow air stream; and
4. A highly adjustable mucociliary system and blood supply.
The physiological significance of these characteristics will be discussed in Chap. 4.

The nasal septum divides the nasal passage into two roughly equal but rarely wholly symmetrical parts. It begins at the nostrils and terminates in the nasopharynx where the two airways merge into one. The narrow constriction, including the nostrils, is collapsible, as is readily seen in sniffing. It is this factor which limits the rapidity with which air can be taken in through the nose. The convolutions of the turbinates account for the complex nature of the main airway with its narrow air stream and large surface area. The blood vessels in the turbinates and septum compose a rich network with erectile characteristics similar to that in the genitalia. It is this network and its neural control which makes it possible for the nasal tissues to become engorged with blood and swollen or relatively free of blood and shrunken. The significance of this to the air conditioning system will be referred to again in Chap. 4.

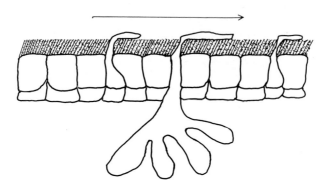

Fig. 10. Diagram of respiratory mucous membrane showing from below upward, convoluted mucous gland with duct extending to surface, basal cells, ciliated cells with goblet cells interspersed, cilia bathed in periciliary fluid, patches of mucus coming from glands and goblet cells, and arrow indicating that ciliary beat drives surface fluids in a specific direction (see Fig. 26)

The lining of the nasal airway begins with the skin at the nostrils leading to mucous membrane within the main passage (2, 14—16). Most of that mucous membrane is secretory and ciliated and this fact is also essential to air modification (Fig. 10). In the upper portion of the passage is the olfactory membrane enabling us to exercise the sense of smell. Some 10 to 14 cm posterior to the nostrils the nasal turbinates and septum end and the airway becomes a single one. At this point, the nasopharynx, the passage bends downward. It is also in the nasopharynx that the adenoids lie and the eustachian tubes, communicating with the middle ears, enter.

On either side and above the nasal passages are the paranasal sinuses (Fig. 11), air spaces in the bones of the face, which are also lined with mucous membrane and which communicate with the nasal airway through small openings. These air spaces may serve a number of physiological purposes, but one of these is the provision of resonators for the voice.

After the nasal passage the airway of the pharynx lies between the palate and tongue in front and the pharyngeal wall in back and on either side. Whereas the nasal passage is a relatively rigid structure the pharynx is capable of a wide range of shape changes related to movements of the tongue and palate. Such shape changes have important effects upon the character of sound originating in the larynx.

At the base of the tongue on either side lie the tonsils. The tonsils and adenoids are lymphoid structures of importance in the development of immune processes. We can note here that the adenoids lie in the path of the inspiratory air stream and the tonsils in the path of all that we swallow.

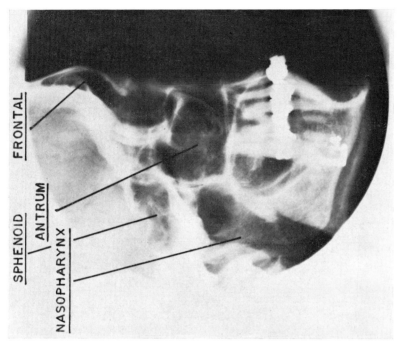

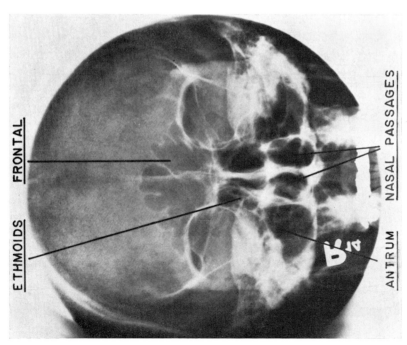

Fig. 11. Radiographs of paranasal sinuses from the front (left) and in profile (right). The dark grey and black areas are air spaces. Note that the sinus air spaces surround the nasal passage and extend half way through the head. (Used with the permission of Marcel Dekker, publisher [New York] from Brain, Proctor, and Reid [1977]: Respiratory Defense Mechanisms)

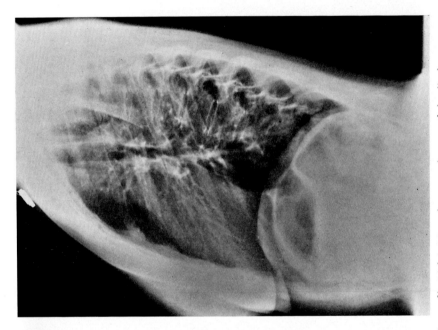

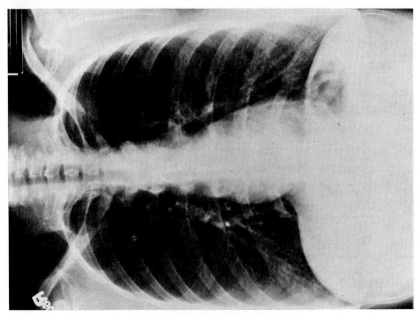

Fig. 12. Radiographs of the chest from the front (left) and in profile (right). Note the upward curve of the diaphragm, even in this film taken at the end of a deep inspiration. At lower lung volumes this curve is more pronounced and the diaphragm rises higher in the chest

The pitted character of their surfaces (crypts) permits the accumulation of small quantities of ingested or inspired materials. Within these crypts a rich network of blood vessels and lymphoid tissue is thus exposed to inhaled or ingested foreign matter.

We can, of course, choose to breathe through the mouth. This generally occurs when we are required to markedly increase the flow of air in and out of the lungs as with heavy exercise. But the oral airway is also resorted to when a variety of conditions block the nasal passage, and this is the principle airway employed during speech or song. When the lips are only slightly parted and the tongue lies close to the palate this can be a narroy airway, but, on marked opening of the mouth, lowering the mandible, and depressing the tongue, it can be quite wide.

Beyond the pharynx lies the larynx and between the vocal folds the airway is ordinarily triangular in shape and undergoes some widening and narrowing during breathing. We will return in a moment to the laryngeal anatomy involved in its function as a valve or a source of sound.

The Lower Airways

Below the vocal cords lies the cylindrical trachea dividing some 12 cm below into the two main bronchi which in turn divide again and again, narrowing all the while, until there are over a million of them leading into the several million alveoli. Like the nose the tracheobronchial airways are lined with respiratory mucous membrane. Their caliber is influenced by smooth muscle in their walls which can, as in asthma, markedly narrow them. The lungs surrounding the intrapulmonary branches of the bronchi contain an extensive mesh of elastic tissue which plays an important role in breathing mechanics and is especially important in holding the airways open. We will return to that subject, an understanding of which is vital to comprehending both breathing and phonation, in Chaps. 3 and 6.

Thus the conducting airways consist of either the double passage of the nose, or the single passage of the mouth, leading into the single pharynx and trachea and then fanning out like the branches and twigs of a great tree to finally arrive at the alveoli. Much of the airway surface is lined by mucous membrane with certain physiological characteristics which we will enlarge upon a bit later.

The Breathing Pump

Now let us consider the pump which provides the force needed to move air to and fro in these passages (Fig. 12). A passive portion of this pump is the elastic tissue of the lungs. Its nature is such that the lung, freed of its surrounding structures, tends to seek a volume approximating that reached with lungs in the living chest after we have squeezed out all the air we can. When we breathe in, this elastic tissue is stretched so that its tendency to make the lung smaller becomes greater with increasing lung volume. The chest wall itself also has an elastic behavior which, when it is freed of other forces, makes it seek a volume somewhat higher than that at which we normally breathe. When expanded to a volume larger than that by inspiration it has an elastic tendency to become smaller and when contracted to a smaller volume by expiratory effort its elastic tendency is to become bigger. When no other force is applied to the system the lung rests at a volume where the lung elastic forces, directed toward expiration, exactly balance the chest elastic forces, working in an inspiratory direction. This is the state of affairs at the end of every quiet relaxed breath. The two structures, chest and lung, are prevented from pulling apart by the thin layer of fluid which fills the pleural space surrounding the lungs on all sides.

It may be easier to consider these structures in the form of a simple model (Fig. 13). In the diagram is shown a simple bellows with certain modifications to simulate the human breathing mechanism. The handles of the bellows have a spring (E) interposed which will restore them to a given position after they have been either spread apart or pushed together. Within the bellows is a balloon (L) of such a nature that a pressure must be applied to its interior to make it fill the bellows interior. If we apply that pressure to the balloon interior (at M) and, as it inflates, allow the air surrounding it to escape at (b) and leave only a thin layer of fluid between balloon and bellows interior, close (b) and remove the pressure used to inflate the balloon, its elastic walls will cause it to contract somewhat, the bellows will grow a little smaller and the whole system will come to rest when the expansile force of the bellows spring (E) exactly equals the contracting elastic force of the balloon. In this model the fluid lined space between balloon and bellows is the pleural cavity and the force required to move the bellows arms represents that of the respiratory muscles. We will return to that model in Chap. 3.

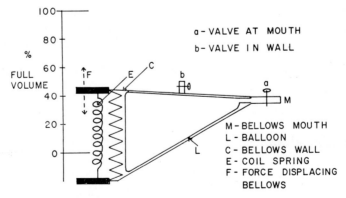

Fig. 13. Diagram of bellows and balloon described in text. The bellows is intended to represent the chest wall, the balloon the lungs, and the space between the two the pleural cavity. See text for explanation

Omitted from this model are the abdominal contents, the abdominal wall, and the diaphragmatic muscle which controls the relative shape and size of the abdominal and thoracic cavities. When not contracting the position of the diaphragm is determined by the elastic pull upward of the lung (across the pleural space) and the weight of the abdominal contents which, in the erect posture, pull downward. Thus, in an upright position, the latter force pulls the diaphragm downward expanding the lungs. If we stand on the head the reverse occurs, and on lying down a mid position is achieved.

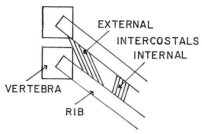

Fig. 14. Highly diagrammatic representation of the rib attachments of the intercostal muscles. Contraction of the external set tends to raise the ribs in relation to their vertebral attachment, while contraction of the internal set tends to bring the ribs together (lowering them)

A number of muscles are involved in the various breathing maneuvers in which we indulge. The diaphragm is a dome shaped muscle lying between the chest and abdomen. Its contraction flattens this dome shape and thus enlarges the thoracic cavity from below. Its action can be influenced by the various muscles of the abdominal wall which are capable of compressing the abdominal contents. Thus, abdominal muscle contraction can push the diaphragm upward or, when balanced with diaphragmatic activity can control the relative size of the thoracic cavity and shape of the abdominal contents. Between the ribs lie two sets of muscles, the internal and external intercostals (Fig. 14). The contraction of one set, the external, elevates the ribs (increasing thoracic volume) and the other set, the internal, depresses the ribs (decreasing thoracic volume) (6).

During quiet breathing enlargement of the lungs is accomplished by contraction of the diaphragm and external intercostals. When deep breathing is required these muscles contract to a greater degree in inspiration, expiratory muscles (including those of the abdominal wall) contract in forced expiration, and another group, the accessory muscles can elevate the clavicles, alter the shape of the curvature of the spine, and supplement the intercostals in moving the ribs.

Among the muscles which can be brought into play in breathing are the sternocleidomastoids, the trapezius, the scalenus muscles, the pectorals, the serratus group, the lastissimus dorsi, and the rectus abdominus, transverse abdominis, and external and internal oblique abdominal muscles (Fig. 15). Details of their anatomical arrangement are not essential here. The curious reader is referred to any standard textbook of anatomy. Their important role in phonation will be discussed in Chap. 7. We shall see (in Chaps. 3 and 7) how all of these forces are controlled to provide the deep inspirations and controlled expirations required for phonation.

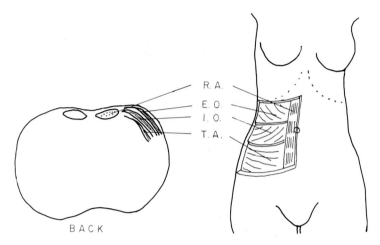

Fig. 15. The muscles of the abdomen chiefly involved in compression of abdominal contents. Right—as seen from the front, and left—seen in cross section. When the diaphragm is relaxed contraction of these muscles pulls the abdominal wall in and pushes the diaphragm upward in the chest. *R.A.* rectus abdominis, *E.O.* external oblique, *I.O.* internal oblique, *T.A.* transverse abdominis

The Larynx

The larynx is composed of a group of cartilages held together by ligaments and muscles (Fig. 16) and suspended in the neck by muscles leading from it to the sternum and clavicles below and the hyoid and jaw above (8, 9, 10) (Fig. 17). A group of muscles (the constrictors) (Fig. 16, left, 1) hold the larynx against the vertebrae thus closing the opening into the esophagus (1). Their relaxation is an essential factor in swallowing (3). The larynx is in part also lined by ciliated mucus secreting epithelium. Its interior is exposed to airway fluids swept upward by ciliary action from the tracheobronchial tree. Mucous glands exist in the larynx itself, especially in the ventricles (the region between the true and false vocal folds). The presence of these fluids is essential for maintaining a moist lubricated surface. But the vocal folds themselves are covered with a delicate squamous epithelium.

The suspension of the larynx in the neck (involving ten muscle groups) is important both in stabilizing it against up and down motion and in producing such motion when required (Fig. 17). You have only to place a finger in the midline of your neck to note the motions the larynx undergoes during swallowing, breathing, and phonation. We will see later that these extra-laryngeal (neck) muscles can also affect the pitch of the voice.

A number of muscles are involved in this laryngeal suspension; but, like the accessory respiratory muscles, a full understanding of them is not essential to the purpose of this monograph. Again, the curious reader is referred to any anatomical text. Among them are the digastric, the hyoglossus, the geniohyoid, the mylohyoid, the omohyoid, the stylohyoid, the thyrohyoid, the sterno-hyoid, the sternothyroid, and the pharyngeal constrictors (Fig. 17).

The keystone of the larynx is the cricoid cartilage which forms a complete strong ring. It articulates with the thyroid and arytenoid cartilages and attaches below to the first cartilage of the trachea. The ability of the laryngeal cartilages to move on one another is essential to the role of the larynx both as a valve and as an organ of phonation. To appreciate this we must first consider the vocal cords which stretch from the arytenoid posteriorly to the inner surface of the thyroid in front. The cords join in front (the anterior com-missure) but can be parted in back (the posterior commissure) to form the triangular glottic airway.

The arytenoid cartilages rest on sliding joints on the top of the cricoid (Fig. 18). They can slide to and from each other, can rotate from side to side, and can tilt upward and backward. Their exact position at any one time is determined by the balance of pull of several muscles. Normally, during breathing, they lie apart from one another.

Although the numerous muscles acting within the larynx and those acting upon it from without seem too complex for easy analysis they are readily understood if considered as functional groups (12). As already mentioned one group suspends the larynx in the neck and a second group holds the larynx firmly against the vertebrae. A third group closes the larynx as a valve. And, finally, one muscle pair alone opens the vocal folds. Of special interest to us is the fact that those closing the larynx as a valve work together for strong closure during swallowing or when maximum elevated intrathoracic pressure is required, but can work in delicate balance to achieve an exact lesser degree of closure of the vocal folds alone during phonation.

As pointed out by Fink (8) the total valve mechanism is composed of a series of folds. These folds, apposed for tight closure, bring together the true cords (or folds), the false cords (vestibular folds) and the aryepiglottic folds (3). In addition the epiglottis is folded backward over the glottis. In phonation the vocal folds alone are apposed.

During swallowing the laryngeal valve is closed by contraction of:
1. the interarytenoid muscles which pull the arytenoids together in back,
2. the cricoarytenoid lateralis muscles which rotate the arytenoids and hold their vocal processes together in front, and 3. the thyroarytenoid and aryepi-glottic muscles bringing together and tensing their folds. The valve is opened by the cricoarytenoid posticus muscles alone which, on relaxation of the other muscles, pull the arytenoids laterally-apart. One more set of muscles is important especially in phonation. They are the cricothyroid muscles which pull the thyroid cartilage forward and rotate it downward in the front toward the cricoid. This action lengthens the vocal cords (Fig. 19).

The same set of muscles and cartilages are involved in phonation but their mass action as a valve must, of course, be modified to permit the periodic escape of air required for sound production.

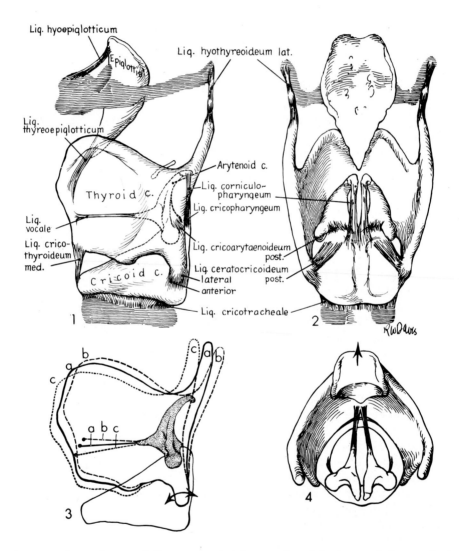

Fig. 16. Left—cartilages and ligaments, and right—muscles of the larynx. Left—note in 4
the vocal ligaments stretching from arytenoids to the thyroid cartilage. Left: *1* seen from the
left side; *2* from the back; *3* tilting of cartilages of cricothyroid joint (see Fig. 19); *4* from
above, arrow at epiglottis. Right: *1* seen from the right; *2* from the back; *3* thyroid cartilage

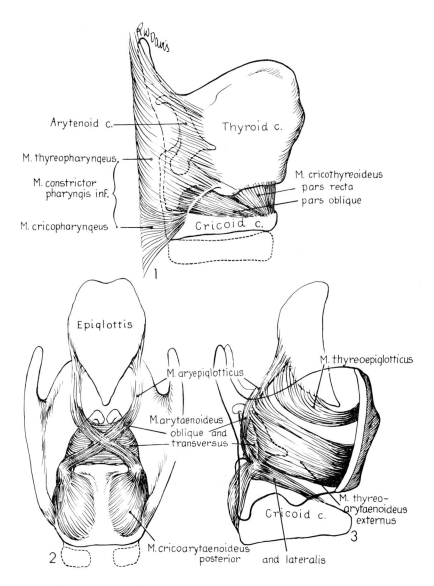

cut away to view interior muscles. See text for explanation. (Used with the permission of the Editors, Handbook of Physiology, Respiration I [Fenn, W. O., Rahn, H., eds.], Am. Physiol. Soc., 1964; from Chap. 8, Proctor, D. F.: Physiology of the upper airway)

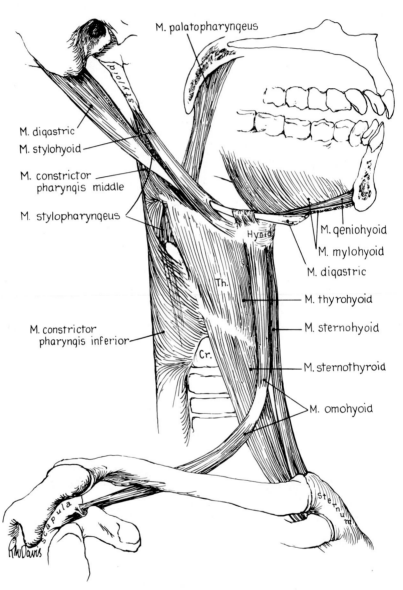

Fig. 17. Some of the extrinsic laryngeal muscles controlling the position of the larynx in the neck in relation to jaw, vertebral column and the chest. The cricoid cartilage is indicated by *Cr.*, the thyroid underlies *Th.* (Used with the permission of the Editors, Handbook of Physiology, Respiration I [Fenn, W. O., Rahn, H., eds.], Am. Physiol. Soc., 1964; from Chap. 8, Proctor, D. F.: Physiology of the upper airway)

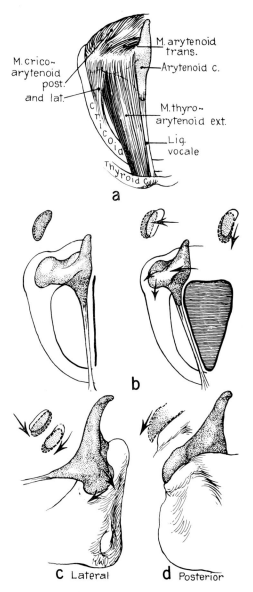

Fig. 18. The cricoarytenoid joint the key to glottic function as a valve and in phonation. *a* its muscular attachments; *b* left: the arytenoid in midline with glottic closure, and right: its lateral motion to open the glottis; *c* and *d* the nature of the joint permitting rotation of the arytenoid as well as sliding from midline laterally. (Used with the permission of the Editors, Handbook of Physiology, Respiration I [Fenn, W. O., Rahn, H., eds.], Am. Physiol. Soc., 1964; from Chap. 8, Proctor, D. F.: Physiology of the upper airway)

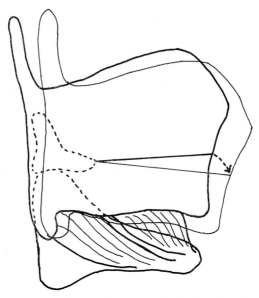

Fig. 19. Cricothyroid motion (see Fig. 16 for comparison). As the cricothyroid muscle contracts the thyroid cartilage moves forward and tilts downward carrying the anterior attachment of the vocal folds with it (arrow). This lengthens the vocal folds

The many other structures involved in breathing and phonation need not be detailed here. We must mention the fact that the larynx like other organs of the body is equipped with sensory nerves which convey to the brain not only pain and touch but also information on the position and motion of the joints (15). The nerve which supplies motor activity to all the laryngeal muscles but one is the recurrent laryngeal (5). The superior laryngeal nerve carries the sensory fibers, and the motor supply for the cricothyroid muscle. One other point on neuromuscular activity is the presence of muscle spindles in both laryngeal muscles and in the intercostals (11). These assure especially fine control of the muscles in which they are found.

References

1. Batson, O. V. (1955): The cricopharyngeus muscle. Ann. Otol. *64*, 47—54.
2. Biondi, S., Biondi-Zappala, M. (1974): Surface of laryngeal mucosa seen through the scanning electron microscope. Folia Phoniatr. *26*, 241—248.
3. Bosma, J. F. (1956): Myology of the pharynx of the cat, dog and monkey with interpretation of the mechanism of swallowing. Ann. Otol. *65*, 982—992.
4. Bosma, J. F. (1975): Anatomic and Physiologic Development of the Speech Apparatus. In: The Nervous System, Vol. 3°. Human Communication and Its Disorders (Tower, D. B., ed.), 489—491. New York: Raven Press.
5. Bowden, R. E. M. (1974): Innervation of Intrinsic Laryngeal Muscles. In: Ventilatory and Phonatory Control Systems (Wyke, B., ed.), Chap. 22. London: Oxford Univ. Press.
6. Campbell, E. J. M. (1968): The respiratory muscles. Ann. N.Y. Acad. Sci. *155*, 135 to 140.

7. Fink, B. R. (1975): The Human Larynx, a Functional Study. New York: Raven Press.
8. Fink, B. R. (1974): Folding mechanism of the human larynx. Acta Otolaryngol. *78*, 124—128.
9. Fink, B. R. (1974): The thyroid cartilage as a spring. Anesthesiology *40*, 58—61.
10. Fink, B. R. (1974): Spring mechanism in the human larynx. Acta Otolaryngol. *77*, 295—306.
11. Grim, M. (1967): Muscle spindles in the posterior cricoarytenoid muscle of the human larynx. Folia Morphol. (Praha) *15*, 124—131.
12. Kanthack, A. A. (1891—1892): The myology of the larynx. J. Anat. Physiol. (London) *26*, 279—294.
13. Negus, V. E. (1962): The Comparative Anatomy and Physiology of the Larynx. New York: Hafner.
14. Ryan, R. F., McDonald, J. R., Devine, K. D. (1956): Changes in laryngeal epithelium: relation to age, sex, and certain other factors. Proc. Mayo Clin. *31*, 47—52.
15. Suzuki, M., Kirchner, J. A. (1968): Afferent nerve fibers in the external branch of the superior laryngeal nerve in the cat. Ann. Otol. *77*, 1059—1071.
16. Tucker, J. A., Vidic, B., Tucker, G. F., jr., Stead, J. (1976): Survey of the development of laryngeal epithelium. Ann. Otol. *85* (Suppl. 30), 1—16.

3 Breathing Mechanics

Speaking and singing are by-products of expiratory airflow when that flow passes through sufficiently adducted vocal folds to produce audible waves. Thus breathing and the mechanism which produces it are fundamental factors in phonation. Anyone who wishes to understand the process of voice production must have a reasonable comprehension first of normal breathing mechanics and second of the modifications of that system necessary for speech and song. The first is the subject of this chapter and the second of Chaps. 5 and 6.

The respiratory mechanism provides the airflow and subglottic pressure necessary for the generation of sound in the larynx. In both speech and song a relatively deep breath in is followed by a controlled flow of air out between vocal folds which have been brought together in the midline. That phase of breathing mechanics will be discussed in Chap. 6. This chapter is devoted to a description of the process of breathing without phonation (13, 17, 18, 20, 23). To follow this discussion it is essential for the reader to understand a few terms and appreciate a few of the methods employed in the study of breathing. Among the terms and methods which are used to describe and study breathing mechanics are those related to lung volumes, airflow, and pressures in the airways.

Lung Volume, Airflow, and Air Pressure

After a maximum effort to expel as much air as possible the lungs still retain a volume of gas referred to as the residual volume (R.V.). The total volume of gas in the lungs at the end of a quiet expiration is called the functional residual capacity (F.R.C.) and the difference between F.R.C. and R.V. is the expiratory reserve volume (E.R.V.). The volume of air moved in and out of the lungs with each breath is the tidal volume (T.V.). When we take in the deepest possible breath the total gas in the respiratory tract is the total lung capacity (T.L.C.). After taking that deepest possible breath the amount of air we can expire down to the residual volume is the vital capacity (V.C.) (13, 14).

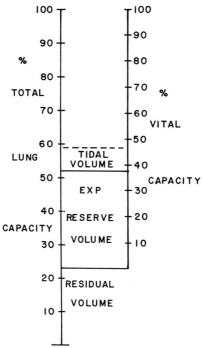

Fig. 20. Lung volume shown as % of the total lung capacity (left) and % of vital capacity (right). Residual volume is that remaining in lungs at the end of a maximum expiratory effort. The tidal volume shown is that characteristic of quiet breathing

Fig. 20 shows the usual volumes in these categories expressed as percent of T.L.C. and of V.C. These percent values vary somewhat among normal individuals, are changed with body position, and also vary somewhat with age. Except when the vital capacity is extremely low, or when the residual volume is large such variations have little significance. Vital capacity in the normal adult ranges between about 3 l in the small female to over 6 l in the tall male. As we shall see later the size of the vital capacity is one determinant of how long a musical phrase can be sung with a single breath. The vital capacity is largest in the upright position and smallest if the head is down, with intermediary values in the sitting and supine positions. Those changes are reflections of the movement of the diaphragm related to the weight of the abdominal contents, downward when standing and upward when lying.

Airflow is generally described in terms of liters per minute (l/min) or per second (1000 ml = 1 l). These terms refer to the amount of air moved in or out per unit time (15). Since, in various parts of the airways, this air moves through relatively wide or narrow airways the speed of each particle of air must increase to negotiate a narrow passage (as we shall see in the nose in Chap. 6), and slow when the passage widens (as in the trachea). That speed of individual particles is referred to in terms of meters per second (m/sec).

The pressure of air in the airways is generally spoken of in relation to atmospheric pressure. Thus a fall or rise in the pressure of air within the airways is described as centimeters of water pressure above or below atmospheric pressure ($\pm$ cm H_2O).

Methods of Study of Breathing Mechanics

One of the simplest tools used in measuring breathing is the spirometer. This is a cylinder (resting in water) in and out of which the subject breathes. As air leaves the lungs the cylinder rises and as it is breathed in again the cylinder falls. Its movements are recorded on a moving piece of paper. That record is a spirogram (Fig. 21). In some circumstances we are especially interested in the moment to moment speed of airflow and then we use the pneumotachometer a device which enables us to record the amount of air moved per unit of time and this is a pneumotachogram. The spirogram is comparable to the chart we would make of a journey if we recorded the distance traveled as a function of time. The pneumotachogram would compare to a chart of the same journey if we noted at each instant the speed at which we traveled.

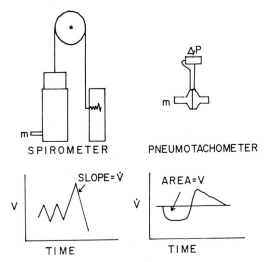

Fig. 21. Two of the methods used in measuring breathing. See text for explanation. $\dot{V}$ airflow, V volume, P is pressure difference, m indicates mouth. Spirometer and spirogram to left and pneumotachometer and pneumotachogram to right

In studying phonation we wish to leave the mouth free of equipment and still measure changes in respiratory volume and the rate of airflow. With both the spirometer and pneumotachometer the subject often wears a nose clip and breathes through a mouthpiece. That system can be replaced by connecting the apparatus to a mask worn over the face. Even with a mask there is some limitation of motion of the jaws and sound is deadened. In order to study breathing during phonation ideally the face should be entirely free. To accomplish this the subject is placed in a sealed box with only the head outside (a modified plethysmograph), and the changes in volume within the box, as the subject changes the volume of air in his thorax, are recorded by connecting the box instead of the face to a spirometer (see Chap. 6, Fig. 39).

Any movement of air results from a pressure difference between one point and another. In the study of breathing mechanics we need to know a good deal about pressure differences and modern pressure transducers are capable of accurately following even very rapid pressure changes. Ideally the pressures we would like to record would be those in the pleural space, alveoli, and trachea (for reasons to be discussed below). Placement of a needle in the pleural space for pleural pressure measurement entails some hazard and therefore we record esophageal pressure instead. Since the thin walled esophagus is surrounded by pleural pressure the pressure within it is a fairly accurate measure of the pressure we want. A long thin flexible tube with a balloon on its end is passed through the nose into the esophagus and, through its connection to a pressure transducer, we record esophageal pressure. In some circumstances we are interested in the pressure below the diaphragm and for that a second balloon is passed in like manner into the stomach. Alveolar spaces are too small to accomodate any instrument so that pressure must be measured indirectly. During quiet breathing with low airflow the alveolar pressure is very close to that in the trachea. Tracheal pressure (subglottic pressure) can be measured through a needle passed through the skin of the neck and the membrane between the cricoid and thyroid cartilage. Methods employed for measuring these pressures in phonation will be further described in Chap. 6.

Consideration of the Static Forces in Breathing

By static forces we mean those which exist when no air is moving through the airways and they may be looked at in three ways, holding the system at rest after a quiet expiration, holding the system at any given position after a breath in or out but with the airways open to the atmosphere, and, after taking a breath in or out, closing the glottis and relaxing respiratory muscle effort (3, 12).

First we will look at the simple bellows model used in Chap. 2 (Figs. 13, 22). Remember, with the valve (a) open we have applied a positive pressure to inflate the balloon until it filled the bellows and then closed the valve. But this time we will leave the valve (b) connected to a pressure transducer to follow pressure in our simulated pleural space surrounding the balloon. When the pressure inflating the balloon is removed the balloon's elastic wall will contract pulling the bellows with it until the bellows spring exerts the

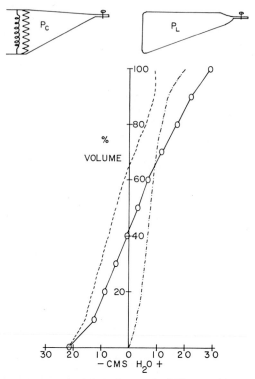

Fig. 22. Compare to Fig. 13. To the left is shown the bellows. The pressure it alone would exert on its contained air against the closed valve at any given volume is indicated by the dashed line. To the right is the balloon and the pressure it alone would exert against the closed valve is shown by the dash-dot line. The solid line shows the sum of those pressures when the balloon and bellows work together as in Fig. 13. Also compare to Figs. 41 and 47

same force outward as the balloon walls do inward. At this point our "pleural" pressure will measure the force with which the elastic balloon is still trying to collapse. We can prove that by attaching a manometer to the bellows mouth (M) and opening the pleural space to the atmosphere. The pressure now in the balloon is the same as the pressure had been in the "pleura" but air has entered the space between the balloon and bellows and the bellows spring has returned to its resting point. That condition can only exist in man if injury or disease has resulted in air entering the normally fluid lined pleural cavity (pneumo-thorax).

Now to return to our original position. No air is moving, the bellows spring and balloon elasticity are equally opposed to one another, and pressure between the two is lower than atmospheric. If we now apply a force to the arm of the bellows to expand it the balloon inside will also expand and, as its elastic walls are further stretched the pressure around it will fall. If we block the bellows mouth and remove the force from the bellows arms the pressure within the balloon will rise. The pressure within the blocked balloon will equal the sum of two elastic forces, bellows and balloon.

When we return to the resting point of the system but now apply force to make the bellows smaller the balloon will also become smaller (less stretched) and the "pleural" pressure less negative. Now, if we block the mouth and remove the force on the bellows, we will find a negative pressure in the balloon, this time the difference between the force of the bellows spring in an expanding direction and the now smaller force of the balloon in a contracting direction.

Thus at any volume of the balloon if its mouth is open and the bellows arms are held steady the "pleural" pressure measures the elastic contractile force of the balloon; and, if the mouth is blocked and the force on the bellows removed, the pressure in the balloon results from and equals the sum of the two elastic forces.

The Dynamic Forces of Breathing

For air to be in motion in or out of the bellows system a pressure difference must be created between the interior of the balloon and the atmosphere. Starting at our resting point, if the bellows are expanded the pressure around the balloon falls and, as the balloon gets larger, the pressure within it falls and air rushes in until atmospheric pressure within the balloon is again achieved. During this process the "pleural" pressure will equal the elastic recoil of the balloon plus the pressure required to overcome the resistance to air flow. To move air more quickly, or if an added resistance to flow is applied at the mouth, a greater pressure drop is required. The reverse is true if air is to move out of this system.

Put in another way, we have a sequence of forces at work. The force moving the bellows arm is comparable to that of our breathing muscles. Its action in making the bellows larger or smaller creates a more negative or positive pressure around the balloon. In response to that pressure change the balloon grows larger or smaller. With change in the balloon volume its contained air is expanded or compressed and the pressure falls or rises. That pressure difference between the air within the balloon and the surrounding atmosphere results in a flow of air in or out through the bellows mouth until the change in volume ceases and the pressure is again equal.

Now if we leave this model and look at the breathing system in life we see that all of the above remains true; the major difference is that respiratory muscles now do the work of the force applied to the bellows arms. To expire below F.R.C. expiratory muscle force is required, and to inspire above F.R.C. inspiratory muscles come into play. After achieving any given lung volume if the glottis is closed and muscular effort is relaxed the pressure within the airways equals the sum of the elastic forces in the chest and lungs (Fig. 22).

In quiet breathing inspiratory muscles enlarge the thorax, the pleural pressure falls, the lungs expand, alveolar pressure falls and air moves into the lungs, the usual tidal volume being about 500 cc. When alveolar pressure is again atmospheric inspiratory effort relaxes and the imbalance in the elastic forces causes the chest to contract and the diaphragm to rise and air to move out until they are again in balance. If we need to move more air more quickly, as in exercise, greater muscular force is employed producing greater pressure swings, more rapid airflows, and larger volume changes (23).

Ordinarily, in the average adult, quiet breathing is accomplished with airflows of 0.3—0.5 l/sec produced by pressure drops of 1—3 cm H₂O. But, in heavy exercise, we employ much greater pressure drops producing flows of 1—3 l/sec or more. Even heavy exercise does not overload the muscular power of the breathing muscles (13). If we deliberately choose to breathe in or out as fast as possible flows of 10—12 l/sec can be achieved. And if we take a deep breath in and forcefully apply expiratory muscle effort against a closed glottis (23) pressures within the lungs can be raised to about 100 cm H₂O. Actually this maneuver is only used physiologically in forceful attempts to expel abdominal contents, as in defecation, urination, parturition, or vomiting.

We have referred to the fact that the pressure required to produce airflow is related to the desired speed of flow and the resistance opposed to the airstream. In Chap. 2 we mentioned a narrow constriction of the airway at the nasal entrance, and we will discuss it further in Chap. 4. At this point we should note that when we choose to breathe through the nose, as we usually do, that narrow constriction nearly doubles the work of breathing. In other words, if we wish to move air very quickly we can, on the one hand, not reach a flow higher than about 2 l/sec through the nose, and, on the other hand, by opening the oropharyngeal airway wide (opening the mouth, lowering the jaw, and depressing the tongue) that same flow can be produced with half the pressure drop and much higher flows can be achieved (Fig. 23).

What are the muscles employed in breathing? Quiet inspiration is accomplished by a contraction (flattening) of the diaphragm and elevation of

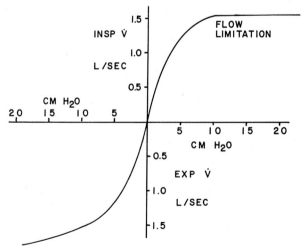

Fig. 23. Diagram of pressure-flow relations in nasal breathing. Note that in inspiration there is a limit to nasal airflow regardless of the increasing pressure produced by effort. (Used with the permission of the Editor, Amer. Rev. Respir. Dis.; from Proctor, D. F. [1977]: The Upper Airways I, *115*, 97—129)

the ribs through contraction of the inspiratory intercostal muscles (10, 11). Relaxation of these muscles is followed by expiration. It is possible voluntarily to make more or less use of either the intercostals or the diaphragm. Thus we can hold the chest fixed and breathe in and out with the diaphragm, keep the diaphragm relatively still and breathe in and out with chest motion, or, without using either diaphragm or intercostals, move the diaphragm up and down through changing pressure on abdominal contents with the abdominal muscles (5, 6). Any or all of the accessory muscles of respiration can be brought into play to increase ventilation. We should note that maximum effort in either an inspiratory or expiratory direction entails muscular maneuvers which are clearly noticeable to an observer. If we wish to move air quickly without giving the appearance of effort, maximum action by the diaphragm and intercostals must be only minimally supplemented by the accessory muscles. If we wish to breathe in deeply toward full lung capacity (T.L.C.) the action of the sternocleidomastoid muscles is of special importance in elevating the clavicles and sternum, and with them, the entire rib cage.

It is worthy of emphasis that all of these complex muscular activities, at rest and during exercise, are brought into play more or less unconsciously. We shall see in subsequent chapters that their use in phonation differs somewhat from their use in ordinary breathing. If you stand in front of a mirror without clothes on it is easy to observe how many "tricks" you can perform with these muscles if you try hard enough. While holding the breath you can compress the chest and expand the belly or vice versa. But changes in the contours of the thorax and belly must be equal and opposite if the breath is held. That is, as the thorax gets smaller the diaphragm is pushed downward and the belly protrudes (16). The diaphragm attaches to the lower part of the thoracic cage and therefore its state of contraction in part determines the basic position of the thorax. For optimum use and control of the breath during singing there is an optimum relationship between thoracoabdominal shapes (1, 2, 7, 8, 15, 25, 26).

From the point of view of the respiratory physiologist it is only fair to say that our knowledge of the action and interaction of the muscles of breathing is still imperfect. There is some debate still over the exact role of the internal and external intercostals. For our purposes resolution of that debate is not essential. In this and subsequent chapters I shall usually only differentiate between "inspiratory" and "expiratory" intercostals. The exact role of the diaphragm and intercostals is of great importance in applying our knowledge of breathing mechanics to understanding the right and wrong way to sing. I will go into that at greater length in Chap. 6.

From time to time suggestions are made that body build and/or sex alters these factors (27). Except in the case of severe obesity this is not so. Only when the abdomen is severely restricted by a girdle are these forces affected. Any ideas that the strong, full voice is only possible in the robust individual should have been fully dispelled by the beautiful voices of a number of lithe and delicately formed women who have had important operatic careers in modern times.

As we shall see in subsequent chapters the processes of phonation do not require the employment of flows and pressures greatly in excess of those employed in quiet breathing. Only in the quick inspirations interspersed in rapid conversation or the very quick and deep inspirations employed in professional singing is greater effort brought into play.

Role of the Larynx

The larynx developed phylogenetically as a valve separating the lungs from the digestive tract during swallowing and it has a role in breathing distinct from its role in phonation (5, 15, 21, 24, 28, 29). The muscles suspending it in the neck prevent excessive motion upward or downward during breathing. The vocal folds part slightly during inspiration but remain sufficiently parted during expiration to prevent significant interference with airflow. Only during swallowing, or when a rise in intrathoracic pressure is required as before cough or during the expelling of abdominal contents, does the laryngeal valve fully close. Under those circumstances the true vocal folds as well as the false, and the aryepiglottic folds approximate forcefully.

A factor, which will be discussed again later, is the lubrication of the laryngeal surfaces (9, 19, 22). Portions of these surfaces and the pharynx are covered with a squamous epithelium, not the ciliated, secretory, respiratory epithelium characteristic of the other airways. There are mucus secreting glands strategically located within the larynx (9, 19) which help to assure its moist surface. But, in addition, the larynx is normally continually washed by secretions coming up from the lungs and the pharynx by those coming down from the nose.

Thus, ordinarily the larynx functions purely as a valve interrupting breathing when closed and offering minimal airflow resistance when open. Its function in phonation will be considered in Chaps. 6, 7, and 8 (29).

References

1. Agostoni, E., Rahn, H. (1960): Abdominal and thoracic pressures at different lung volumes. J. Appl. Physiol. *15*, 1087—1092.
2. Agostoni, E., Sant'Ambrogio, G., Portillo Carrasco, H. del (1960): Electromyography of the diaphragm in man and transdiaphragmatic pressures. J. Appl. Physiol. *15*, 1093 to 1097.
3. Agostoni, E., Mead, J. (1964): Statics of the Respiratory System. In: Handbook of Physiology, Respiration I (Fenn, W. O., Rahn, H., eds.), 387—409. Washington: Amer. Physiol. Soc.
4. Andrew, B. L. (1955): The respiratory displacement of the larynx: A study of the innervation of accessory respiratory muscles. J. Physiol. *130*, 474—487.
5. Bishop, B. (1968): Neural regulation of abdominal muscle contraction. Ann. N.Y. Acad. Sci. *155*, 191—200.
6. Bishop, B. (1974): Abdominal Muscle Activity During Respiration. In: Ventilatory and Phonatory Control Systems (Wyke, B., ed.), Chap. 2. London: Oxford Univ. Press.

7. Campbell, E. J. M. (1958): The Respiratory Muscles and the Mechanics of Breathing. Chicago: Year Book Publishers.
8. Campbell, E. J. M. (1974): Muscular Activity in Normal and Abnormal Ventilation. In: Ventilatory and Phonatory Control Systems (Wyke, B., ed.), Chap. 1. London: Oxford Univ. Press.
9. Delahunty, J. E., Cherry, J. (1969): The laryngeal saccule. J. Laryngol. *83*, 803—815.
10. Euler, C. v., Critchlow, V. (1963): Intercostal muscle spindle activity and its motor control. J. Physiol. *168*, 820—847.
11. Euler, C. v. (1968): The proprioceptive control of the diaphragm. Ann. N.Y. Acad. Sci. *155*, 204—205.
12. Euler, C. v. (1974): Control of Depth and Rate of Respiratory Movements. In: Ventilatory and Phonatory Control Systems (Wyke, B., ed.), Chap. 7. London: Oxford Univ. Press.
13. Fenn, W. O., Rahn, H. (1964): Handbook of Physiology, Respiration I. Washington: Amer. Physiol. Soc.
14. Gilson, J. C., Hugh-Jones, P. (1949): The measurement of total lung volume and breathing capacity. Clin. Sci. *7*, 185—216.
15. Jaeger, M. J., Matthys, H. (1968): The pattern of flow in the upper human airways. Respir. Physiol. *6*, 113—127.
16. Konno, K., Mead, J. (1967): Measurements of the separate volume changes of rib cage and abdomen during breathing. J. Appl. Physiol. *22*, 407—422.
17. Mead, J. (1961): Mechanical properties of lungs. Physiol. Rev. *41*, 281—330.
18. Mead, J. (1973): Respiration: Pulmonary mechanics. Ann. Rev. Physiol. *35*, 169—192.
19. Nassar, V. H., Bridger, G. P. (1971): Topography of laryngeal mucous glands. Arch. Otolaryngol. *94*, 490—498.
20. Otis, A. B., Fenn, W. O., Rahn, H. (1950): Mechanics of breathing in man. J. Appl. Physiol. *2*, 592—607.
21. Pressman, J., Kelemen, G. (1955): Physiology of the larynx. Physiol. Rev. *35*, 506—554.
22. Punt, N. A. (1974): Lubrication of the vocal mechanism. Folia Phoniatr. *26*, 287—288.
23. Rahn, H., Otis, A. B., Chadwick, L. E., Fenn, W. O. (1946): The pressure-volume diagram of the thorax and lung. Am. J. Physiol. *146*, 161—178.
24. Schiratzki, H. (1965): The oral and laryngeal components of the upper airway resistance during mouth breathing. Acta Otolaryngol. *60*, 71—82.
25. Sears, T. A., Davis, J. N. (1968): The control of respiratory muscles during voluntary breathing. Ann. N.Y. Acad. Sci. *155*, 183—190.
26. Sharp, J. T., Goldberg, N. B., Druz, W. S., Danon, J. (1975): Relative contributions of rib cage and abdomen to breathing in normal subjects. J. Appl. Physiol. *39*, 608—618.
27. Sheil, R. F. (1962): A study of respiration with relation to somatotype. Ann Arbor: University Microfilms.
28. Widdicombe, J. G. (1975): Reflex control of the larynx. Bull. Physiopath. Resp. *11*, 102—103.
29. Wyke, B. D., Kirchner, J. A. (1976): Neurology of the Larynx. In: Scientific Foundations of Otolaryngology (Hinchcliffe, R., Harrison, D., eds.), Chap. 40. London: Heinemann.

4 The Nose and Air Modification

The word nose is commonly employed to describe that more or less prominent appendage on the front of the face. Physiologically the nasal passage leading backward from the nostrils is the region important to health. In addition although we do not usually think of the nose or nasal passages as a part of the phoniatric mechanism, they are important contributors to the hygiene of the respiratory tract as a whole and vital to normal voice production. Most people who depend upon the speaking or singing voice for the successful pursuit of their careers are well aware of the fact that nasal disease, even a simple common cold, impairs the voice. This chapter is devoted to a discussion of the physiological role of the nose in breathing, protecting the health of the airways, and supplementing the larynx as a resonator for sound (2, 3, 7, 8, 9, 10). Various problems of nasal disease and the voice will be discussed in Chaps. 9 and 10.

Although the main physiological function of the airways and the breathing pump is to ventilate the lungs, and a secondary role is the modification of the breathing process to produce sound, these functions could not continue if the airways did not fulfil another function. That is the alteration of the physical nature, or conditioning, of the inspired air. Ordinarily the air about us is below body temperature and contains relatively little water vapor, that is it has a low relative humidity (R.H.). To protect the delicate membranes which permit exchange of oxygen and carbon dioxide between lung air and blood it is essential that alveolar air be at body temperature and saturated with water vapor (37 °C, 100 % R.H.). In addition our ambient air often contains airborne materials which may be injurious to the interior of the body, gaseous air pollutants, dusts, bacteria, and viruses. During the passage of inspired air those noxious materials are largely removed and temperature and water vapor are adjusted. Most of that modification process normally takes place in the nose (4, 5).

Nasal Air Modification

When we are forced to breathe through the mouth, as during a bad cold, we are all familiar with the fact that certain discomforts ensue, an indication that the mouth, pharynx, and trachea suffer somewhat when forced to take on the job of air conditioning ordinarily carried out in the nasal passages. But, as we shall see a little later, the process of speech or singing involves some degree of mouth breathing. Since the maintenance of healthy air passages is conducive to our ability to speak or sing, as well as to our general well being, let us examine the nasal airways in that light.

The air modification process is dependent upon the relation between the inspiratory air stream and the surfaces over which it passes and the function of the mucous membranes which compose those surfaces. Already we begin to see the significance of the complexity of the nasal airway as described in Chap. 2 (Fig. 9). We will first examine the nature of airflow, note its effect on the fate of inhaled materials, and then consider the role of respiratory mucous membranes.

The nasal air stream entering the nostrils is directed upward and, a short distance within the nose, must pass through the narrow constriction (described in Chap. 2) and negotiate a bend to run backward half way through the head. Just beyond that bend the air flows as a narrow stream through the spaces between the septum and the convolutions of the turbinates. After passing more or less straight back some 7—9 cm the stream bends again, this time downward, to flow through the pharynx into the larynx. The individual particles of air must move very fast to go through the anterior constriction but may then move in a relatively leisurely fashion through the main passage. Whereas the linear velocity of the air stream during quiet breathing is in the neighborhood of 1 m/sec in the main airways, at the anterior nasal constriction it approaches 12—15 m/sec.

Particles in the inhaled air are in large part deposited at the point where the swiftly moving stream makes its initial bend. Water soluble gases, such as sulfur dioxide (2), have an optimum opportunity to be absorbed in surface fluids in the main passage where the air moves relatively slowly in a narrow stream over a large surface area (Fig. 24). The same characteristics of the main passage allow for the adjustment of air temperature and the addition of water vapor to the inspired air.

Thus by the time air has reached the nasopharynx it is within a few degrees of 37 °C and saturated with water vapor (100 % R.H.). The additional change in temperature and the added water to keep R.H. at 100 % is probably largely accomplished in the small airways of the lungs where, once again, the air stream moves slowly through narrow channels.

Of course the condition of our ambient air is subject to large and, sometimes, sudden change. Such change naturally occurs with weather and climate. But sudden changes occur in going in or out of a heated building on a cold day, or in or out of an air cooled room on a hot humid summer's day. The amount of adjustment in nasal mucous membrane which must occur must also

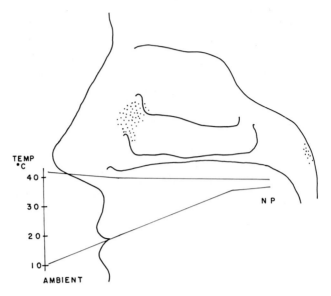

TEMP
°C
40
30   N P
20
10
AMBIENT

Fig. 24. Superimposed on the diagram appearing in Fig. 9 is shown the region of chief particle deposition anteriorly and secondary deposition in the nasopharynx (stippled areas). The main passage between is the site of temperature adjustment and air humidification. Below is indicated the approximate rate of temperature adjustment when breathing warm or cold air

vary to an appropriate degree, and as quickly as one passes through a doorway. This is a remarkably efficient built in air conditioning system with its own set of controls. The adjustments are accomplished through changing the amount of blood flowing through the walls of the nasal passage and altering to the exact degree required the amount of water secreted onto the surface.

Mucociliary Function

Although the nature of airflow to surface relationship is a key part of this system it could not continue to function without the mucociliary system lining the surface (Fig. 10, Chap. 2). This system consists of the cilia which beat in such a manner as to carry surface fluids (and materials deposited on them or absorbed in them) constantly backward to the nasopharynx, and the cells and glands which secrete mucus. At regular intervals, during swallowing and without our consciously being aware of it, the soft palate rises to wipe the nasopharyngeal wall and carry materials into the stomach. Interspersed among the ciliated cells are goblet cells and the ducts of mucous glands. From them the watery and mucous secretions are continually added to the surface. These secretions are also highly adjustable to meet the demands of relatively dry or moist air. The exact mechanism of that adjustment is not known.

Airway Secretions

The quantity of nasal secretions, which are normally swept backward through the nose and swallowed, is also not known. Estimates vary and some have suggested it may amount to a pint (500 cc) per day. Added to this is the quantity of secretions swept upward through the larynx from the lungs, also to be swallowed (Fig. 25). Ordinarily this process is entirely unconscious but in some individuals there develops an awareness of the presence of these fluids normally present in the throat. They then may complain of a "post-nasal-drip". In other individuals the secretions may become relatively thick and sticky, sometimes resulting in a feeling of a dry throat. In some these symptoms are a result of disease, but variations in normal physiological function are more commonly responsible. Fear may trigger a lessening in quantity of secretions which are then more than normally dried by the air conditioning process in the nose. Thus both a feeling of dry throat and "post-nasal-drip" may be a result of one degree or another of stage fright.

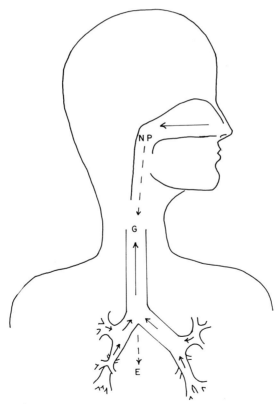

Fig. 25. Diagram of the paths of mucociliary clearance of respiratory surfaces. Nasal fluids are moved backward to the nasopharynx *(NP)* whence, with swallowing, they are carried down the pharynx and dispatched into the esophagus *(E)*. Fluids from the tracheobronchial tree are moved upward through the posterior larynx *(G)*. After passing through the larynx they too are swallowed

These questions will be considered in more detail in later chapters. At this point it is only necessary to emphasize the fact that secretions in the throat are a part of normal physiology. When one becomes overly conscious of them a habit may develop of throat clearing, and even hawking and spitting to clear them instead of swallowing. Those actions can have a serious detrimental effect upon the voice.

In any event the mucociliary character of the respiratory mucous membrane normally provides a continuous moist surface. Thus, although the surfaces of the nasal passage are continually being contaminated with inhaled materials, the ciliated cells provide the power for moving the fluid lining and its contaminants constantly backward into the nasopharynx whence it is swallowed. In that manner the mucosa is kept covered by a fresh self replenishing fluid coat. But ciliated mucous membranes cease to function when they are exposed to dry air and for that reason it has been generally assumed that maintenance of a healthy nasal airway required humidification of the ambient air. Actually many people live in very dry climates, or at high altitude, or in cold climates where the air is very dry without suffering any evidence of nasal disease. Indeed it is commonly said that a dry climate is helpful for patients with respiratory disease and a wet climate harmful.

The fact is that the nose is such an efficient humidifier that, in normal subjects, even the driest of air is made moist enough not to injure mucosal function. Whether there may be some "abnormal" subjects to whom dry air is harmful is not known. With my colleagues in Aarhus, Denmark (Andersen, Lundqvist, and Jensen) we have conducted studies directed at this problem. When normal young adults were confined in an environmental chamber for 78 hours (1) there was no deterioration in mucociliary function even when the ambient air was extremely dry (9 % R.H. at 23 °C). We also found that exposure to moist air (70 % R.H. at 23 °C) failed to improve the rate of mucociliary clearance in those in whom it was ordinarily slow. In another set of similar experiments we did find that when air was either cooled or warmed from an initial 23 °C there was some slowing of nasal mucociliary clearance (9). These findings indicate that normal subjects do not suffer from dry air or benefit from moist air but may have some deterioration in function attributable to temperature change. Thus we can say that ordinarily a normal person need not fear dry air nor seek artificially humidified air but that sudden changes in temperature may have a deleterious effect.

When the singer is performing or when the speaker is engaging in busy conversation or delivering a long lecture the situation is different. As we shall see, under those circumstances a portion of each breath taken in passes through the mouth, not the nose. Note for yourself how awkward it would be to close the mouth to inspire between each phrase of conversation. In the singer this fact assumes greater importance because of the special need for quick breaths during short breaks in song phrases. Thus, in those circumstances, dry ambient air may tend to dry the throat. The air of airplanes is often very dry. With these facts in mind the singer or public speaker traveling by air to an engagement would be wise to eschew prolonged conversation. Let us consider these points a little more carefully.

Nasal vs Mouth Breathing

As we have already pointed out the nose offers a resistance to airflow which is far greater than that offered by an open oropharyngeal airway. This is normal (Fig. 26). There are circumstances (in disease, malformation, or developmental abnormalities) when nasal breathing is difficult or impossible. These will be discussed in Chap. 10. For the moment let us consider the significance of ordinary nasal airflow resistance to problems of phonation.

To a slight degree in talking, but to a much greater degree in singing, it is desirable to take quick deep inspirations between phrases (Figs. 27, 28). We take these breaths unconsciously with the mouth at least slightly parted. It is not only awkward to close the mouth between phrases but it is simply impossible to move large volumes of air into the lungs through the nose in a fraction of a second. Peak inspiratory nasal airflows are in the range of 2 l/sec, while peak flows through the mouth may be as high as 10—12 l/sec. Quite commonly in singing we wish to replenish nearly the entire vital capacity in less than a second (4—5 l/sec). As we have seen, nasal breathing moistens the inspired air and one should be sure to take advantage of this in breathing during longer pauses in phonation.

Finally we should say again that healthy nasal passages and sinuses are conducive to the optimum use of these resonators in producing the best quality of voice (6). We are all familiar with the change in voice quality associated

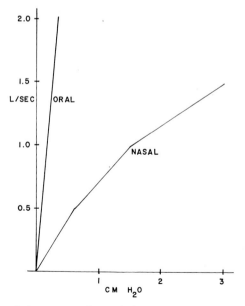

Fig. 26. Comparison of the pressure-flow relations in oral and nasal breathing. Note that with the same pressure drop, produced by respiratory muscle effort, far higher flows occur with mouth breathing. See Fig. 23 for nasal flow limitation

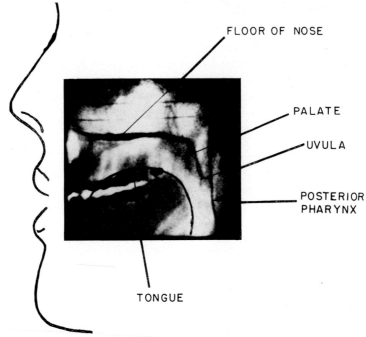

FLOOR OF NOSE

PALATE

UVULA

POSTERIOR
PHARYNX

TONGUE

Fig. 27. This and Fig. 28, and a number of subsequent figures are taken from a cinefluoro-graph of the supraglottic structures during breathing, talking and singing. This figure is intended to orient the reader as to the structures shown

with nasal blockage as with a common cold. Lesser degrees of nasal airway impairment or disease in the paranasal sinuses can result in a more subtle but nonetheless important loss of phonatory quality.

References

1. Andersen, I., Lundqvist, G., Jensen, P. L., Proctor, D. F. (1974): Human response to 78 hours exposure to dry air. Arch. Environ. Health 29, 319—324.
2. Andersen, I., Lundqvist, G., Jensen, P. L., Proctor, D. F. (1974): Human response to controlled levels of sulfur dioxide. Arch. Environ. Health 28, 31—39.
3. Brain, J. D., Proctor, D. F., Reid, L., eds. (1977): Respiratory Defense Mechanisms, Vol. 1, Chaps. 3 and 4. New York: M. Dekker.
4. Cole, P. (1954): Some aspects of temperature, moisture and heat relationships in the upper respiratory tract. J. Laryngol. 67, 449—456, 669—681, 68, 295—307, 613—622.
5. Ingelstedt, S. (1956): Studies on the conditioning of air in the respiratory tract. Acta Otolaryngol. Suppl. 131, 1—80.
6. Lindqvist-Gauffin, J., Sundberg, J. (1976): Acoustic properties of the nasal tract. Phonetica 33, 161—168.
7. Proctor, D. F., Swift, D. L. (1971): The nose—a defense against the atmospheric environment. In: Inhaled Particles III (Walton, W. H., ed.), 59—69. Surrey: Unwin Bros.
8. Proctor, D. F. (1977): State of the Art, The upper airways I. Nasal physiology and defense of the lungs. II. The larynx and trachea. Amer. Rev. Resp. Dis. 115, 87—130, 315—342.

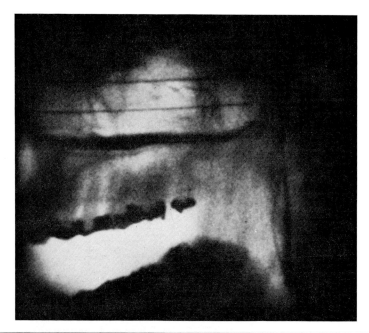

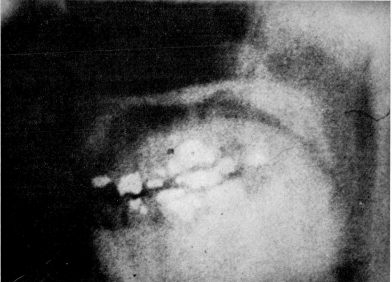

Fig. 28. Two frames from the cinefluorograph to show the difference between the relatively quiet inspiration through parted lips interspersed in conversation (below) and (above) the widened airway when a quick deep breath is taken through the mouth

9. Proctor, D. F., Andersen, I., Lundqvist, G. (1977): Human nasal mucosal function at controlled temperatures. Respir. Physiol. *30*, 109—124.
10. Proctor, D. F. (1964): Physiology of the Upper Airway. In: Handbook of Physiology, Respiration I (Fenn, W. O., Rahn, H., eds.), Chap. 8. Washington: Amer. Physiol. Soc.

5 Sound Production

Breathing, speech, and song are the subjects of this book. Put in another way, our purpose is to examine the combination of airflow and the function of the larynx for the production of sound. Now that we have some understanding of the anatomy and physiology of the respiratory system we can turn our attention directly to its involvement in voice production (2, 4, 23, 24, 32, 37, 54, 55). But first let us consider the nature of sound.

For all of us who are not deaf the world is full of sound. Indeed for certain research purposes, the creation of completely soundproof rooms is a complicated and expensive business. A large part of our world of sound consists of noise which here we can deplore but otherwise ignore. The sounds employed for human communication (speech) or for our entertainment (song, other forms of music, and the theater) are organized in a manner to be intelligible and euphonious. What is sound?

Nature of Sound

Air, like most materials, is elastic. That is to say, when deformed or displaced it has a tendency to resume its former shape or position. If we imbed a steel rod in a fixed base and apply a force at its tip to displace it, when the force is removed the elasticity of the rod comes into play to set up a vibratory movement (Fig. 29). The rate at which the rod vibrates is a function of the length, mass, and stiffness of the rod. The vibration of the rod sets up a disturbance in the air surrounding it and that disturbance travels through the air as a wave. If the frequency of that wave is within the range of our hearing our ears interpret it as sound. The intensity of this sound reaching our ears (loudness) will be related to the amount of energy emanating from its source (the vibrating rod) into the air, the distance at which we are from the source, and the absorbent qualities of surrounding materials (such as walls, rugs, etc.).

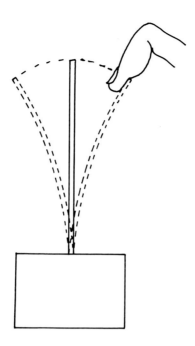

Fig. 29. Vibrating rod as sound source, shown being plucked by a finger

A tuning fork is such a rod doubled and made of the exact length, mass, and stiffness to produce a frequency of vibration usually corresponding to a note on our musical scale (Fig. 30). The loudness of its tone may be increased somewhat by striking it more forcefully. But, if its handle is placed against a flat surface which it can set in vibration, a louder sound can be produced. In like manner, if the fork is held before a container of air of appropriate shape and size to be set in vibration by the fork, an increase in loudness will be noted. In these instances the fundamental frequency and the overtones are amplified by the vibrating surface or the resonating box. Put simply, the tuning fork when plucked or struck is the generator supplying the energy and the fundamental frequency (plus various partials), and the resonator acts as an amplifier increasing the intensity of the sound and lending emphasis to overtones.

Musical Sound

Musical instruments are designed in that manner. The strings of the violin or piano and the reed, or the player's pursed lips, in wind instruments are, when appropriately set in motion, generators. The wooden frame of the violin, the sounding board of the piano, and the air column of the wind instrument are the amplifiers.

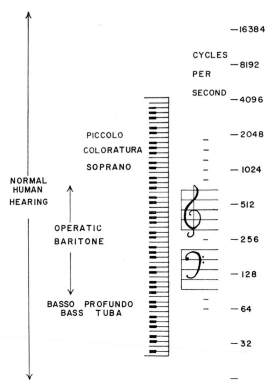

Fig. 30. From left to right, normal human hearing, ranges of human voice and musical instruments, the piano keyboard, and musical notation, all related to pitch in terms of cycles per second, far right

Most of the vibrations set up by musical instruments have a frequency of 30 to 5000 cycles per second (Fig. 30). The perfect human ear in a young person is capable of perceiving vibrations from about 16 to 22,000 cycles per second. Pitch is a word used to describe the subjective correlate of the vibrations perceived by the ear. After the age of 20 most of us gradually lose some of the ability to perceive the higher tones, eventually bringing our useful perception down to a range of 16 to approximately 8000. Our musical scale is set about the frequency of 256 vibrations per second which is middle C on the piano. An octave in that scale represents a factor of two. Thus C above middle C is 512, the C above that 1024, the C below middle C 128, etc. (Fig. 30). The exact frequencies of our musical scale vary slightly from those for reasons we need not go into here.

In the human voice the vibrating vocal folds are the generators of the fundamental frequency and overtones (14, 31, 34, 53), the pressure drop between their under surfaces and the supraglottic space (subglottic pressure) is the force setting them in vibration, the airways above the larynx are the amplifiers (42), and the lips, tongue, and palate tune the amplifiers to produce the subtle variations in sound which compose speech or song.

The Human Voice

Let's review for a moment the anatomical and physiological features of the larynx involved in sound production. The vocal folds are brought together in the midline through the action of the muscles controlling the motion of the arytenoid cartilages over the upper surface of the cricoid (1, 15, 28). Various neurophysiological techniques, including electromyography (6, 7, 8, 20, 39, 59), have led to an understanding of how this takes place. Whereas in swallowing a very tight closure of the airway is accomplished by a mass action bringing together all of the folds (see Chaps. 2 and 3), for voice production only the true vocal folds are apposed, and that in a delicately controlled fashion. We are capable of holding those folds together with a force which will prevent the passage of air even at very high pressure, over 100 cm H_2O (Fig. 31). For phonation their apposition must be such that even low pressures, 2—10 cm H_2O, will result in air moving between them. We will return to that in a moment.

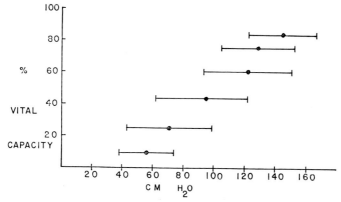

Fig. 31. Ranges of subglottic pressure (horizontal coordinate) among normal subjects which can be produced by expiratory effort at the various lung volumes indicated (vertical coordinate). (Data taken from Rahn, H., Otis, A. B., Chadwick, L. E., Fenn, W. O. [1946]: Pressure volume diagram of thorax and lungs, Am. J. Physiol. *146,* 161 to 178). Note that even close to R.V. pressures well in excess of those employed in ordinary phonation are possible

If we consider the various muscles controlling arytenoid motion (see Figs. 16, 18 in Chap. 2) (1, 15, 28, 33) it is readily apparent that the vocal cords can be brought together in a number of different configurations (21, 27, 50) (Fig. 32). If the action of the cricoarytenoid lateralis outweighs that of the interarytenoid muscles the membranous portions of the folds come together while the cartilaginous portions are apposed only at their anterior ends *(C)*. If the reverse occurs a diamond shaped glottic chink can result and, in the face of this latter condition if the vocalis muscles are relatively relaxed the chink will approach an ellipse *(D)*. This is probably close to the configuration used in whispering, although for that type of phonation even the posterior arytenoids are not brought together. If the cartilaginous portions are held sufficiently firmly together, when the folds part with airflow only their membranous portions will be set in vibration *(E)*. Indeed, if the vocalis muscles are firmly enough tensed under that condition, only the mid portion of the folds may be set in vibration *(F)* (probably the configuration for the falsetto voice).

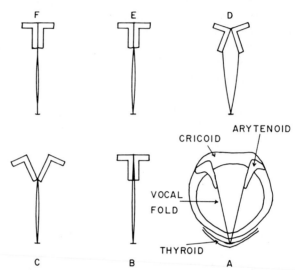

Fig. 32. Diagrammatic presentation of some of the possible configurations of the glottic opening, arytenoids above and anterior commissure below. *A* The normally open glottis; *B* The configuration most compatible with normal phonation making possible vibration of entire length of vocal folds; *C* Improper closure which can lead to erosion of mucosa over tips of arytenoid vocal processes and leakage of air posteriorly; *D* Very loose closure, some variant of which may be used in whispering; *E* Tight approximation of arytenoids, possible mechanism for falsetto voice; *F* High muscular tension in vocalis muscle added to tight arytenoid closure, possible mechanism in high pitched falsetto squeak. Obviously many intermediary positions are possible and, in spite of high speed cinematography, there is still some dispute over exact configuration in optional phonation

Still another possible variant on that theme has been suggested and is theoretically possible, but I have never observed it in action. This involves a tilting of the arytenoids in such a manner that the anterior ends of their vocal processes may project either downward or upward in relation to the natural plane of the vocal folds. For our purposes we can ignore this possibility except to note that it would result from an inappropriate action of the cricoarytenoid posticus muscles.

Since the posterior portion of the vocal folds overlies the cartilaginous vocal process of the arytenoid cartilages, it has been suggested that that part of the folds plays no part in the vibratory motion associated with phonation (19). It is my belief that the entire length of the folds participates in phonatory vibration under normal conditions. The conditions indicated in *E* and *F* (Fig. 32) are to my mind abnormal. The latter is probably the mechanism for the falsetto voice, as employed by some singers to extend their high range. Certainly for the lowest tones of the voice vibration of the whole length of the folds is desirable (29, 51). A change in mechanism in going from such low tones to the higher voice might occasion the "break" discussed later; but I favor the explanation to be discussed in Chap. 8.

Another subject of controversy has been the belief that the airways below the larynx act as important resonators for the voice (19). That there must be a fluctuating pressure in the tracheobronchial tree corresponding in frequency to the pitch of the voice seems to be true. But these small pressure fluctuations can have little effect upon the very large volume of air in the lungs. The use of such terms as "chest register" indicates how firmly some believe in the significance of subglottic resonance. The evidence for or against this view is to my mind incomplete. It is my belief that the tracheobronchial airways offer little significant contribution to the resonance of the voice (52).

Pitch Control

Of all of the various possible configurations of the vocal folds in phonation we will consider here only that in which they are evenly apposed in the midline in such a manner that their entire length may be set in vibration (Fig. 32, B). Some of the other possibilities will be discussed in subsequent chapters in considering voice abnormalities. In this configuration each person will have a natural, resting length and mass of the vocal folds which will determine the natural frequency of the voice (34). That is to say that, with only the muscular effort required to bring the vocal folds to the midline, the frequency which results when they are set in motion by a moderate transglottic pressure will be determined by their dimensions and configuration under those circumstances; and that "natural" frequency will differ among individuals in relation to such factors as age, sex, size, etc. The length of the vocal folds increases as the larynx grows through the age of puberty. The child's vocal folds are short and the folds in a woman are usually shorter than in a man. Although less is known about mass per unit length, this too probably varies with age and sex.

As with any structure involving muscle and elastic tissue, if a force is applied to lengthen it there will be a relation between the lengthening force and the tension developed (Fig. 33). Tension in the vocal folds can also be increased by contraction of the vocalis muscle without any change in length. As has already been described, a change in vocal fold length can be accomplished by contraction of the cricothyroid muscles (see Fig. 19, Chap. 2), bringing their attachment to the thyroid cartilage forward and downward, in relation to the cricoid cartilage. Sonninen has also pointed out that such action can be supplemented by extrinsic laryngeal muscles (44, 45). Both lengthening and tensing of the vocal folds results in a redistribution of their vibrating mass so that it is decreased in relation to unit length.

These factors control the fundamental frequency (often spoken of as "pitch") of the voice. The natural length and mass of the vocal folds result in the natural frequency of the voice and changes from that natural one result mainly from a shortening or lengthening and/or a decrease in their tension

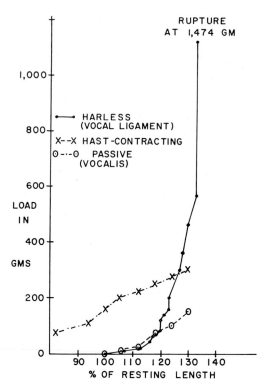

Fig. 33. Some of the data available on the change in length of vocal cord with changing force applied. The solid line is taken from Harless' data (17) which shows that relatively little force was needed to stretch the vocal ligament to 120 % of resting length. Very large force produced only a small further change and then rupture. The other two lines come from Hast's data (19) and show that in the passive vocalis muscle a 30 % increase in length was achieved with a relatively small force while the actively contracting muscle (which started at 80 % of resting length) also could be stretched to 130 % of resting length without unreasonable force. A 30 % increase in vocal fold length is believed to occur in the human vocal fold in going from low to high pitched singing voice

plus a redistribution of mass per unit length. The pressure across the vocal folds also affects the frequency of their vibration to a small degree. During a crescendo (produced by a rising subglottic pressure) the frequency of vibration would rise (and with it the perceived pitch of the voice) unless internal adjustment of elastic forces in the folds has occurred proportionately. The degree to which lengthening or tensing are involved in achieving the highest pitches of which one's voice is capable is a difficult and controversial matter. It will be discussed in subsequent chapters.

The combination of factors involved in this determination of frequency of vibration of the vocal folds can be described by a mathematical equation (45). The frequency in cycles per second *(F)* equals a constant *(C)* multiplied by the square root of an elastic factor *(K)* divided by the mass of the fold per unit length *(M)* : *(F = C \/ K/M)*. The constant *C* includes not only natural dimensions and characteristics of the individual larynx but also the influence of subglottic pressure. The elastic factor K is a combination of the natural elasticity of the folds, set by the elastic tissue they contain, plus an added elasticity which is dependent upon the tone of the vocalis muscle and any stretch of the folds beyond their natural length (Fig. 34). The mass per unit length M can be redistributed either by contraction of the vocalis muscle or by stretching or relaxing to a greater or lesser length (11, 13). Thus, while variations in the resting dimensions of the larynx and in subglottic pressure may result in a rise or fall in the natural resonant frequency, an increased elastic tension raises the frequency and an increase in mass per unit length decreases it. In other words each of us possesses certain anatomical character- istics affecting the ordinary pitch of the voice, but increasing voice intensity by raising subglottic pressure, making the folds more taut by stretching them or tensing them, or thinning their mass per unit length (usually a result of stretching or tensing) will all raise the perceived pitch by increasing the fundamental frequency.

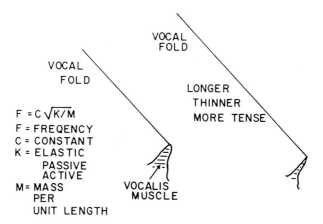

Fig. 34. Factors controlling pitch. As the vocal fold lengthens (right), whether through passive stretching by cricothyroid activity or by vocalis muscle contraction, its tension increases and its mass per unit length decreases. Formula describing relation of forces to pitch is at left

Although the control of all the muscles involved in phonation is obviously a complex of phenomena, that control is in large part a more or less unconscious one evidently learned in infancy as speech is acquired (30). Still we know we are capable of consciously modulating the quality of the voice and do so in achieving emphasis, especially in conveying emotional meaning to what we are saying. Both the conscious and unconscious controls involve, even for a simple sound, a steady flow of messages from the larynx to the brain and back to the larynx again (20). The complex sounds resulting in speech require messages to and from the supraglottic organs in addition. Certainly there are sensory nerves which convey to the brain the exact position of the laryngeal cartilages as well as the state of contraction of their attached muscles.

Neural Feedback

Intervening in this family of neuromuscular actions is a feedback mechanism from our hearing (43). Our auditory perception of the sounds we make can be used to modify the brain's response to the sensory information it receives. If we are exposed to noise the voice responds by becoming louder and when the noise stops we reduce the voice volume appropriately, sometimes after an embarrassing gap of a few seconds. There is much still to be learned about this feedback system. The trained singer can produce a more or less unimpaired voice even when his ears are exposed to noise drowning out all other auditory perception (personal communication J. Kirchner, Yale University, New Haven). Perhaps he has learned to make maximum use of the sensations arising in his vocal tract and can, at least for short periods, ignore auditory sensation. But the adult with perfectly normal speech if stricken with total deafness may suffer marked impairment in speech. Such persons require assistance from a speech teacher to maintain an intelligible speech. Some years ago in an experiment to measure subglottic pressure during phonation some of the anesthetic, in the needle tract through the cricothyroid membrane, was accidentally injected into my trachea. It apparently numbed the mucosa of my vocal cords, and, although I could talk intelligibly, I could no longer sing in an acceptable fashion. To me this signifies that some more delicate control is required for singing than talking and that sensory feedback from the mucosa of the vocal cords is a part of that control (10).

The power source for setting the vocal fold generator in action is the breathing apparatus and this will be discussed in Chap. 6. At this point we need only examine how the subglottic pressure produced by the breathing mechanism activates the vibratory motion of the folds (12, 17, 22, 25, 36, 38, 48, 53).

Some years ago it was suggested that vocal fold vibration resulted from rhythmic contractions of the vocalis muscle at the frequency of the desired pitch. This was labeled the neurochronaxic theory and was soon laid to rest by many who realized that such rapid contractions of a muscle are not physiologically possible. The current explanation is called the myoelastic theory (57). Simply stated this postulates the following series of actions. The vocal folds are approximated in the midline with just sufficient force for the build up of the desired subglottic pressure. When that pressure is achieved the folds part slightly and air flows between them. Immediately the elasticity of the folds combines with a negative pressure force in the airstream resulting from airflow (known as the Bernoulli effect) to bring the folds together (56). This process repeats itself at the frequency of the desired pitch, that frequency being determined by the factors discussed above. All of this occurs almost instantaneously so that we are generally unconscious of a time factor involved in the onset or continuance of phonation. Obviously the force with which the folds are approximated must be exactly that to match the desired subglottic pressure prior to the initiation of phonation if a sound of a given intensity is to result. The use of high speed recordings, especially high speed cinematography, has cast useful light on these events (26, 49).

Sound Intensity

The degree to which subglottic pressure is raised determines the energy with which the vibratory motion of the cords is instituted and maintained (36). Thus it controls the intensity or loudness of the tone that vibration engenders. For a constant intensity the mean subglottic pressure must be held constant in spite of the escape of air with each parting. Of course there will be very brief transitory falls in that pressure with each escape of air. Although

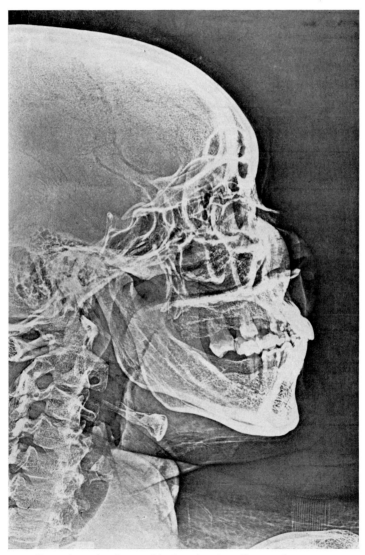

Fig. 35. Xeroradiograph (as in Fig. 8), this time showing all supraglottic structures. Pharynx and oral cavity are adjustable while nasal cavity and paranasal sinuses are relatively fixed resonators. Lowering of larynx in neck will lengthen the total supraglottic airway. See text and Fig. 36

this relationship between subglottic pressure and sound intensity holds generally true there are two exceptions. First, the pressure required for a given intensity will vary somewhat with the pitch of the tone being produced. In general somewhat higher pressures are required for higher tones, a fact probably related to the increased tenseness in the folds. Second, although we are capable of producing very high subglottic pressures (up to 100 cm H_2O and more), even the loudest tone requires no more than 50—60 cm H_2O and only seldom are pressures over 20 cm H_2O needed. Thus, excessive subglottic pressures may be inappropriate to phonation and result in abnormal use of the voice.

For efficient use of the breath, airflow through the vibrating vocal folds should be kept to a minimum (3, 35). In ordinary speech and song those flows range between 60 and 400 ml/sec. In most speech and song these phonatory airflows are less than the average flow during quiet expiration. The amount of flow varies somewhat with the intensity of the tone and with its pitch. Very low tones produced through relatively relaxed vocal folds require higher airflows. For reasons not entirely clear, but probably partly related to the subglottic pressures required, very soft and very loud tones require somewhat higher flows. In making speech sounds some consonants are produced at the expense of a momentary excess escape of air. The same is true of singing, but the trained singer learns to minimize that extra loss of air.

Resonance

Finally we must consider the role of the supraglottic spaces and organs in sound production (Fig. 35). The tuning fork (held in the air with no appropriate resonating chamber) produces a thin sound only audible a short distance away. The larynx (if activated outside the body) produces an ill defined buzz like sound. Within the body the fundamental frequency and its overtones produced in the larynx act upon the resonant chambers above and the result is the sound we know as voice. These resonant chambers react to various harmonics of the fundamental frequency and amplify them. Groups of these amplified harmonic vibrations are spoken of as formants (10). The nature and number of formants (within a certain frequency band) is determined by the length and shape of the air spaces made to resonate by the fundamental tone arising from the vibrating vocal folds. Ordinarily at least two such formants are clearly audible and make up part of perceived speech. In special circumstances additional formants play an important part in forming the total sound of the voice.

Speech

As we all know, we can produce a number of sounds with the tongue and lips with the vocal folds open and playing no active role in the sound production. We can make a blowing sound through pursed lips or a whistle on combining proper tongue and teeth position. We can click or trill the tongue against the palate and alveolar ridge. In fact a wide variety of sounds, including the well known "raspberry", can be produced by variations on these maneuvers. When sound originates in the larynx, appropriate positioning of tongue, palate, lips, and pharynx results in the various vowels and consonants necessary to speech. The vowels are a result of various combinations of formant frequencies coming from appropriate larynx, tongue, lip, and palate placements. Variations in such placement add the consonant sounds. For some sounds in addition to the subglottic pressure (40), a pressure drop across one or another closure above the glottis will result in an intraoral pressure (40).

Differences between the speech of different people are related to the natural fundamental tones arising in the larynx, the shape (and change in shape) of the resonant air column above, and especially the manner in which the tongue, lips, palate, and pharynx are employed during phonation. Poor diction may be simply a matter of laziness in using the various muscles involved. Deliberate immobilization of the parted lips will result in barely intelligible speech, and clearly intelligible speech is produced only when optimum use of appropriate muscles is employed. The role of the breathing mechanism in all of this will be taken up in Chaps. 6 and 7.

For the moment let us examine in more detail the events involved in producing a sustained tone. If we sing "ah" at a pitch somewhere in the comfortable middle register of the voice we find that we can vary the sound in a number of ways. The loudness can be increased by increasing the subglottic pressure. By changing the shape of the supraglottic air space we can change the ah (as in "calm") to a (as in "have") to aw (as in "ball"). The same is true for the other vowel sounds. Airflow can be held quite constant or can be increased by a change in the nature of apposition of the vocal folds. This can result in a "breathy" quality to the sound. Whether or not a configuration of the apposed vocal folds permitting escape of air through their posterior portion (see Fig. 32) should be included in "normal" phonation is to me an open question. There can be no question that that mechanism is sometimes employed; but, to my mind, this "waste" of air is incompatible with efficient sound production.

Whereas the variance in the shape of the supraglottic air column accounts for the various vowel sounds, the consonants depend upon the modification of sounds produced by the appropriate placement and movement of the lips, tongue, and palate (Fig. 36). Each consonant is produced by a particular action. In English the tongue, soft palate and lips are chiefly involved, but in other languages the uvula and pharynx probably play an essential part. Developments in exploration of the oceans and space have sometimes required the mixture of helium with the respired gases. The consequent change in gas density in the lungs affects airflow and results in a thin, high pitched voice difficult to understand (5, 41, 58).

Thus far we have covered some of the facts pertinent to an understanding of the mechanics of breathing, the nasal air conditioning system, and the larynx as an organ of sound production. Now let us turn to the application of these facts to an understanding of the role of breathing in voice production.

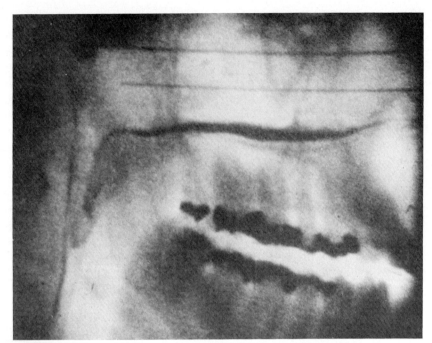

Fig. 36. Frame from cine during speech (compare with Figs. 27 and 28)

References

1. Ardran, G. M., Kemp, F. H. (1966): Mechanism of the larynx: Movements of arytenoid and cricoid cartilages. Brit. J. Radiol. *39*, 641—654.
2. Cavagna, G. A., Margaria, R. (1965): An analysis of the mechanics of phonation. J. Appl. Physiol. *20*, 301—307.
3. Cavagna, G. A., Margaria, R. (1968): Airflow rates and efficiency changes during phonation. Ann. N.Y. Acad. Sci. *155*, 152—164.
4. Cavagna, G. A., Camporesi, E. M. (1974): Glottic Aerodynamics and Phonation. In: Ventilatory and Phonatory Control Systems (Wyke, B., ed.), Chap. 6, 76—87. London: Oxford Univ. Press.
5. Cooke, J. P. (1964): Communication and sound transmission in helium and various gases at reduced pressures. Aerospace Med. *35*, 1050—1053.
6. Faaborg-Andersen, K. (1956): Action potentials from internal laryngeal muscles during phonation. Nature *177*, 340—341.
7. Faaborg-Andersen, K. (1957): Electromyographic investigation of intrinsic laryngeal muscles in humans. Acta Physiol. Scand. *41*, Suppl. 140.
8. Faaborg-Andersen, K. (1965): Electromyography of Laryngeal Muscles in Human. Basel: S. Karger.
9. Freedman, L. M. (1955): The role of the cricothyroid muscle in tension of the vocal cords. Arch. Otolaryngol. *62*, 347—353.
10. Gould, W. J., Tanabe, M. (1975): The effect of anesthesia of the internal branch of the superior laryngeal nerve upon phonation. Folia Phoniatr. *27*, 337—349.
11. Harless, E. (1853): Stimme, Handwörterbuch der Physiologie, Vol. 4, 562. Braunschweig: F. Vieweg.
12. Hast, M. H. (1961): Subglottic air pressure and neural stimulation in phonation. J. Appl. Physiol. *16*, 1142—1146.

13. Hast, M. H. (1967): Physiologic mechanisms of phonation: Tension of the vocal fold muscle. Acta Otolaryngol. *62*, 309—318.
14. Hirano, M. (1974): Morphological structure of the vocal cord as a vibrator and its variations. Folia Phoniatr. *26*, 89—94.
15. Hirose, H. (1976): Posterior cricoarytenoid as a speech muscle. Ann. Otol. *85* (3 pt. 1), 334—342.
16. House, A. S., Stevens, K. N. (1958): Estimation of formant band widths from measurements of transient response of the vocal tract. J. Speech Hearing Res. *1*, 309—315.
17. Isshiki, N. (1964): Regulatory mechanism of voice intensity variation. J. Speech Hearing Res. *7*, 17—29.
18. Kay, R. H. (1966): The independence of vocal frequency vibrato from the tuning of the vocal resonators. J. Physiol. *186*, 5—6.
19. Khambata, A. S. (1977): Anatomy and Physiology of Voice Production: The Phenomenal Voice. In: Music and the Brain (Critchley, M., Henson, R. A., eds.), Chap. 5, 59—77. Springfield: Charles C Thomas.
20. Kirchner, J. A., Wyke, B. D. (1965): Articular reflex mechanisms in the larynx. Ann. Otol. *74*, 749—768.
21. Koike, Y., Hirano, M. (1973): Glottal-area time function and subglottal-pressure variation. J. Acoust. Soc. Amer. *54*, 1618—1627.
22. Ladefoged, P. (1960): The regulation of subglottic pressure. Folia Phoniatr. *12*, 169—175.
23. Ladefoged, P. (1962): Elements of Acoustic Phonetics. Univ. Chicago Press.
24. Ladefoged, P. (1974): Respiration, Laryngeal Activity and Linguistics. In: Ventilatory and Phonatory Control Systems (Wyke, B., ed.), Chap. 18, 299—306. London: Oxford Univ. Press.
25. Lamm, H., Schaffrath, H. (1967): Druckwechselvorgänge in der gesunden menschlichen Kieferhöhle beim Singen und Sprechen. Z. Laryngol. Rhinol. *46*, 403—409.
26. LeBel, C. J., Dunbar, J. Y. (1951): Ultra speed recording for acoustical measurement. J. Acoust. Soc. Amer. *23*, 559—563.
27. Leden, H. v., Moore, P., Timcke, R. (1960): Laryngeal vibrations: measurements of the glottic wave. Arch. Otolaryngol. *71*, 16—35.
28. Leden, H. v., Moore, P. (1961): The mechanics of the cricoarytenoid joint. Arch. Otolaryngol. *73*, 541—550.
29. Lieberman, P. (1968): Vocal cord motion in man. Ann. N.Y. Acad. Sci. *155*, 28—38.
30. Lind, J. (Ed.) (1965): Newborn Infant Cry. Uppsala: Almqvist and Wiksell.
31. Malcolm, J. E. (1974): Resonant Cavities, Dipole Resonance and Phonation: a Description of the Upper Respiratory Tract in Engineering Terms. In: Ventilatory and Phonatory Control Systems (Wyke, B., ed.), Chap. 16, 265—270. London: Oxford Univ. Press.
32. Margaria, R., Cavagna, G. (1959): Il rendimento meccanico della fonazione. Boll. Soc. Ital. Biol. Sper. *35*, 2075—2077, 2077—2079.
33. Martensson, A. (1968): The functional organization of the intrinsic laryngeal muscles. Ann. N.Y. Acad. Sci. *155*, 91—97.
34. McGlone, R. E., Richmond, W. H., Bosma, J. F. (1966): A physiological model for investigation of the fundamental frequency of phonation. Folia Phoniatr. *18*, 109—116.
35. McGlone, R. E. (1967): Air flow during vocal fry phonation. J. Speech Hearing Res. *10*, 299—304.
36. Mead, J., Bouhuys, A., Proctor, D. F. (1968): Mechanisms generating subglottic pressure. Ann. N.Y. Acad. Sci. *155*, 177—181.
37. Negus, V. E., Neil, E., Floyd, W. F. (1957): The mechanism of phonation. Ann. Otol. *66*, 817—829.
38. Perkins, W. H., Koike, Y. (1969): Patterns of subglottal pressure variations during phonation. Folia Phoniatr. *21*, 1—8.
39. Portmann, G., Robin, J. L., Laget, P., Husson, R. (1956): La myographie des cordes vocales. Acta Otolaryngol. *46*, 250—263.
40. Proffit, W. R., Fogle, J. L., Heitlinger, L. W., Christiansen, R. L., McGlone, R. E. (1966): Dynamic calibration of lingual pressure transducers. J. Appl. Physiol. *21*, 1417—1420.
41. Sergeant, R. L. (1968): Voice communication problems in spacecraft and underwater operations. Ann. N.Y. Acad. Sci. *155*, 342—350.

42. Shelton, R. L., Bosma, J. F., Sheets, B. V. (1960): Tongue, hyoid and larynx displacement in swallow and phonation. J. Appl. Physiol. *15*, 283—288.
43. Siegel, G. M., Pick, H. L., jr. (1974): Auditory feedback in the regulation of voice. J. Acoust. Soc. Amer. *56*, 1618—1624.
44. Sokolowsky, R. R. (1943): Effect of the extrinsic laryngeal muscles on voice production. Arch. Otolaryngol. *38*, 355—364.
45. Sonninen, A. A. (1956): The role of the external laryngeal muscles in length-adjustment of the vocal cords in singing. Acta Otolaryngol. Suppl. *130*, 1—102.
46. Stevens, K. N. (1964): Acoustical Aspects of Speech Production. In: Handbook of Physiology, Respiration I (Fenn, W. O., Rahn, H., eds.), Chap. 9, 347—356. Washington: Amer. Physiol. Soc.
47. Stevens, K. N., Klatt, D. H. (1974): Current Models of Sound Sources for Speech. In: Ventilatory and Phonatory Control Systems (Wyke, B., ed.), Chap. 17, 279—291. London: Oxford Univ. Press.
48. Strenger, F. (1960): Methods for direct and indirect determination of the subglottic air pressure. Studia Linguistica *14*, 98—112.
49. Tanabe, M., Kitajima, K., Gould, W. J., Lambiase, A. (1975): Analysis of high-speed motion pictures of the vocal folds. Folia Phoniatr. *27*, 77—87.
50. Timcke, R., Leden, H. v., Moore, P. (1959): Laryngeal vibrations: measurements of the glottic wave. Arch. Otolaryngol. *69*, 438—444.
51. Titze, I. R. (1976): On the mechanics of vocal-fold vibration. J. Acoust. Soc. Amer. *60*, 1366—1380.
52. Van den Berg, J. (1955): Transmission of the vocal cavities. J. Acoust. Soc. Amer. *27*, 161—168.
53. Van den Berg, J. (1956): Direct and indirect determination of the mean subglottic pressure. Folia Phoniatr. *8*, 1—24.
54. Van den Berg, J. (1956): Physiology and physics of voice production. Acta Physiol. Pharmacol. Neerl. *5*, 40—55.
55. Van den Berg, J. (1957): Microphonic effect of the larynx. Nature *179*, 625—626.
56. Van den Berg, J., Zantema, J. T., Doornenbal, P. (1957): On the air resistance and the Bernoulli effect of the human larynx. J. Acoust. Soc. Amer. *29*, 626—631.
57. Van den Berg, J. (1958): Myoelastic-aerodynamic theory of voice production. J. Speech Hearing Res. *1*, 227—244.
58. Wather-Dunn, W., Michaels, S. B. (1968): Some effects of gas density on speech production. Ann. N.Y. Acad. Sci. *155*, 368—378.
59. Wustrow, F., Wieck, H. H. (1963): Elektromyographische Untersuchungen am menschlichen M. vocalis und ihre Bedeutung für die Theorie über die Entstehung der Stimmlippenschwingung. Z. Laryngol. Rhinol. *42*, 118—129.

Breathing Mechanics and Phonation   6

We have now devoted five chapters to a discussion of morphology and function, a discussion necessary to any depth of understanding of the human voice. Now we must go on to the application of that information to the problems of speech and song. In this chapter our purpose is to examine the modifications of the process of breathing necessary for normal sound production.

In his excellent chapter in "Music and the Brain" Sears (28) makes the following comment:

"Most descriptions of breath control during singing somehow manage to obscure the fact that it is the sub-glottal pressure which plays the vital role in regulating sound intensity ... the voice teacher must inevitably resort to descriptions of the airflow and its control and attempt to relate these to where he expects the singer to perceive the location of his sense of vocal effort in order to achieve the desired vocal end result."

It is indeed the control of subglottic pressure which is the key to the major problem of breathing in phonation, especially in artistic singing and I shall return to it again and again. In this chapter I will discuss the way in which the breathing mechanism is employed to control that vital factor in phonation (2, 16, 26, 27, 32). But first let us consider some of the ways in which breathing in connection with phonation differs from that more simple use of the mechanism described in Chap. 3.

Phonation and Respiration

The primary purpose of breathing is the ventilation of the alveolar spaces at such a rate as to maintain constant blood gas pressures. We do not have to learn that process. In the healthy subject a variety of homeostatic physiological mechanisms drive the breathing pump at just the appropriate rate to accomplish this whether at rest or during exercise. When we utilize the breath for phonation we are voluntarily interfering with these vital controls. In doing so to whatever degree we disturb alveolar ventilation our blood gases will be altered; and, if that occurs to more than a mild degree (hypo- or hyperventilation), unpleasant symptoms will ensue. Thus, in considering the application of breathing mechanics to phonation we are confronted with two problems. First, how relatively normal alveolar ventilation is maintained, and second, how breathing mechanics are modified for optimum application to the production of speech and song.

It turns out that the first of these is not a serious problem. Evidently the body's homeostatic mechanisms override our voluntary efforts to distort them and dictate a breathing-with-phonation pattern which prevents any gross alteration in blood gases. This override usually results in a slightly excessive adjustment so that, if anything, we slightly hyperventilate with speech and probably with song (3, 24, 25). Some of the minute volumes required for various phonatory maneuvers are shown in Fig. 42.

In the excellent investigations by Bunn and Mead (3, 21) they found that the hyperventilation accompanying reading aloud reduced blood CO_2 from the level of 39 mm Hg found in quiet breathing to about 37.5 mm Hg. This was not accompanied by any sensation of hyperventilation. In the same study they found that the increase in pulmonary ventilation normally following exposure to CO_2 (in this case 3—4 %) was obtunded when the exposure occurred during phonation. Thus slight hyperventilation accompanied phonation but the ventilatory response to elevated CO_2 was reduced. In regard to phonation with exercise they comment that, "if at rest speech tends to come in paragraphs, during exercise the unit tends toward the sentence and, in heavy exercise, the gasped phrase". The hyperventilation accompanying speech is partially compensated for by "quick nonphonated expirations", and (at the end of speaking) periods of apnea might occur as long as 18 seconds.

The problem is complex when we phonate during exercise. Under that condition two phenomena are of interest. First, for talking during vigorous exercise we use shorter phrases interspersed with deeper breaths. In extreme conditions phonation becomes difficult as the physiological demands for pulmonary ventilation reach the maximum of which we are capable (see Ref. 51 in Chap. 7). Second, is the action we choose when we are using the muscles of the upper extremities for heavy work. Their optimum implementation is facilitated by a fixation of their attachments to the chest wall. We automatically take a deep breath and close the glottis in wielding a heavy blow with an axe. Often that action is followed by a grunt as the ensuing expiration occurs. It is a common practice for groups working together to engage in singing as seen in chaingang songs or sea chanteys. Some of our folk music has such an origin. The song serves two purposes. It provides a rhythm to assure appropriate concerted effort. It also provides a relatively fixed chest during loud singing to facilitate the optimum use of the arms.

Breathing Mechanics in Phonation

Now let us return to the physiology of breathing mechanics discussed in Chap. 3. In its application to phonation multiple factors need to be considered. First, we need to breathe in (between phrases) enough air to keep up with the demands of respiration and to enable us to produce the next phrase without an awkward pause in the flow of speech or song. Second, we need to have enough air in the lungs to readily sustain phonation during the completion of a phrase. As a general rule we are physically more comfortable at a lung volume near to or above F.R.C. than at lower lung volumes. This matter of simple comfort probably partly accounts for the fact that phonation is generally initiated after a greater than usual breath (14, 18). Third, we need to control the subglottic pressure at the level required for the desired sound intensity (30, 31, and Ref. 34 in Chap. 5). Fourth, we wish to limit airflow to that necessary for sound production to facilitate completion of the phrase without the necessity for an inappropriate pause for a new breath and to avoid a thin "breathy" tone (16, 24). Cavagna (see Ref. 3 in Chap. 5) has shown that it is possible to produce similar tones with widely varying airflows. But to my mind only one flow can be correct. That is the minimal flow compatible with the pitch and intensity desired. All of these factors are relatively simple problems in ordinary conversation, somewhat more complex for the deliverance of a speech, and far more complicated for effective singing.

Lung Volumes

Let us give some further consideration to the first factor mentioned above. Even in quiet conversation we usually begin talking at a lung volume some-what higher than that at the end of a normal quiet inspiration. Since we are anxious to proceed from phrase to phrase without undue interruption, this volume of inspired air is taken in rather quickly. The lips are parted in speaking and they remain so during the interspersed inspirations. Thus at least part of the inspiratory airflow is through the mouth (Fig. 37). The main-tenance of a relatively constant subglottic pressure and the conservation of expiratory airflow are of minor importance in quiet speech and we need give them little attention here. We should strive for a euphonious and intelligible speech, and effective voice production is of special importance to those whose livelihoods require a great deal of talking, but we shall return to this in Chap. 7. For public speaking the production of a relatively loud voice, effective use of phrasing, and uninterrupted flow of idea are essential. To accomplish these, somewhat deeper breaths are required and the main-tenance of an appropriate subglottic pressure and conservation of airflow are more important (4, 12, 13, 14).

Hoshiko (13) studied the lung volume chosen for initiation of speech in 30 male and 30 female subjects. He found this volume to approximate 50 %

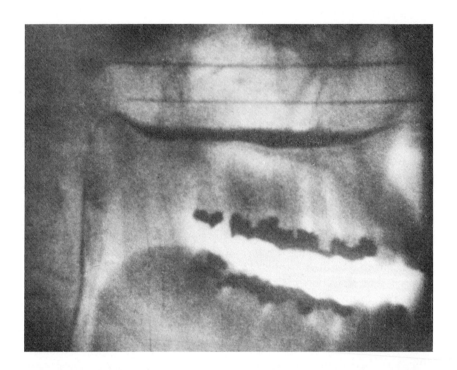

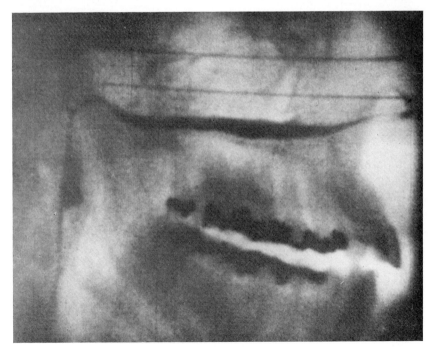

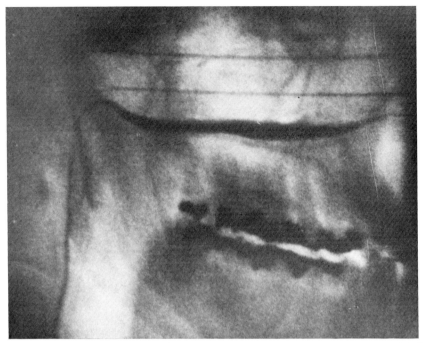

Fig. 37. Frames from cine during talking and singing (compare Figs. 27, 28, 36). Left below, during an inspiration concluding song phrase and, left above, during voluntary hyperventilation. In the breath associated with singing the tongue is drawn downward and forward widening the airway but this is an intermediary position between the extreme wide airway of deep breathing (left above) and the narrow airway for breathing in conversation (above)

of the V.C. but the standard deviation among his subjects amounted to 9 to 12 %. I would suggest that those who chose the larger volumes were making more effective use of breathing in phonation and those who chose the lower volumes were relatively ineffective speakers.

Isshiki *et al.* (15) have pointed out that, owing to the positive airway pressure, even with maximum expiratory effort there is more air in the chest at the end of phonation than after forced expiration with the glottis open. That means that one cannot continue quite to R.V. while phonating, and the higher the subglottic pressure at that point the larger must be the volume of air left in the lungs.

As we shall see later on, singing is most easily and effectively accomplished at the higher lung volumes, although the trained singer can continue singing nearly down to his R.V. when necessary (Fig. 38). For that reason the singer begins to sing very near to his full lung volume (T.L.C.) and returns as closely as possible to it each time he is able to do so (that is whenever time between phrases permits). Since inspirations during a song must often be taken during very brief pauses (sometimes imperceptible to an audience) they take place through a widened low resistance oropharyngeal airway (Fig. 37). Although the singer is anxious to achieve a deep inspiration in a minimum of time he is equally anxious to avoid the awkward appearance of effort. A maximum quick breath in is accomplished by adding all the accessory muscles of breathing to the diaphragm and the inspiratory intercostals. The singer learns to employ those latter two to maximum advantage while minimizing the use of other muscles, employment of which is readily visible to the onlooker.

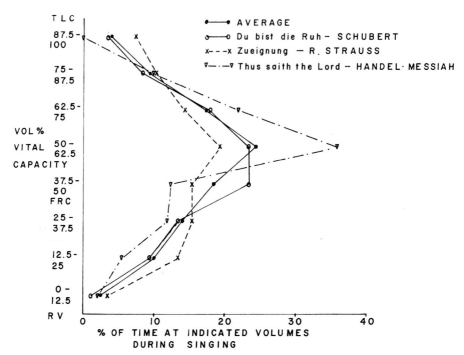

Fig. 38. Percent of time spent during the singing of the three indicated songs at the volumes indicated on the left (figures refer to volume ranges, 87.5 to 100 % V.C., etc.). On the average (solid line, closed circles) most time is at 50 to 62.5 % of vital capacity, but about 3 % of time is spent at volumes below 12.5 % and about 5 % above 87.5 % of vital capacity. The shorter phrases of the recitative from "Messiah" and the longer phrases of "Zueignung" are reflected by less time at low volumes in the former and greater than average in the latter

Muscle Control

As promised in Chap. 3 this is a good place to elaborate a little on the employment of the diaphragm and the abdominal muscles in phonation, especially in the performance of the well trained singer. We have already mentioned that the singer must learn to use the diaphragm and inspiratory intercostals with great efficiency. Although only occasionally is an inspiration to T.L.C. necessary in a fraction of a second, exercises directed at perfection of this rapid deep inspiration through a widened oropharyngeal airway are essential. The lips need not be widely separated. One does not wish to present the unesthetic appearance of a fish out of water in which this would result; but the base of the tongue is lowered and moved forward to provide a low resistance passage (see Figs. 28, 37, and 52). Actually these are some of the characteristics of the supraglottic airway for optimum resonance and therefore should come naturally to the accomplished performer.

Once full, or nearly full, lung volume is achieved and the vocal folds are approximated for phonation the diaphragmatic activity ceases and this muscle becomes a relatively flaccid membrane interposed between the intercostals and abdominals which take over at that point. Subtle changes in airflow and subglottic pressure are largely controlled by a balance between expiratory and inspiratory intercostal muscle activity, particularly at lung volumes above F.R.C. (see Ref. 19 in Chap. 1). Relatively loud tones (requiring high subglottic pressures) at all lung volumes, and continuance of even soft singing at lung volumes between F.R.C. and R.V. require abdominal muscle activity.

Although the intercostal muscle action seems to be more or less unconscious it is desirable that abdominal muscles be consciously controlled. When one feels a sense of strain in the upper chest and neck during full crescendos or at the end of long phrases, improper technique is being employed. Instead, with the onset of crescendo, or as lung volume decreases, a distinct feeling of easy compression of the abdominal wall should begin low down and move progressively upward. As the abdominal wall moves inward there should be a sense of absolutely effortless swelling or continuity of tone. In that manner only can relatively high subglottic pressures be achieved and low lung volumes be used without any awkward appearance or feeling of "squeezing" on the chest. To accomplish these ends very fine control of abdominal muscles must be achieved. In these respects especially, breathing in phonation differs grossly from that with exercise. In the latter the forces of breathing mechanics are directed at one main object, increase in pulmonary ventilation. Usually no more than 50 to 75 % of the vital capacity is employed, airflow is rapid, and any awkward appearance of effort is relatively unimportant. In phonation there is no need for increase in minute ventilation, nearly all of the vital capacity is employed, airflows are kept low, and a graceful effortless appearance is highly desirable.

There is no doubt in my mind that mastery of this sort of muscle control is a major factor characterizing the skilled vocal performer. Most experienced singers can recall the satisfaction which came with the development of the easy use of the abdominal wall muscles to provide the necessary supplementary force required for full, rich tones and for the graceful completion of long musical phrases on a single breath. These points are also of importance in maintaining the low subglottic pressure during the sustaining of tones of low intensity. One puzzling point about the use of lung volumes in actual performance is the fact that certain phrases, of a duration well under the time during which a performer is capable of sustaining a single tone, are quite difficult to negotiate in a single breath. I remember such difficulties in several phrases in the recitative "Thus saith the Lord" and the aria "But who may abide" in Handel's "Messiah". In the former the final "and the desire . . .", and in the latter "and who shall stand when He appear . . . eth?" are typical of this phenomenon. Actually the phrases in these selections have durations from only 10 to 19 seconds and I could readily sustain a single tone for 45 seconds. It appears to me that the vocal maneuvers necessary in such songs are almost inevitably associated with some air leakage. Indeed, unless the music will not permit it, the smoother a legato employed in such phrases the more readily they can be negotiated on a single breath. In any event it is clear that phrases longer than 20 seconds in duration are quite rare.

Although most of what I have just written in this section on muscle control is to my mind more or less beyond dispute, our physiological knowledge of the exact events is still incomplete. Dr. Jere Mead wrote to me in June, 1977, ". . . ironically, our approach to measuring chest wall mechanics . . . has never really been put to adequate use in singing. . . . The thought that I have had that I would pursue is that singers are taught to breathe in with their bellies and sing from belly-out posture so that the diaphragm may be maintained as slack as possible throughout phonation. Once the passive diaphragm comes under tension it exerts an inspiratory influence against which the phonator must strain . . ." (Personal communication from Dr. J. Mead, Harvard School of Public Health, Boston). It seems obvious to me that, if maximum use of the abdominal muscles is to be made, they should be nearly fully relaxed (belly-out) at the end of full inspiration.

In a letter from Dr. Beverly Bishop in 1977, in response to my suggestion "that the singer relaxes his diaphragm almost immediately as sound begins, and the control of airflow and subglottic pressure is left to a balance between intercostal and abdominal muscle activity", she makes the following comments. "The diaphragm, in comparison to the other major respiratory muscles, has relatively weak segmental control. . . . From observations on diaphragm activity in anesthetized cats, I have always been impressed with the instantaneous responsiveness of the diaphragm to even the slightest ventilatory perturbation. . . . In contrast, the expiratory activity of the abdominal muscles is stereotyped and limited." In view of these facts it is quite clear that the inactivity of the diaphragm and the carefully controlled strong action of abdominal muscles during sound production are, in the view of respiratory physiology, "unnatural" acts. They must be learned in the process of voice training. It is my feeling that the inactive phonatory role of the diaphragm is in part learned early in life with the beginning of speech; but the control of the abdominals may never be learned unless it is given careful attention. Dr. Bishop then goes on to say, "It is true that the intercostals, diaphragm and abdominal muscles all attach to the ribs. This 'tethering', as you called it, mechanically couples them and provides a mechanism by which each 'can know' what the others are doing through neural feedback" (personal communication from Dr. B. Bishop, Department of Physiology, State University of New York at Buffalo). It is worthy of emphasis that further investigation is necessary before we fully understand all the differences between proper and improper singing in these respects.

For those especially interested in the question of relative thoracoabdominal movement in speech and song I recommend the long but splendid papers of

Hixon, Mead and co-workers (9, 10). Their techniques permit them to write with authority on the subject, although even their work leaves some questions incompletely answered. In one paper (9) they conclude that during the utterance of speech "... forces were operating to make the rib cage larger and the abdomen correspondingly smaller than they were during relaxation at the prevailing volume." This could reflect the important role of abdominal muscles, with or without inspiratory intercostals, in maintaining the required subglottic pressure. In a later report (10) they conclude that "... the abdomen occupies an especially important role in running conversational speech in that it mechanically tunes the diaphragm to increase the latter's inspiratory efficiency and thus enables man to minimally interrupt his ongoing speech for needed inspiratory pauses." That "tuning" is apparently accomplished through maintenance of expiratory tone in the abdominal muscles during inspiration. Such expiratory tone must not be sufficient to interfere with the "belly-out" posture mentioned above after the quote from Dr. Mead. This is a matter of delicate and exact balance.

But now let us return to the forces brought to bear on the airways after the individual has taken in a maximum deep breath. To understand this we need to go back to the integration of forces described

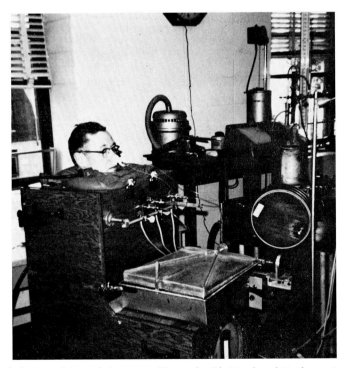

Fig. 39. Technique used in experiments at Harvard with Mead and Bouhuys. Author seated in plethysmograph with airtight seal around neck and nasal catheters leading to esophageal and gastric balloons. (Used with permission of Editor, J. Appl. Physiol., from Bouhuys, A., Proctor, D. F., Mead, J. [1966]: Kinetic aspects of singing, *21*, 483—496)

in Chap. 3. Some years ago Drs. Jere Mead, Arend Bouhuys and myself engaged in studies of breathing during phonation carried out at the Harvard School of Public Health. The findings, combined with the pioneering work of many other investigators, now enable us to speak objectively about this complex subject.

Physiological Studies

Numerous methods have been employed to study respiratory events during phonation (30, 31). An esophageal balloon placed high in the esophagus behind the trachea yields a rough measure of subglottic pressure. A needle passed through the cricothyroid space into the trachea gives an accurate measure of subglottic pressure but involves some discomfort in its passage and in connection with singing. Airflow can be measured with a pneumotachometer attached to a face mask, and that mask can be divided to give separate measures of nasal and oral airflow. Unfortunately no such mask has yet been designed to avoid interference with phonation. Cineradiographic techniques can be used to visualize the structures in the supraglottic regions and the film can be synchronized with physiological measurements. The X-ray exposure involved limits such studies to a very brief time in any one subject. Special methods have been employed to follow relative motion of chest and abdomen (9, 10, 22). Electromyographic recordings yield information on the activity of individual muscles (11, 12, 13, 19). Most studies of details of laryngeal neuromuscular physiology are conducted in the experimental animal (17), but some are done in man (see Ref. 58 in Chap. 5).

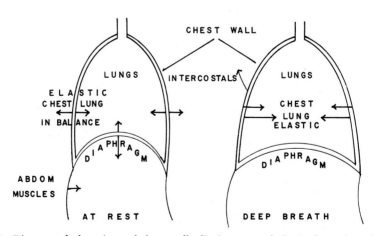

Fig. 40. Diagram of alterations of chest wall, diaphragm, and elastic forces in going from F.R.C. (left) to T.L.C. (right). Note abdominal muscles must relax to accomodate downward movement of diaphragm. When diaphragm is relaxed abdominal muscles influence relative change in lung volume. (Used with permission of the Editor, N.Y. Acad. Sci., from Proctor, D. F. [1968]: The physiologic basis of voice training, *155*, 208—228)

In our studies the subject was seated in a body plethysmograph (Fig. 39) through which lung volumes and airflow could be accurately followed (2, 27). Esophageal and gastric balloons enabled us to measure subglottic and transdiaphragmatic pressure. Before and after each tone, phrase, or song a vital capacity was performed so that volume events could be related to it. As the subject of many of the experiments I can testify that the procedure did not make performance difficult or uncomfortable.

In Chaps. 2 and 3 I have used a simple model (balloon-bellows) to point out the nature of the forces involved. Now let us substitute the thoracic cage for the bellows and the lungs for the balloon (Figs. 40 and 41). In these figures we see a diagram of the forces (Fig. 40) and in Fig. 41 pressures are represented as seen in the pleural space resulting from the elastic force of the lungs (solid line) and the elastic force of the chest wall (dashed line). Without

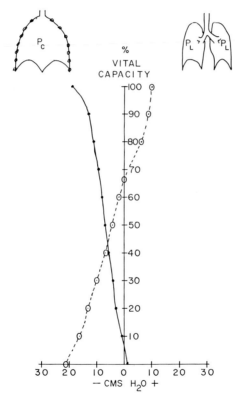

Fig. 41. Compare with Figs. 13, 22. In this figure the solid line shows the pressure around the lungs necessary to inflate them to the indicated volume, and (dashed line) the pressures necessary to place the rib cage at indicated volumes. With the lungs within the thorax the negative pressure in the pleural space required to inflate the lungs (produced by inspiratory muscle force) becomes a positive pressure within the lungs when inspiratory muscle force is relaxed against the closed glottis. Thus subglottic pressure (at any given lung volume) will equal the pressure indicated in the dashed line (chest) plus the lung pressure (solid line) but now with a reversed sign (+ 28 cm H_2O at 100 % V.C., + 9 cm H_2O at 66 % V.C., 0 cm H_2O at 43 % V.C., and —14 cm H_2O at 10 % V.C.)

muscular effort it is the sum of these two pressures which is available at any given lung volume from elastic forces alone to produce air flow or, with the glottis closed, to produce subglottic pressure. Thus, at full lung volume, some 25 to 30 cm H_2O positive pressure arise from that source alone, while at 10 % of the vital capacity some 15 cm H_2O pressure (this time negative) are applied. In this subject at about 43 % of V.C. the sum of the pressures is zero and this is F.R.C. Shortly we will apply these facts to the problem of creating subglottic pressure in phonation. For the moment let us consider their significance to the employment of the breathing muscles in phonation.

For most speech the lung volumes employed are those not very far removed from F.R.C. with only some 40 to 50 % of the V.C. involved. Therefore, the inspiratory muscles are brought into play only a little in excess of their use in quiet breathing and expiratory effort supplements the forces available from elastic sources alone largely for purposes of emphasis. Minute volumes are only moderately in excess of those in quiet breathing while in singing they may, over short periods, range from relatively low to a quite high value (Fig. 42).

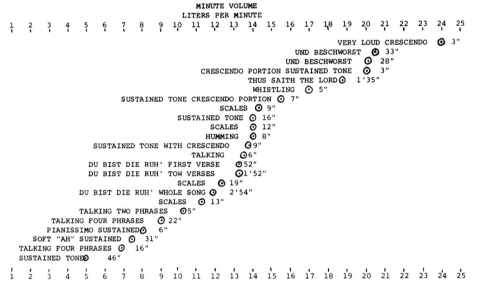

Fig. 42. Minute volumes (expiratory) under varying conditions of phonation. The times occupied by each maneuver are indicated in min and sec to the right. Thus the "sustained tone" (9th from top) occupied 16 sec. The two verses of "Du bist die Ruh'" (10th from bottom) occupied 1 min 52 sec. Very small airflow, less than 90 cc/sec, is indicated for the sustained tone (bottom), while high flow occurred for the loud tone (top) 400 cc/sec

But in singing, where nearly the whole of the vital capacity may be required, we have a different story. This is epitomized in the singing of a single tone of low to moderate intensity, that is with relatively low subglottic pressure (Fig. 43). From the facts shown in Fig. 41 it is apparent that, for such a maneuver, it is necessary to counteract the elastic forces at the top of V.C.

with inspiratory effort, to steadily reduce that effort as positive elastic forces reduce with falling lung volume, and finally to bring in increasing expiratory effort to sustain the tone at lower lung volumes.

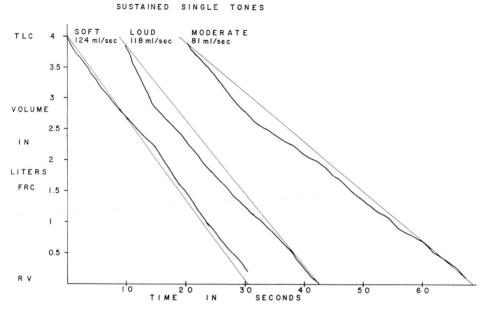

Fig. 43. Chart of volume change during the singing of three single tones. In each nearly the full vital capacity was employed. The lowest flow occurred in the tone of moderate intensity (right) thus enabling its sustaining for 46 sec, while for the tone sung softly (left) higher flows limited it to 30 sec. Had the tones been sung more perfectly the actual volume changes (wavy lines) would have been closer to the constant flow indicated by the straight lines. (This figure and Figs. 38, 44, 47, 49, 50 used with the permission of the Editor, from Proctor, D. F. (1974): Breathing Mechanics During Phonation and Singing. In: Ventilatory and Phonatory Control Systems [Wyke, B., ed.], Chap. 4. London: Oxford Univ. Press)

To appreciate these events we must now return to the subject with which this chapter opened, subglottic pressure. As shown in Fig. 44, phonation never demands the pressures which we are capable of producing (see Fig. 32 in Chap. 5). Subglottic pressure in singing varies between about 5 and 35 cm H_2O (rarely going as high as 50 to 60). If we are to produce a sound of exactly the desired intensity the muscular force required must be exactly applied in relation to the elastic force available, in turn related to the lung volume at any given moment (15, 23). Ladefoged (19) has shown this beautifully in relation to a single sustained tone (Fig. 45). At D is shown diaphragmatic activity supplemented by the external intercostals (E) for the inspiration preceding and following the tone. Since the elastic forces available to produce subglottic pressure are in excess of the pressure required at the top of V.C. inspiratory effort must counteract them (11). The diaphragm, a major inspiratory muscle, plays no part in this and remains a passive structure until the next breath in. The external intercostals are equipped with muscle

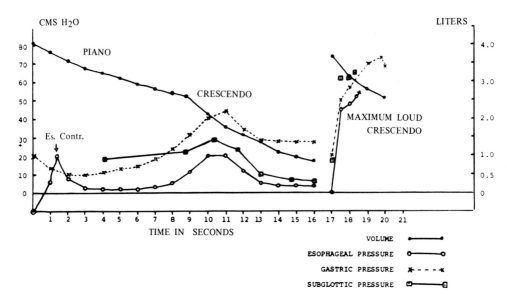

Fig. 44. Chart showing changes in volume, esophageal pressure, gastric pressure, and sub-glottic pressure during the singing of a soft tone leading into a crescendo (left) and a maximum loud crescendo (right). *Es. Contr.* indicates an artifact owing to esophageal contraction. Note the maximum subglottic pressure of some 60 cm H_2O during the loud crescendo, the highest recorded during our studies

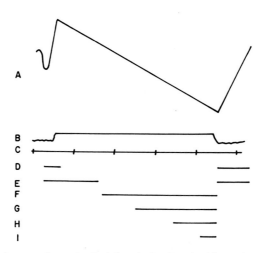

Fig. 45. Redrawn from a figure in Ladefoged, P. (1967): Three Areas of Experimental Phonetics, London: Oxford University Press. Ladefoged recorded pressure and volume events simultaneously with electromyograms from the indicated muscle groups. *A* volume, *B* subglottic pressure, *C* time, *D* diaphragm, *E* external intercostals, *F* internal intercostals, *G* abdominal external oblique, *H* rectus abdominis, *I* latissimus dorsi. See text for interpretation

spindles, which make their fine control comparable to the delicate muscles of the fingers (see Ref. 11 in Chap. 7), and supply the required inspiratory effort. As lung volume decreases that effort is no longer needed and the now necessary expiratory supplementation of the elastic forces comes first from the internal intercostals, in turn supplemented by abdominal muscles and finally, to some degree, accessory muscles.

If we now return to our pressure diagrams (Fig. 46) we see the diminishing inspiratory effort and increasing expiratory effort required for the singing of a soft tone (hatched areas). For a very loud tone elastic forces must be supplemented by expiratory effort from the moment of attack and that effort must be delicate at first, steadily increase, and be very strong indeed to continue this intensity near R.V.

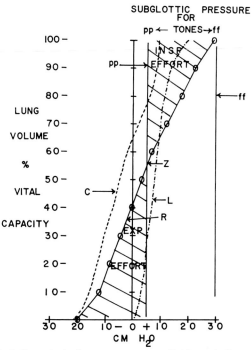

Fig. 46. The dot-dash line *(L)* indicates pressure available at indicated volumes from lung elastic force, the dashed line *(C)* that from chest elastic, and the solid line *(R)* the sum of the two (the subglottic pressure produced against a closed glottis with total muscle relaxation). The two vertical lines *(pp* and *ff)* represent the subglottic pressures required for a soft and a loud tone. The hatched areas show the inspiratory and expiratory muscle force required for the soft tone (zero at Z volume). For the loud tone increasing expiratory force would be required from the onset

It has been suggested that control of expiratory flow during the performance of a long musical phrase may be effected by laryngeal muscle tone (1, 5). But any change in the tone of the key muscle which would be so involved, the vocalis or thyroarytenoid, will affect pitch. It is my view that appropriate

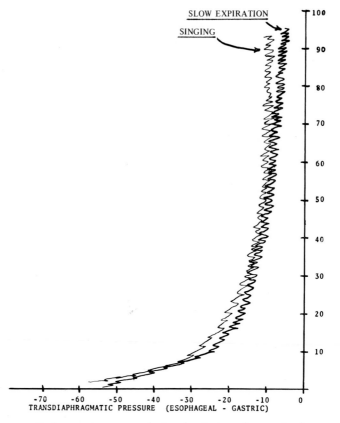

Fig. 47. The transdiaphragmatic pressure during the singing of a sustained tone compared to that during a slow expiratory vital capacity, a maneuver where the diaphragm is known to be relaxed

flow in phonation at lower lung volumes can only be accomplished by fine control of the abdominal muscles and/or the intercostals.

Thus we see that the production of a tone of any given intensity requires the appropriate subglottic pressure. This is accomplished by the exact blending of inspiratory and expiratory muscle effort with the elastic force associated with the lung volume at the time. This blending is largely produced through a balancing of the abdominal muscles against or with those of the chest wall across a relaxed diaphragm, occasionally supplemented by accessory expiratory muscles. Evidence for the passivity of the diaphragm is shown in Fig. 48 (9, 10, 21, 22, 29). Here the transdiaphragmatic pressure during the singing of a sustained tone is compared to that pressure during a maneuver known to be associated with diaphragmatic passivity, a slow expiratory vital capacity (Fig. 47). Their near identity is obvious (see Ref. 2 in Chap. 3).

Figs. 48 and 49 show other data from our studies casting further light on these problems. In Fig. 49 is charted a maneuver in which the esophageal pressure is recorded during the singing of an interrupted tone through the

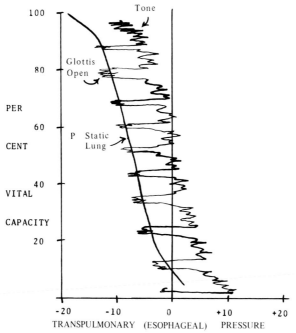

Fig. 48. The esophageal pressure compared to that resulting from lung elasticity (P Static Lung) during the singing of a tone, interrupted at intervals. Distance between the recorded pressure (Tone) and the P Static Lung line equals the subglottic pressure. The fluctuations in the pressure trace (right) are attributable to heart beats

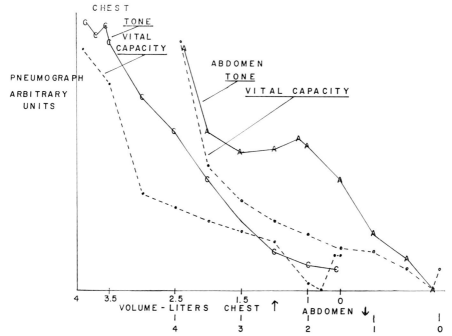

Fig. 49. Changes in chest and abdominal girth during the singing of a sustained tone and the performance of an expiratory vital capacity. Chest girth is shown at left and abdominal at right. Solid line indicates "tone" and broken line "vital capacity". See text for interpretation

vital capacity. The return of that pressure to the static pressure line (lung elastic) during each interruption is shown, and the difference between the pressure and that line during singing is a measure of the subglottic pressure.

The data obtained for Fig. 49 were obtained with the singer wearing pneumographs around the abdomen and chest. The more or less parallel reduction in chest and abdominal girth during a vital capacity is compared with that occurring during the singing of a sustained tone. It is evident that during singing a sharp early reduction in abdominal girth (probably associated with an initial rise in the passive diaphragm) is followed by a period in which chest girth alone is reduced and finally, as F.R.C. is passed, steadily decreasing abdominal girth.

Muscle Training

An interesting question has been raised by Gould. How far is it possible to increase breathing capacity and efficiency with training? Indeed we might begin with another question, is it necessary for a person to have a certain minimum breathing capacity to become a successful singer? It appears that anyone with an average normal lung capacity and function can perform adequately (see Ref. 27 in Chap. 8 for substantiation of this statement). The larger lung capacities will make the management of long phrases easier, and a very low capacity might prevent the performance of phrases lasting over 20 seconds, of which there are very few in music. The size of the chest and lungs has nothing to do with the resonance of the voice. Gould believes that the process of voice training results in an alteration of lung volumes (6, 7). The key factor in such an alteration would be a change in the R.V./T.L.C. ratio (increase in V.C.). From a study comparing a group of professional singers with a comparable group of voice students and a group of non-singers Gould has concluded that the R.V./T.L.C. ratio is reduced during the process of voice training. If so this would mean that either inspiratory muscles had increased their ability to take air in to a volume greater than the initial vital capacity or that expiratory muscles had increased their ability to squeeze air out of the lungs to a volume below the initial residual volume. Although his figures are suggestive of such a change, as he himself points out, it may be that during the process of voice training and professional singing those with ordinary R.V./T.L.C. ratios tend to fall by the wayside. Another study indicates that there are no major differences in lung volumes between professional singers and non-singers (8). Leith (20) has shown that, indeed, ventilatory muscle strength can be increased by training. It seems likely that the process of voice training accomplishes this to some degree; but the learning of appropriate use of muscles certainly far outweighs in importance any increase in their strength.

To my mind a more important consideration is whether or not the process of voice training includes those exercises best calculated to lead to the optimum use of lung volumes and respiratory muscles in singing in the individual voice student. Some voice teachers utilize complicated maneuvers in the hope of so training their students. As we shall see in Chap. 8 very simple vocal exercises are far more likely to lead to the desired result.

A question remains as to how much knowledge of the fundamentals of breathing mechanics is desirable in the teacher and the student. To my mind the more the teacher knows the more successful he will be with his pupils. As to the student, he certainly should know that the diaphragm is not the abdominal wall (a surprisingly common misconception) and he will probably learn more quickly if he appreciates the simpler aspects of lung volumes and the production of subglottic pressure.

At this time we might briefly refer to a subject dealt with later in Chap. 8, since it is both a key point in the art of singing and a factor related to the breathing mechanism. In an important paper published in the Scientific American, Sundberg (see Ref. 27 in Chap. 8) describes the importance of the shape of the supraglottic air spaces. He says that, through lowering the larynx and widening the pharynx, the trained singer is able to add a fourth formant to the voice. An important part of this maneuver is wide opening of the jaws yielding a sensation somewhat like yawning. The average distribution of energy in orchestral sounds appears to be in the vicinity of 450 C.P.S., and the fourth "singing formant" lies well above that frequency. As Sundberg says, thus "... the singer achieves audibility without having to generate extra air pressure" even in the face of the full orchestra. Sundberg says that "Pop" singers substitute for this a dependency on electronic amplification.

In this same paper the author clearly addresses the important question as to whether the accomplished singer must possess some unique anatomical or physiological characteristics. To quote from Sundberg, "There are ... a few morphological specifications that probably have some effect on the ease with which someone can learn to sing well" but "It is in the complex of knowledge, talent and musical instinct that is summed up as 'musicality', rather than in the anatomy of the lungs and the vocal tract, that an excellent singer's excellence lies." I emphatically agree.

In conclusion of this chapter let us look at some further comparison of ordinary breathing with that during phonation (Fig. 50). Quiet breathing involves the use of only a small amount of the vital capacity. Conversation offers a slight increase in that amount, public speaking a considerable increase, and singing employs nearly the whole V.C. Alveolar pressure (quite close to subglottic during phonatory maneuvers) fluctuates only a few cm H_2O in quiet breathing, but ranges from high negative pressures during inspiration to relatively high positive during phonation. Airflow rate is also relatively low in quiet breathing and expiratory flows are also low in speech and singing, but higher inspiratory flows must be associated with speech and much higher still associated with singing. Not shown on this diagram are pressures and flows in exercise or maximum breathing effort. It is worthy of repetition here that phonation never demands either pressures or flows approaching those values. Phonation involves delicate use of the breathing mechanism. The control of breathing in connection with phonation in the presence of disease affecting the respiratory tract will be considered in Chap. 9.

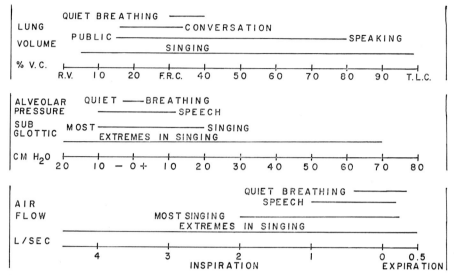

Fig. 50. Comparison of ranges of volumes (as % of V.C. above) pressures (middle), and flows (below) during phonation with those characteristic of quiet breathing. Extremes in maximum effort without phonation (not shown) are well above those shown with the exception of the use of lung volume

References

1. Bartlett, D., jr., Remmers, J. E., Gautier, H. (1973): Laryngeal regulation of respiratory airflow. Respir. Physiol. *18*, 194—204.
2. Bouhuys, A., Proctor, D. F., Mead, J. (1966): Kinetic aspects of singing. J. Appl. Physiol. *21*, 483—496.
3. Bunn, J. C., Mead, J. (1971): Control of ventilation during speech. J. Appl. Physiol. *31*, 870—872.
4. Draper, M. H., Ladefoged, P., Whitteridge, D. (1959): Respiratory muscles in speech. J. Speech Hearing Res. *2*, 16—27.
5. Gautier, H., Remmers, J. E., Bartlett, D., jr. (1973): Control of the duration of expiration. Respir. Physiol. *18*, 205—221.
6. Gould, W. J., Okamura, H. (1973): Static lung volumes in singers. Ann. Otol. *82*, 89—95.
7. Gould, W. J., Okamura, H. (1974): Respiratory training of the singer. Folia Phoniatr. *26*, 275—286.
8. Heller, S. S., Hicks, W. R., Root, W. S. (1960): Lung volumes of singers. J. Appl. Physiol. *15*, 40—42.
9. Hixon, T. J., Goldman, M. D., Mead, J. (1973): Kinematics of the chest wall during speech production: volume displacement of the rib cage, abdomen, and lung. J. Speech Hearing Res. *16*, 78—115.
10. Hixon, T. J., Mead, J., Goldman, M. D. (1976): Dynamics of the chest wall during speech production: function of the thorax, rib cage, diaphragm, and abdomen. J. Speech Hearing Res. *19*, 297—356.
11. Hoshiko, M. S. (1960): Sequence of action of breathing muscles during speech. J. Speech Hearing Res. *3*, 291—297.
12. Hoshiko, M. (1962): Electromyographic investigation of the intercostal muscle during speech. Arch. Physical Med. Rehabil. *43*, 115—119.

13. Hoshiko, M. S., Berger, K. W. (1965): Sequence of respiratory muscle activity during varied vocal attack. Speech Monographs *32*, 185—191.
14. Hoshiko, M. S. (1965): Lung volume for initiation of phonation. J. Appl. Physiol. *20*, 480—482.
15. Isshiki, N., Okamura, H., Morimoto, M. (1967): Maximum phonation time and airflow rate during phonation: simple clinical tests for vocal function. Ann. Otol. *76*, 998—1007.
16. Judson, L. S. V., Weaver, A. T. (1965): Voice Science. New York: Appleton-Century-Crofts.
17. Kirchner, J. A., Suzuki, M. (1968): Laryngeal reflexes and voice production. Ann. N.Y. Acad. Sci. *155*, 98—109.
18. Koike, Y., Hirano, M., Leden, H. V. (1967): Vocal initiation: acoustic and aerodynamic investigations of normal subjects. Folia Phoniatr. *19*, 173—182.
19. Ladefoged, P. (1967): Three Areas of Experimental Phonetics. London: Oxford Univ. Press.
20. Leith, D. E., Bradley, M. (1976): Ventilatory muscle strength and endurance training. J. Appl. Physiol. *41*, 508—516.
21. Mead, J., Bunn, J. C. (1974): Speech as Breathing. In: Ventilatory and Phonatory Control Systems (Wyke, B., ed.), Chap. 3. London: Oxford Univ. Press.
22. Mead, J., Hixon, J., Goldman, M. D. (1974): The Configuration of the Chest Wall During Speech. In: Ventilatory and Phonatory Control Systems (Wyke, B., ed.), Chap. 5. London: Oxford Univ. Press.
23. Murry, T., Schmitke, L. K. (1975): Airflow onset and variability. Folia Phoniatr. *27*, 401—409.
24. Otis, A. B., Clark, R. G. (1968): Ventilatory implications of phonation and phonatory implications of ventilation. Ann. N.Y. Acad. Sci. *155*, 122—128.
25. Otis, A. B. (1974): Some Ventilation Phonation relationships. In: Ventilatory and Phonatory Control Systems (Wyke, B., ed.), Chap. 20. London: Oxford Univ. Press.
26. Pommez, J. (1967): Respiration et phonation. Rev. Laryng. (Bordeaux) *88*, 465—472.
27. Proctor, D. F. (1974): Breathing Mechanics in Phonation and Singing. In: Ventilatory and Phonatory Control Systems (Wyke, B., ed.), Chap. 4. London: Oxford Univ. Press.
28. Sears, T. A. (1977): Some Neural and Mechanical Aspects of Singing. In: Music and the Brain, Studies in the Neurology of Music (Critchley, M., Henson, R. A., eds.). London: Heinemann.
29. Sewall, H. (1890): On the relations of diaphragmatic and costal respiration with particular reference to phonation. J. Physiol. *11*, 159—178.
30. Siegert, C. (1969): Der intrathorakale Druck und seine Beziehungen zur Stimmfunktion. Folia Phoniatr. *21*, 98—104.
31. Warren, D. W., Wood, M. T. (1969): Respiratory volumes in normal speech: a possible reason for intraoral pressure differences among voiced and voiceless consonants. J. Acoust. Soc. Amer. *45*, 466—469.
32. Yanagihara, N., Koike, Y., Leden, H. v. (1966): Phonation and respiration. Folia Phoniatr. *18*, 323—340.

7 The Speaking Voice

Thus far we have considered the structure and function of the portions of the respiratory system involved in phonation, some of the basic principles of sound production, and the special adaptation of the breathing mechanism for the voice. It now remains for us to examine the processes by which vocal sound is converted into speech and further refined for song. In this chapter our attention will be turned especially upon a consideration of what is good speech, how teaching can be brought to bear on the improvement of speech, questions of special importance to those whose livelihood is more or less dependent upon speech, and finally a few speech problems.

Importance of Speech to Man

In his opening talk at the 1968 international symposium on "Sound Production in Man" Wallace Fenn said (13), "... talking is like walking. Both are taken for granted. We know how to do both rather well, and we think we understand the relatively simple basic mechanisms of both ..." Indeed speech is simply a matter of superimposing a number of actions in the upper respiratory tract upon the action of the larynx (in producing a fundamental tone) to result in audible modifications of that sound in appropriate sequence. For the vowel sounds mere changes in the shape of the resonating supraglottic airway result in transition from one vowel to another; and, for the consonants, the tongue, lips, and palate perform a variety of maneuvers to interrupt or modify the vowels in the manner suitable to the language being spoken.

Still this simple function, so easy a child can do it, is one of the most marvelous accomplishments of man. The development of speech marked the point in evolution when the use of symbols enhanced the power of the brain to think. Through speech, and the written language which followed, man has been able to engage in abstract thought, profit and learn from spoken and written records, and enjoy a separate art form in the literature of story, play, and poetry. Yet most of us, most of the time take this great gift for granted and use it almost unconsciously. Only when we observe the infant learning to talk, when we are learning a foreign language, when we are exposed to either a particularly attractive or unattractive way of speaking, or when we are unable to understand one whose speech is insufficiently audible or comprehensible, only under such circumstances do most of us give thought to the process of speaking. Yet I would have to agree with Fenn (13) when he said, "Without the ability to communicate ideas orally, human culture would be non-existent".

No special knowledge is required on the part of either a normal parent or infant to accomplish the speech learning process, and most good school teachers are quite capable of building on that beginning to assure a child's development of relatively adequate speech habits. Obviously neither this chapter nor the long list of papers and books devoted to the subject are intended or needed to teach the average person how to speak. They are intended to provide some background of knowledge of use in understanding and remedying speech problems when they develop, and in aiding those whose livelihood depend upon their voices. The whole gamut of these problems will not be discussed here. Many are included in other monographs in this series and in the vast pertinent literature, some of which is listed in the references cited in this book (14, 15, 21, 24, 30, 35, 36, 37, 39, 40, 46). Our principle attention will be directed toward the factors involved in producing speech which is audible, intelligible, and euphonious.

Respiratory Mechanisms in Speech

Proper breathing is the sine qua non of proper speech. This fact underlies all of the popular dicta about speech including Hamlet's famous instructions

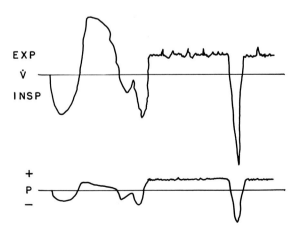

Fig. 51. Recording of subglottic pressure (below) and airflow (above) during casual speech. Period of conversation shown at right

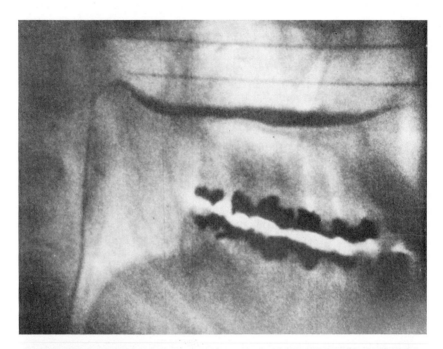

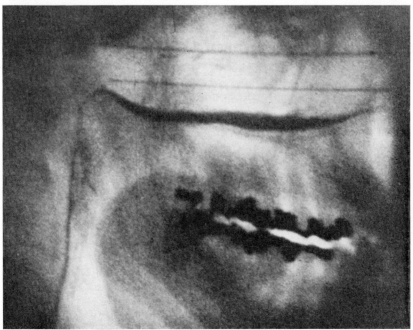

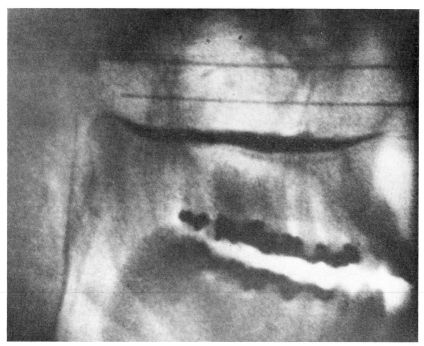

Fig. 52. Frames from the cinefluorograph mentioned previously. Upper left, during the sounding of "a" as in the word "shape"; bottom left, the sound "o" as in the word "of"; right, breath between phrases of conversation. See also Fig. 27 for orientation

(Shakespeare, Hamlet, Act III, Scene III) "Speak the speech, I pray you, as I pronounced it to you, trippingly on the tongue; . . . Nor do not saw the air too much with your hand, . . . suit the action to the word, the word to the action . . ."

Clearly speech demands vary with the connection in which speech is employed. I mentioned in Chap. 6 that, under certain circumstances such as the demands of respiration during heavy work, speech is difficult. It becomes even more difficult when the organism is heavily stressed by other environmental factors. One example of this appears in Wyndham's treatise on heat exposure (51). He describes the sensations accompanying the necessity to carry out heavy work in severe heat and notes among other problems that, "Conversation dwindled to requests for water, the time, etc." and says that later on, "talking was a distinct effort".

The demands upon an actor are different from those whose livelihood depends upon deliverance of frequent lectures or performance in the theatre to those of salesmen or others whose work demands constant use of the voice throughout the 40 hour work week (16). But despite these different demands all of us could find a single answer in arriving at optimum employment of the phonatory mechanism for speech at all times. Of what does that optimum consist?

Some of that answer can be deduced from what has been said in previous chapters. We know that a sound of sufficient intensity to be heard in a small room or a large hall can be produced with a relatively small subglottic pressure provided with relatively little effort by the breathing mechanism (Fig. 51). Indeed we have seen that delicate control of the phonatory and breathing mechanism is required rather than heavy effort (2, 43, 44, 49, 50). We have seen also that a resonant quality and carrying power is related to control of the supraglottic air spaces. I have already referred to the use of radiography in the study of the supraglottic organs during phonation (33, 38, 41). In Fig. 52 are shown some frames from the cinefluorograph illustrating some of the variations there with speech sounds.

Thus proper sound production per se is merely a matter of taking a breath in and modulating the ensuing expiration effectively. One need only listen to and care about the quality of the ensuing sound to be able to modify it with simple adjustments.

We have already discussed breathing and the production of sound. The conversion of sound into speech is another matter, and the production of speech which is audible, intelligible, and euphonious under widely varying circumstances another matter still. But without the effortless emission of sound of a good quality the best directed attempts to arrive at effective speech will fail (Fig. 53). Certain points deserve special emphasis here.

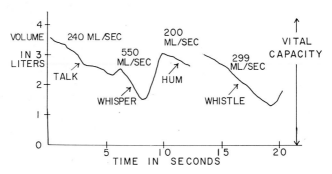

Fig. 53. Volume events and airflows associated with spontaneous talking, whispering, humming, and whistling (from left to right)

Lung Volumes for Speech

The first of these is the respiratory volume at which speech is initiated. Hoshiko (Ref. 14, Chap. 6) in a study of 60 males and females found that speech was initiated on the average at about 50 % of the vital capacity. In these subjects the expiratory reserve volume was about 30 % of V.C. Thus, on the average a breath about twice that of the ordinary tidal volume preceded the initiation of speech. But, among these subjects, this volume varied between about 40 and 60 % of V.C. It is probable that speech is best begun at the higher of these volumes and that the average speaker starts with a handicap by failing to achieve it. Thus I would advise the speaker to seek a comfortably large volume of air in the lungs before beginning to speak and in each breath interspersed between phrases.

Subglottic Pressure

A second point involves the pressure producing the sound (11, 25, 34, 42, 45). Speech, audible speech, can be produced with subglottic pressures as low as 2—3 cm H_2O (31, 32). For louder speech, to attract attention or to carry any distance, larger pressures are required up to 10 to 20 cm H_2O but even that pressure is achieved with minimal effort at higher lung volumes. The common error is to employ high pressures to produce a loud sound thus attempting to overcome poor intelligibility by loudness. That is a waste of effort and traumatic to the larynx. Certain speech sounds require, in addition to the subglottic pressure a rise in intraoral pressure (2, 16, 47) of as much as 10 cm H_2O (as for the "t" in "time"). Here again this is accomplished with minimal effort at the higher lung volumes.

We have already mentioned the role of the intercostal muscles in moderating subglottic pressure. We shall see in the succeeding chapter how important this is in song; but, in speech too, if the speaker is willing to use the higher lung volumes this is a key factor. It appears that, especially in speech, an interplay of the internal and external intercostals produces the fine variances in both pressure and flow necessary for intelligible enunciation of speech sounds. In an excellent paper Adams (1) has analyzed the muscle activity related to speech. She especially stresses the role of the intercostal muscles in articulation. "The internal intercostal muscle activity pattern appeared to be related mainly to the speaker's degree of linguistic proficiency." In other words this expiratory muscle group came into play in opposition to the external intercostals in producing the changes in subglottic pressure and flow necessary to clear enunciation. Adams goes on to note that there appeared to be ". . . phasic activity related to speech . . ." in the external intercostals, but uniform activity decreased at the end of long phrases (when inspiratory effort was no longer required for modification of the positive elastic forces). Some of the volume and pressure events are portrayed in Figs. 51 and 53.

Phrasing and Emphasis

Phrasing in speech is of importance in the delivery of the idea to be conveyed. As we punctuate and paragraph in writing so we phrase in speech. This is only possible in comfort and at ease if proper breathing is employed. The breathing must be appropriate to the length of the ensuing phrase and the intensity of sound required. One study shows how this can be accomplished (Fig. 54). As is readily seen this speaker employed quite different breathing patterns when going from ordinary conversation to reading in a loud voice (Ref. 2, Chap. 6). In that study one of three subjects was a trained singer. While reading aloud he employed a smaller percentage of his vital capacity (55 % compared to 80 % in another subject); but during loud reading he exhibited a lower airflow rate (0.25 l/sec compared to 0.5 l/sec in another subject). This may represent a more efficient use of the breath in speech. This same subject uses nearly the whole of his V.C. in singing. Numerous other methods are available today for special studies of speech physiology and pathology (10, 33, 38, 48). Although such studies are not feasible for use in large numbers of subjects, the lessons learned from them can and should be applied in assisting those whose speech is important to their careers.

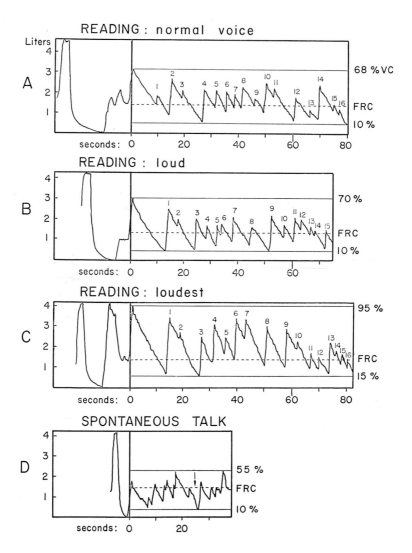

Fig. 54. For this figure a subject was directed to read the same passage three times, in a normal voice (top), loud voice (second from top), and loudest voice (third from top). He then engaged in spontaneous conversation (below). Volume events are shown in relation to the vital capacity (left). The arrow in "spontaneous talk" indicates the subject laughing. (Used with permission of the Editor, J. Appl. Physiol., from Bouhuys, A., Proctor, D. F., Mead, J. [1966]: Kinetic aspects of singing, *21*, 483—496)

Teaching of Speech

Whereas learning to speak is a natural process, once certain speech characteristics have been acquired they are difficult to modify. As described in
Shaw's "Pygmalion", and later in the musical "My Fair Lady", certain speech
characteristics may seriously handicap a person's path in life. These handi-
capping features consist in part of bad grammar and limited vocabulary; but
sound quality may also mark an individual in an undesirable manner.
Shaw's character's voice stamped herself as cockney; but, also, her whining
nasality gave a raucous and sometimes obsequious connotation to everything
she said. Regional accents and voice quality may indeed be desirable and
attractive unless they are so extreme as to make speech unintelligible to
those of different regions or walks of life. Certainly the enjoyment of conversation would be severly limited if all of us used the same sound quality and
enunciation. But, if speech is to be an asset rather than a handicap in life it
should, on one hand, be an expression of an individual's character and, on the
other hand, pleasant to hear and intelligible to the listener.

In his paper on "voicing control" Hirose (20) emphasizes the complexity
of activity in the intrinsic laryngeal muscles in speech (49, 50). He found that
the posterior cricoarytenoid muscle (ordinarily only brought into play to
open the glottis) and the reciprocal action of the interarytenoid play key
roles in speech production. Some of the possible results of inappropriate action
of these and other intrinsic laryngeal muscles were depicted in Fig. 26, Chap. 5.

Certain "abnormalities" of the speaking voice may, in some instances,
be justifiable. A number of actors and actresses are famous for the husky,
rough, or other unusual quality of the voice. As long as this voice quality
is not the result of a process leading to an eventually failing voice it may
be not only not reprehensible but even desirable. Most of us find certain accents
pleasant to listen to. Both regional accents, such as those characteristic of the
Southerner or the New Englander in the United States, and the accent of one
speaking a non-native tongue may be desirable as long as they do not
interfere with intelligibility. That requires at least a minimum attention to
diction.

Diction

The primary yardstick for measuring diction is the ease with which one's
speech is understood (5, 28). If it is understood a secondary consideration is,
is it pleasant to hear? In a well printed book it is possible to cover half of each
letter and still read with ease. In a similar manner clearly enunciated speech
will be comprehensible to the listener in noisy surroundings, or to the listener
with impaired hearing. Accomplishment of this requires four speech characteristics. Sound intensity must be adequate to the circumstances. Excessive
rapidity of speech is to be avoided. Consonants must be enunciated fully, not
barely touched upon. And vowel sounds must be true and clear.

Nearly everyone suffers from certain regrettable speech habits, particularly evident in phrases frequently employed as a matter of form. "Thank you" becomes "ku" for instance. Some of this is acceptable and even inevitable but such short shrift or even total neglect of certain sounds (especially consonants) must be kept from spreading from simple phrases such as "thank you" to speech as a whole. We should all take pride in the sound of our voices and in the ease with which we are understood by strangers or under difficult circumstances. It is absolutely vital for those whose income is associated with speech but, even in ordinary casual conversation, the trouble taken to speak clearly should be considered a common courtesy. Carried to extremes this attention to clear enunciation could lead to a stilted artificiality of speech. In modifying speech habits the individual character of speech should be maintained. It is a matter of eliminating serious speech faults from, and adding essential features to one's natural voice.

Although the consonants are the chief constituents of speech making sound intelligible as language, the clarity of the vowels is not only important to intelligibility but essential to speech beauty (5). The major characteristic of the more unpleasant regional accents is the distortion of vowel sounds. I live in Baltimore and the fact that natives of this city often refer to it as Bawlmer is notorious. There can be no doubt that the pronunciation of the "ti" and the good round "o" sound in the "more" not only make the word more easily understood but turn an ugly sound into one of beauty. In the same way the attractive name of our State Maryland is often reduced to a mere "Merlun". Good speech habits come from hearing one's own voice, noting the desirable and undesirable in the voices of others, and taking the trouble and time to appropriately modify one's own speech. Obviously this is relatively easy to do in childhood and far more difficult when habits have been developed over years.

Song and Speech

In singing the regular and rhythmic progression from speech sound to speech sound and the necessity to use clear vowels are self evident. Song makes some poor speech habits difficult or impossible. In our state song one cannot fit "Merlun" into the phrase "Oh, Mar-y-land my Mar-y-land". With a little introspective thought we can thus use song as a path to good speech. The proper setting of the supraglottic air spaces and the correct use of lips and tongue and palate can in that manner be noted, practiced, and become an unconscious part of everyday speech (Ref. 5, 20, Chap. 5, and 26, 27 this chapter). In Fig. 52 some of these facets of speech and song are depicted. Unless we develop good speech habits and use them habitually we are unlikely to resort to them when occasion demands. The constituents which make up good speech habits are:

1. The use of breaths in which are appropriate for the delivery of the desired phrase;

2. The control of subglottic pressure to produce sound of intensity appropriate to the circumstances (screaming and yelling are examples of the inappropriate use of high subglottic pressures producing sounds no more audible, in the face of noise or at a distance, then far smaller pressures properly employed);
3. The proper shaping of the supraglottic air spaces to modulate the resonance of the voice and produce the desired vowel; and
4. The active use of the lips and tongue to impose clear consonant constituents of speech.

In some languages, notably Welsh, the mere process of speaking the language at all makes the proper use of the four requirements listed above almost inevitable. The naturally beautiful singing voices of the Welsh are well known. But in most languages relatively acceptable speech can be produced in the face of relative neglect of one or more of them. In those cases good speech habits must be learned through conscientious attention or taught by skilled teachers. As a general rule if we desire to improve our speech we can learn through listening to ourselves and that learning process can be facilitated by listening to a recording of one's own voice. Most people are struck with surprise when first confronted by a recording of their own voices. Our own auditory system fails to appreciate the full character of speech during its production. Noting faults as heard on a recording can often lead to their correction, and practice reading aloud can facilitate that process. The final product can only be judged by the listener, and only when it is produced in the varying circumstances the speaker is likely to encounter in real life. Thus the actor and lecturer must be judged by the audience, the salesman by his success with the buyer and his ability to go on talking week after week.

As one who has attended perhaps too many medical meetings I am entirely in sympathy with the following comment of Calnan (9). "The simple fact is that although doctors read aloud badly ... most can learn to speak spontaneously and with animation; but this requires time and effort, both of which are donated in a miserly way. The successful lecturer is generous and considerate of his audience—a rare being at medical meetings."

Sometimes I wonder if sufficient attention and time are devoted in our schools to the teaching of speech. One study found an incidence of 24.6 % speech problems among over 10,000 eleven year old school children (10). There could be no better training ground than the classroom in which the pupil can become accustomed to standing on his feet and reciting in a well ordered manner and in a pleasant, audible, and intelligible voice. If from the early grammar grades onward this were a regular part of school life good speech habits in most could be acquired relatively painlessly and along with them would come the confidence necessary for the effective use of speech throughout life. Attention should be given to the quality of the voice, the purity of diction, and well phrased melodic delivery. The subject should learn to modulate the pitch of the voice (32). It is relatively easy to learn to deliberately choose a lower pitch for emphasis in some phrases. Varying tempo will also relieve monotony. Certain phrases call for deliberate slow enunciation while in others a faster pace may be employed. It is difficult to make a habitually slow speaker speed up but what is more important, teaching the overly fast speaker to slow down, can be accomplished.

For those whose career in life will demand public speaking, the orator, the actor, one whose career demands presentations in public, and even the salesman, that early start in school can be a great help. But some will need further help when the special demands on their speaking voice bring out problems. In some instances that help should be sought from a speech therapist or pathologist. In other instances work with a singing teacher may be beneficial. The production of clear and clean vowels, the control of the breath, ease in public appearance may all be conveyed by a skillful singing teacher. Certain problems should be referred to a laryngologist and more will be said of this in Chaps. 9 and 10.

Speech Problems

When a speech problem develops the question of to whom to turn for help may be difficult. A good speech therapist should be able to manage the majority of problems; but, when sound quality is poor and especially when faulty breathing is suspected, an interested singing teacher should be considered. Speech problems should be considered as potentially multidisciplinary in nature. In addition to the speech therapist and/or pathologist, the laryngologist, audiologist, and psychiatrist may all be needed.

Communication problems are multidisciplinary of necessity (12, 19). Over thirty years ago in Maryland in conjunction with the State Health Department we began a statewide program for conservation of hearing and speech in school children. They were periodically screened for difficulties, laying special stress on the slow child or the emotionally disturbed. Such children were seen by an audiologist, a speech therapist, and an otolaryngologist. Once the source of the difficulty was identified appropriate action could be taken as to therapy.

Some of the more common faults which each of us can look for in our own speech are:

1. Lack of rhythm and emphasis (1, 8, 31, 47) (monotony is boring and pleasantly varied speech receives attention);
2. Laziness in the use of lips and tongue resulting in the slurring of sound;
3. Failure to interpose sounds which add to intelligibility (especially in public speaking the use of "hoow-" in the "wh-"words, the placement of a vowel between words ending and beginning in consonants as in what-[a]-to-do);
4. Failure to speak in punctuated sentences and employment of useless sounds and phrases in lieu thereof (the notorious "um", "uh", "er ah", and "you know");
5. Failure to face the listener (everyone uses what he sees as well as what he hears in apprehending what is spoken);
6. Covering the mouth with the hand during speech; and

7. Dependence upon and misuse of electronic amplification (everyone should be capable of audible speech without amplification, and appropriate modulation of sound when amplification is used is absolutely essential; try the system in advance whenever possible).

In public speaking there should be continual communication between speaker and audience. Even when reading a speech the speaker must frequently look up, at, and about the audience. Only thus can he sense boredom, loss of interest, or incomprehensibility and alter his delivery as needed to win his listeners over. Leonardo da Vinci gave this wise advice in one of his notebooks, "... when addressing men whose good opinion you desire, either cut short your speech when you see these evident signs of impatience (yawning), or else change the subject; ..." Brevity is the soul of wit. It is also the secret of holding an audience and making your point.

The person deriving a living from the theater stage or the lecture platform has a special problem in being required not only to perform with excellence but to do so night after night. For these people it is absolutely necessary to foster the ability to use the breath and the subglottic pressure in an optimum manner and to habitually employ diction which assures understanding of even the quietly spoken voice. Except for those blessed with a natural talent in speaking, such individuals would be wise to seek the assistance of professionally competent teachers early in their careers (17). A special problem in this connection exists for the singer taking part in musical shows requiring speech. Sometimes even the skilled singer may find speech more wearing on the voice then song (7).

Now let us consider some special problems which may confront the speech teacher. Poor enunciation or hoarseness in childhood are indications for consultation with an otolaryngologist. Only after defective hearing or laryngeal pathology have been ruled out or corrected can speech be restored to normal. In adolescence almost all boys pass through a period when adjustment to the changing size of the larynx lags behind growth and the cracking breaking voice results. Time alone will permit suitable adjustment to occur. In some men that adjustment does not occur and a high pitched squeaky voice persists into adult life. In each of the patients who have consulted me about that problem I have found a completely normal male larynx. The problem is functional and susceptible to correction with a patient skilled teacher.

Hoarseness in the adult smoker of cigarettes should always suggest the possibility of cancer. That diagnosis can only be established or ruled out be direct laryngoscopy and biopsy. Since this is one of the most curable forms of cancer in its early stages it is a real tragedy to see such a patient subjected to prolonged attempts to relieve symptoms prior to resort to laryngoscopy. Cigarette smoking is unwise in anyone and is a common cause of hoarseness. Certainly this cause for a hoarse voice deserves primary consideration.

Laryngitis is a frequent complication of the common cold, flu, or less obvious chronic respiratory infection. Voice rest during laryngitis will hasten the return of a normal voice and protect the inflamed vocal folds from injury. Persistent or frequently recurring laryngitis is an indication for laryngological consultation. More will be said of this in Chaps. 9 and 10.

7*

Speech Impediments

This is not the place for a full discussion of the causes and treatments of speech impediments (3, 4, 18, 23, 48) but a few remarks are appropriate to the subject of this and the succeeding chapter. Regardless of its origin (frequently in some complex of emotional stresses) once stammering or stuttering has developed the fear in speaking which they engender clouds the mind and brings to the speaker a dread of each speech experience. The attention, which should be focused on what is being said, is now directed solely to looking ahead toward the next dreaded obstacle. The actor imitating the stutterer will often make it a source of amusement with his interspersed whistles and gestures. To the sufferer from the impediment it is anything but amusing. It is shameful and agonizing. How can our considerations of the normal speech process help in the relief of these people? Having been at one time a stammerer I have some special appreciation of the problem.

Like many stammerers I found special difficulty with certain sounds, especially when speech had to be initiated with them. Once the flow of speech was begun less difficulty was encountered but there remained the looking ahead toward a sound which would be difficult. I was a singer and noted that there was never even a thought of stammering in song. I also could read aloud in groups with no trouble. These facts are almost universally true of even severe stammerers and stutterers.

When I reached the point in my career when speaking in public became necessary I found a way to solve my problem, taking my cue from the lack of difficulty in singing. First I chose to begin a speech with a sound presenting no difficulties. The sound "s" was one of them and it was no problem to choose an initial sentence beginning with "Some of . . .", "Since the . . .", etc. Next I went through my text and marked it for stress and rhythm much as a piece of music is annotated. Simple underlining of certain syllables, words, and phrases sufficed. I soon found that, in speaking, my attention was now directed toward the production of well phrased rhythmic and euphonious speech and the impediments gradually disappeared. Finally I found it possible to use the same attention toward effective speech in spontaneous talks without a written text.

When reading aloud in unison the fear of a block is eliminated because the individual knows that if he simply stops no one need notice. The rhythm employed in group reading is also important. The use of this exercise to demonstrate to the sufferer from an impediment that he is physically and mentally capable of normal, uninterrupted and even euphonious speech may be a useful beginning in rehabilitation. In singing a different mechanism is involved. The attention of the subject is taken away from the impending hazard of stumbling over a coming sound and directed toward the regular breathing, production of clear pitch, and clear enunciation of sound which is characteristic of even the simplest singing. Hutchinson (22) emphasizes the fact that the use of rhythm is of help not in distracting the attention of the speaker from his problem, but in attracting his attention to the beauty of speech. This is a key point.

In my own case not only was confidence in being able to speak restored but I gradually became a speaker who took pride in being easily understood and whose delivery was enjoyable to the audience. In a sense this is a matter of singing speech, or at least making speech melodious. There is nothing new about these ideas. Many speech teachers have long recognized that the superimposition of rhythm is one way to help the sufferer from speech impediments. I do wonder if sufficient thought has been given to the use of singing as a path to that end.

References

1. Adams, C., Munro, R. R. (1973): The relationship between internal intercostal muscle activity and pause placement in the connected utterance of native and non-native speakers of English. Phonetica 28, 227—250.
2. Arkebauer, H. J., Hixon, T. J., Hardy, J. C. (1967): Peak intraoral air pressures during speech. J. Speech Hearing Res. 10, 196—208.
3. Barbara, D. A. (1954): Stuttering—A Psychodynamic Approach to Its Understanding and Treatment. New York: Julian Press.
4. Barbara, D. A. (1965): New Directions in Stuttering. Springfield: Charles C Thomas.
5. Bogert, B. P. (1953): On the band width of vowel formants. J. Acoust. Soc. Amer. 25, 791—792.
6. Bole, C. T., II, Lessler, M. A. (1966): Electromyography of the genioglossus muscles in man. J. Appl. Physiol. 21, 1695—1698.
7. Brodnitz, F. S. (1954): Voice problems of the actor and singer. J. Speech Hearing Dis. 19, 322—326.
8. Brown, W. S., jr., McGlone, R. E. (1974): Aerodynamic and acoustic study of stress in sentence productions. J. Acoust. Soc. Amer. 56, 971—974.
9. Calnan, J. (1976): A lecture on lecturing. Med. Educ. 10, 445—449.
10. Calnan, M., Richardson, K. (1976): Speech problems in a national survey: assessments and prevalences. Child Care Health Dev. 2, 181—202.
11. Draper, M. H., Ladefoged, P., Whitteridge, D. (1960): Expiratory pressures and air flow during speech. Brit. Med. J. 1, 1837—1843.
12. Falck, F. J., Falck, V. T. (1961): Communicative disorders: A multidisciplinary problem. J.A.M.A. 178, 290—295.
13. Fenn, W. O. (1968): Perspectives in phonation. Ann. N.Y. Acad. Sci. 155, 4—8.
14. Flanagan, J. L. (1968): Source-system interaction in the vocal tract. Ann. N.Y. Acad. Sci. 155, 9—17.
15. Gray, G. W., Wise, C. M. (1934): The Bases of Speech. New York: Harper and Bros.
16. Gutzman, H. (1954): Die Beurteilung und Behandlung von Kehlkopfveränderungen bei Rednern und Sängern. Münchner Med. Wschr. 96, 671—673.
17. Hardy, J. C. (1967): Techniques of measuring intraoral air pressure and rate of airflow. J. Speech Hearing Res. 10, 650—654.
18. Healey, E. C., Mallard, A. R., III, Adams, M. R. (1976): Factors contributing to the reduction of stuttering during singing. J. Speech Hearing Res. 19, 475—480.
19. Henner, R., Pollack, F. J., Campanelli, P. A., Philips, D., Judiesch, M. (1956): The team approach to hearing and speech disorders. J.A.M.A. 161, 957—960.
20. Hirose, H., Gay, T. (1972): The activity of the intrinsic laryngeal muscles in voicing control. An electromyographic study. Phonetica 25, 140—164.
21. Hixon, T. (1966): Turbulent noise sources for speech. Folia Phoniatr. 18, 168—182.
22. Hutchinson, J. M. (1976): A review of rhythmic pacing as a treatment strategy for stuttering. Rehabil. Lit. 37, 297—303.
23. Jain, C. K., Kishore, B., Manchanda, S. S. (1968): Functional speech defects. A study of 90 children with stammering, stuttering and babbling. Arch. Child. Hlth. (Bombay) 10, 87—96.

24. Kaplan, H. M. (1960): Anatomy and Physiology of Speech. New York: McGraw-Hill.
25. Kelman, A. W., Gordon, M. T., Simpson, I. C., Morton, F. M. (1975): Assessment of vocal function by air-flow. Folia Phoniatr. 27, 250—262.
26. Kenyon, E. L. (1927): Relation of oral articulative movements of speech and of extrinsic laryngeal musculature in general to function of vocal cords. Arch. Otolaryngol. 5, 481—501.
27. Kenyon, E. L. (1928): Action and control of the peripheral organs of speech. J.A.M.A. 91, 1341—1346.
28. Klatt, D. H., Stevens, K. N., Mead, J. (1968): Studies of articulatory activity and air flow during speech. Ann. N.Y. Acad. Sci. 155, 42—55.
29. Ladefoged, P. (1968): Linguistic aspects of respiratory phenomena. Ann. N.Y. Acad. Sci. 155, 141—151.
30. Lawson, F. D. (1944): The Human Voice. New York: Harper and Bros.
31. Lieberman, P. (1960): Some acoustic correlates of word stress in American English. J. Acoust. Soc. Amer. 32, 451—454.
32. Lieberman, P., Knudson, R., Mead, J. (1969): Determination of the rate of change of fundamental frequency with respect to subglottal air pressure during sustained phonation. J. Acoust. Soc. Amer. 45, 1537—1543.
33. Lubker, J. F., Moll, K. L. (1965): Simultaneous oral-nasal airflow measurements and cinefluorographic observations during speech production. Cleft Palate J. 2, 257—272.
34. Lubker, J. (1973): Transglottal airflow during stop consonant production. J. Acoust. Soc. Amer. 53, 212—215.
35. Luchsinger, R. (1950): New researches on the field of the physiology of voice and voice construction. Folia Phoniatr. 2, 61—67.
36. Luchsinger, R. (1953): Physiologie der Stimme. Folia Phoniatr. 5, 58—127.
37. Luchsinger, R., Arnold, G. E. (1965): Voice—Speech—Language. London: Contable & Co.
38. Macmillan, A. S., Kelemen, G. (1952): Radiography of the supraglottic speech organs. Arch. Otolaryngol. 55, 671—688.
39. Malmberg, B., ed. (1968): Manual of Phonetics. Amsterdam: North Holland Publ. Co.
40. Margaria, R., Cavagna, G. (1959): Il Meccanismo della fonazione. Boll. Soc. Ital. Biol. Sper. 35, 2075—2077.
41. Perkell, J. S. (1969): Physiology of Speech Production. Cambridge: MIT Press.
42. Rothenberg, M. (1977): Measurements of airflow in speech. J. Speech Hearing Res. 20, 155—176.
43. Smith, W. R., Lieberman, P. (1964): Studies in pathological speech production. Data Sci. Lab., Air Force Cambridge Res. Lab.
44. Subtelny, J. D., Worth, J. H., Sakuda, M. (1966): Intraoral pressure and rate of flow during speech. J. Speech Hearing Res. 9, 498—518.
45. Subtelny, J. D., McCormack, R. M., Subtelny, J. D., Worth, J. H., Cramer, L. M., Runyon, J. C., Rosenblum, R. M. (1968): Synchronous recording of speech with associated physiological and pressure-flow dynamics: Instrumentation and procedures. Cleft Palate J. 5, 93—116.
46. Travis, L. E. (1917): Handbook of Speech Pathology. New York: Appleton-Century-Crofts.
47. Vallancier, B., Gautheron, B. (1974): Speech melody and articulatory melody. Folia Phoniatr. 26, 265—274.
48. Wingate, M. (1969): Sound and pattern in "artificial" fluency. J. Speech Hearing Res. 12, 677—686.
49. Wyke, B. (1969): Deus ex machina vocis. An analysis of the laryngeal reflex mechanisms of speech. Brit. J. Commun. 4, 3—25.
50. Wyke, B. (1974): Respiratory Activity of Intrinsic Laryngeal Muscles: An Experimental Study. In: Ventilatory and Phonatory Control Systems (Wyke, B., ed.), Chap. 24. London: Oxford Univ. Press.
51. Wyndham, C. H. (1970): Adaptation to Heat and Cold. In: Physiology, Environment, and Man (Lee, D. H. K., Minard, D., eds.), 188—189. New York: Academic Press.

The Art of Singing   8

Nearly all of mankind, regardless of the degree of civilization, indulges in and derives pleasure from song. Whereas some seem to have little capacity for singing in a manner pleasant to the listener and others exhibit remarkable talent in this direction, there are many capable of producing merely an acceptable singing voice whose performance can be appreciably improved by training. It is my purpose here to discuss some of the factors involved in converting the singer to the artist. In this chapter I shall present to you findings from research done at the Harvard School of Public Health in collaboration with Drs. Arend Bouhuys and Jere Mead, discuss my own personal experiences as a voice student and a singer, and try to provide some definition of those factors which are involved in artistic performance (10, 11, 16, 21, 22, 30, 31, 32).

Of what does the art of singing consist? Hector Berlioz wrote in 1862 (1):
A singer able to sing so much as sixteen measures of good music in a natural, well-poised and sympathetic voice, without effort, without affectation, without tricks, without exaggeration, without hiatuses, without hiccuping, without barking, without baa-ing—such a singer is a rare, a very rare, an exessively rare bird . . .
If she can strike a low G or F like a death-rattle and a high F like the shriek of a little dog when you step on its tail, the house will resound with acclamations.

This presents a negative approach, what not to do. In 1974 Carroll wrote (6):
The art of being a "singing teacher" is a special talent and an extraordinary gift, with which few people are blessed . . .
She then implores us to stop making a mystery of singing and says:
The science of singing consists simply of palate up, tongue down, larynx as low as is comfortably possible, and phonating vowels as close as possible to the point where the sound originates. Then, after inhaling abdominally, one allows the sound to float in one continuous stream on the breath with no interference from the consonants.

Offhand it might seem simple to eschew the errors listed by Berlioz and a little less simple to follow the directions of Carroll; but, as Berlioz says, the successful performer is an extraordinarily "rare bird". In the final analysis the measures of success are winning the audience, holding their attention, arousing in them an enthusiastic appreciation of the song, and being able to do it with reasonable regularity at performance after performance, year after year. In that sense one might say that many "pop" singers, who would not themselves claim to be artists in singing, are successful. For our purposes we must add to the definition of success the ability to sing great music, receive acclaim from a critical audience, and protect the integrity of the voice. In other words the professional singer must be able to produce the optimal vocal product and at the same time preserve the machine producing it.

In any event the simple ability to sing correctly, to stay on pitch, keep the proper tempo, produce tones of correct intensity properly modulated is not enough. Something more must be added to differentiate between a correct performance and an inspiring one. We will consider first those factors involved in correct singing and second those which elevate it to the level expected of a successful artist.

Physiological Studies

In 1963 and 1964 Drs. Bouhuys, Mead and I engaged in a series of weekend studies in Dr. Mead's laboratory at Harvard directed at an examination of the breathing mechanisms involved in singing (2, 23). Although it is possible to measure the pressures involved in phonation through a needle inserted into the trachea just beneath the vocal folds, and measure the characteristics of breathing with a mask over the face, these methods involve interference with the performance of the singer. For that reason we elected to use the following technique in our studies.

The subject was seated in a body plethysmograph (see Fig. 39 in Chap. 6) with the head uncovered. To reiterate some of what has already appeared in Chap. 6, a seal about the neck was accomplished by a collar filled with fine sand which set into a firm seal when exposed to negative pressure. Although this might be thought to provide some interference with free movement of the head and neck in fact, when properly positioned, it was perfectly comfortable and offered no interference. To measure the significant pressures two balloons were passed through the nose, one lying in the esophagus and one in the stomach. This also entails very little discomfort and the fine catheters leading to them, lying behind the larynx, offered no interference with singing. Since the body was sealed in an airtight box all movements of air in and out of the lungs could be accurately measured by a spirometer attached to the box. A vital capacity was recorded at the beginning and ending of each passage of singing in order to know at what volume the singer performed.

In addition, the elastic properties of the subject's breathing mechanism were measured through the performance of a slow expiratory vital capacity and recording of esophageal (pleural) pressure in conjunction with the volume tracing. Since airflow resistance is negligible during slow airflow, from that record we could calculate the exact force available from the sum of lung and chest elasticity at all lung volumes. Fortunately, all proper singing is accomplished with very low airflows and, therefore, the pressure in the alveoli is nearly identical to that just beneath the vocal folds (subglottic pressure) during singing. Thus variations in esophageal pressure from those related to elastic forces alone, at any given lung volume, could be used as a measure of subglottic pressures.

Finally the simultaneous recording of gastric and esophageal pressure yielded a measure of the pressure across the diaphragm, an index of diaphragmatic activity. This pressure difference was measured during the performance of a slow expiratory vital capacity (a condition in which the diaphragm is known to be relaxed) and compared with the transdiaphragmatic pressure during singing (Fig. 47).

One other maneuver was included separately. This was the use of chest and abdominal pneumographs to register relative changes in chest and abdominal circumferences. That measure has since been greatly refined with improved techniques by Dr. Mead's group, and their findings in this respect have been fully reported (see Refs. 9, 10, 22, Chap. 6).

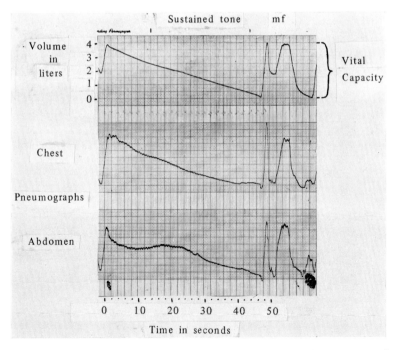

Fig. 55. Sustaining a single tone for 46 seconds. Volume changes above (compared to the V.C.—right). Changes in chest circumference (middle) and abdomen (below). See text for explanation. Compare to Fig. 49. This and Fig. 63 used with the permission of the Editor, Ventilatory and Phonatory Control Systems (Ref. 56, Chap. 1)

An example of the sort of record obtained is seen in Fig. 55 where we see the events observed during the singing of a single tone as reflected in the volume trace and the pneumographs. As we see this particular tone (which was in the singer's comfortable mid-range at moderate intensity) was sustained for 46 seconds, began very near the top of lung capacity, and continued virtually down to R.V. Airflow (which averaged 81 ml/sec) was a little higher during the first ten seconds but, even during that time averaged only 100 ml/sec. We see from the remaining 36 seconds that the tone can be maintained at a flow of only 75 ml/sec. If the subject (myself) had been in more perfect command of his performance the tone could have been sustained for an additional 4 seconds. We will return to this later in this chapter but for now let us note that, although long passages on a single breath rarely demand the full lung capacity, efficient use of the voice should demand the optimum of the breathing apparatus and voice at all lung volumes. Analysis of the esophageal pressure record showed that the subglottic pressure necessary for this tone of moderate intensity was about 10 cm H_2O.

In the same figure we see a recording of relative thoracoabdominal motion with the pneumographs. It is readily apparent that the chest wall grows smaller in circumference at a remarkably steady rate throughout most of the time. This fall in circumference begins about 2 seconds after the tone is attacked and almost completely ceases during the last 7—8 seconds. In contrast, although the abdominal circumference immediately decreases on the attack of the tone, it then remains more or less constant until the mid-lung volume has been reached, from which point on it steadily becomes smaller. Fig. 49 compares these thoracoabdominal movements with those observed in going over the same lung volume change with the glottis open (performance of a vital capacity). That they differ from one another is clearly seen; and that difference has been explained in Chap. 6.

In these two simple Figs. (49 and 55) lies one of the most significant facts regarding breathing related to singing, a fact to which I have alluded in both Chaps. 3 and 6 but which is of such importance as to warrant its reiteration here.

Elastic Forces and Muscle Control

At full lung volume (total lung capacity) the elastic forces of the chest and lungs alone (with all muscles relaxed) combine to produce a pressure of about 25 to 30 cm H_2O or more against a closed glottis. In most singing this far exceeds the pressure desired, in the case of the tone in Fig. 55 by 15 to 20 cm H_2O. Inspiratory effort is required to counteract these elastic forces and reduce subglottic pressure. In Figs. 49 and 55 we see, at the attack of the tone, the chest momentarily held in position while the abdominal wall moved inward slightly. The chest wall is fixed by the inspiratory intercostal muscles, probably assisted by the sternocleidomastoids which fix the clavicles. The diaphragm relaxed its recently completed inspiratory contraction and moved upward accounting for the initial airflow and the movement inward of the abdominal wall. The notch in the chest curve is probably a slight readjustment of the chest configuration when the inspiratory pull of the diaphragm was released. During the ensuing 20 seconds the steady reduction of the inspiratory intercostal activity accounts for the steady reduction in chest size and the airflow accompanying the tone (see Fig. 45). By this time the expiratory elastic forces have reached the point where they exactly equal the 10 cm H_2O subglottic pressure required for this tone intensity (24). To sustain that pressure now the abdominal muscles begin contracting, pushing the diaphragm upward and thus reducing lung volume. This is accompanied by further reduction in chest size in which expiratory intercostals come into play. Finally, during the last few seconds, the chest wall ceases to move and the abdominal muscles alone maintain airflow and subglottic pressure down to R.V. (13).

If the singer were to try to consciously control all these varied and complexly related muscle activities, or if the teacher were to say, do this or that with your chest or abdomen, with your inspiratory or expiratory intercostals, one could hardly expect the smooth transition from one muscle group to the other which is necessary in producing such a smoothly flowing tone production. How do you consciously relax your diaphragm? How do you consciously control the intercostals? Fortunately these maneuvers are roughly accomplished unconsciously as seen in the study of untrained singers, probably because similar actions develop in infancy and early childhood in learning to talk. But, in the untrained singer these actions do not achieve the perfection required for optimal singing. We will come to a simple exercise calculated to lead to perfection in a moment.

What is the evidence for relaxation of the diaphragm during tone production? That evidence comes from many sources. It was first pointed out in the classical paper of Draper et al. (see Ref. 4, Chap. 6). Electromyography has demonstrated the relative action of the intercostals and diaphragm. In our own studies it is shown in Fig. 47 which compares transdiaphragmatic pressure during the singing of a single tone and during a slow expiration (where it is know that the diaphragm is relaxed), both from T.L.C. down to R.V. Actually we might have predicted that the diaphragm could not perform such a delicate task while the intercostals could. As mentioned in Chap. 2, the difference lies in the presence of muscle spindles in the latter muscles, enabling fine control.

Now we are ready to reexamine the pressure-volume diagram once more (Fig. 46). Here are shown two single tones, one very soft requiring only 5 cm H_2O subglottic pressure, and the other a very loud tone requiring nearly 40 cm H_2O. For the first, at the attack, the inspiratory intercostals must supply a force resulting in a reduction of about 20 cm H_2O in the subglottic pressure which would have resulted from static elastic forces alone. As air begins to move out of the lungs this inspiratory muscle force must be immediately and steadily reduced until, at about 50 to 60 % of lung volume, it is zero. But then immediately and steadily the abdominal muscles must come into play and increase their force until, near R.V., they are supplying that needed for some 30 cm H_2O, 25 now counteracting the elastic forces and

5 for the subglottic pressure. In contrast, for the very loud tone, from the very beginning of the attack the abdominal muscles must supplement elastic forces and that supplementation must steadily increase as lung volume decreases. To further complicate matters, if the soft tone involves a smooth crescendo in intensity to the very loud tone and then a diminuendo back again to the soft again, appropriate adjustments all along the way are required to achieve the exact subglottic pressure desired.

Vocal Exercises

What is the simple exercise through which perfection in such performance can be learned? I well remember my first teacher, David Melamet, carrying me through that exercise over and over again (Fig. 56). He would give me a tone on the piano in my mid range and ask me to begin it softly, crescendo and then dimuendo, and continue the tone as long as I could. Each tone was exactly timed with the second hand on his large pocket watch. Each part of the exercise had to be done just right. The attack had to be soft but clear and on pitch, the crescendo smoothly carried out followed by the diminuendo calculated to just arrive at the initial intensity as the tone ended. But, most of all, the entire tone must be of maximum duration. I soon learned that the deepest possible breath was an essential beginning and equally essential was to begin the actual sound of the tone with the very first escape of air. It was also quite evident that, if the tone were to begin softly, I had to do something to control its intensity. When I was successful in doing that it turned out that I had a sensation as though I were breathing in instead of out although air was obviously moving out of my larynx. Finally, in order to gain his grudging approval (rarely accompanied by even a small smile) it was necessary that I go on singing smoothly and clearly until there was no breath left, but complete the tone cleanly, not breathlessly. Before long I found that the last of these required careful application of the muscles of my abdominal wall. I should stress here that Melamet did not give me any complicated descriptions of respiration physiology. He only told me what the product should be and indicated how near I came to fulfilling his goals.

If in doing this simple exercise one can gradually learn to increase the duration of the tone from 20 to 25 to 30 to 35 seconds or longer, maintaining good tone quality, that time increase is the best possible measure of the efficiency of breath usage and muscle control in singing. It is not necessary to use complicated maneuvers or apparatus, or to concentrate upon this or that muscle group (except for the period when one is first learning the importance of fine control of the abdominals). The second hand on the watch is the measure and to meet its challenge learning the proper use of the breath is essential.

It may appear that I have overstressed these points, but it is surprising to find how frequently the control of the breath is misunderstood by singing teachers and misinterpreted in books on singing. In one, otherwise excellent

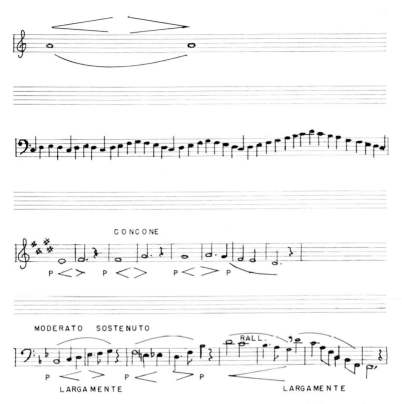

Fig. 56. Above, as described in text, the prolonged crescendo and diminuendo in a tone sustained as long as possible. Second line, the sort of scales used to overcome the "break" in the voice. Below, exercises from Concone, to be sung with a simple vowel. The first is a modification of the single tone above; the second intended to acquire smooth changes in tone intensity while going from tone to tone (Concone, Vol. 243, Schirmer Music Publ.)

text (8), there appears the phrase that air is "compressed into the diaphragm", to me a totally meaningless wording. In the same book appears the statement that, "Rationing the breath expulsion is always exceedingly dangerous, and there is convincing proof on all sides to support the claim that throatiness is the natural result of controlled expiration". I feel justified in saying again and again that in controlled expiration lies the very essence of fine singing.

Two points are notably difficult to learn, the beginning of a soft tone with the very first escape of air, and the continuance of the tone throughout the full lung volume without waste of air or wavering from the desired pitch and intensity (9, 14, 20). Teachers use a variety of expressions to facilitate the first (12). To me the most helpful are, "You must feel at the moment of attack almost as though you are breathing in, not out", and "Try to feel as though you are plucking the tone out of the air, not expelling it." As for the second point, I don't know how it is learned. One does learn quickly to avoid a "breathy" quality and achieve absolute clarity, but the inexorable value read from the watch's second hand is the key factor. You work and work until you know you cannot achieve a longer time. It is my opinion that there is nothing the teacher and student of voice can do which will equal the value of this simple exercise in learning the use and control of the breathing mechanism in singing. When it is extended from the upper middle range to the lower notes of the voice and various degrees of moderate crescendo are employed, a process involving months of study, the student will have achieved a sense of confidence and mastery which is essential if he is to be able to concentrate on song interpretation and leave the breathing mechanism to be controlled by well developed habit. The singing teacher often uses the phrase "support of the tone". That should refer to the correct use of the abdominal muscles to provide the control of subglottic pressure in the most effortless manner.

Another dividend from this exercise is the habitual seeking a full lung volume before beginning to sing, and the recognition of the fact that singing at volumes from T.L.C. down to a little below F.R.C. is more comfortable than at the volume from F.R.C. to R.V. The reasons for this relative discomfort at low lung volumes are complex and incompletely understood.

The "Break" in the Voice

As valuable as it is repeated performance of the exercise just discussed can be boring. As a reward the teacher will permit scales and more interesting and, in a sense, more challenging exercises (Figs. 56 and 57). In the singing of a scale from mid range up into the higher notes of the voice (not the highest but about three to four full tones below it) most singers find that the voice tends to "break" at some point. My own baritone range is from a low E to a high G sharp and the break tends to occur at about middle C to the D above. The scales should extend just above that breaking point. The nature

Fig. 57. Some of the simpler exercises in Vaccai combining the mastery of intervals and the enunciation of speech sounds (Vaccai, Vol. 1911, Schirmer Music Publ.)

of this "break" is not entirely clear but I have my own opinion. As explained in Chap. 5 the higher tones of the voice are reached by increasing tension and length of the vocal folds (25, 26). It is quite clear that the trained singer employs an increase over the resting length up to perhaps 30 % in reaching the highest tones. There can be no doubt that when the voice is well trained and kept in perfect condition such a "break" is absent or at least imperceptible (1, 17, 18).

It is my opinion that one naturally uses increased tension to raise pitch and that mechanism is instinctively employed until the pitch will go no higher. Increase in tension of the folds is a normal part of the action for tight glottic closure when the larynx is carrying out its ordinary function as a valve. To reach the next higher note (after that accomplished through raised tension alone) the mechanism of length increase is then suddenly brought into play (involving the cricothyroid and the strap muscles of the neck). What is learned in good voice training is the bringing in of length increase to supplement tension at a lower pitch than absolutely necessary and thus avoid any abrupt transition from one mechanism to the other. We have no voluntary control of the muscles involved. Our only recourse is the performance of such scales (covering the breaking point) in a quiet (but not breathy) clear tone, striving for a perfectly smooth legato, and reducing any sense of effort to an absolute minimum. With the help of the good teacher's ear one thus learns by trial and error, so to speak, the optimum transition from mid to upper range.

There is perhaps more debate over this than any other subject in the field of voice training. Unfortunately a number of terms have come into the teacher-student jargon which have no really satisfactory definition, terms such as "head register", "chest register", etc. Even the widely accepted term "covered" or "dark" voice can lead to confusion in the mind of the student if not the teacher. Often there seems a tendency to think that the use of such terms is an adequate substitute for understanding. My explanation for the "break" may not be entirely correct. We have no proof that it is. But it does take into consideration some of the known facts about the organs of voice and the physiological means involved in phonation. Whether one is singing softly or loudly, at a low pitch or high it is the same glottis which sets the air column in vibration, the same breathing mechanism producing the airflow and subglottic pressure, and the same supraglottic spaces acting as the resonant amplifiers. Applying an adjective descriptive of the quality of tone does not really help our appreciation of the function involved.

High Tones

I stress here that these scales which we have been discussing need not, and indeed should not, extend to the highest notes of the voice. It is the transition toward them which should be involved. I shall never forget my learning of that point. For three years Melamet had restrained me from singing beyond the

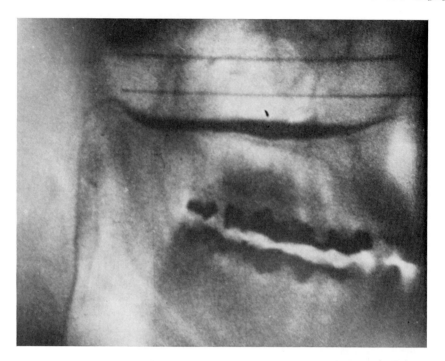

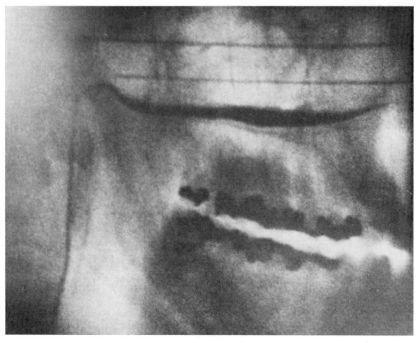

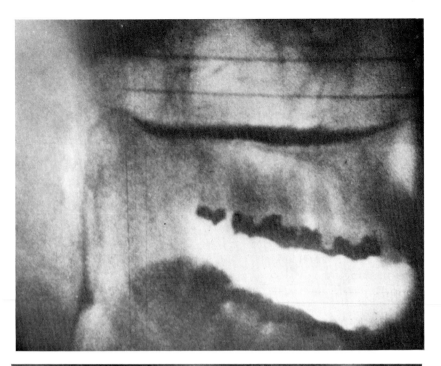

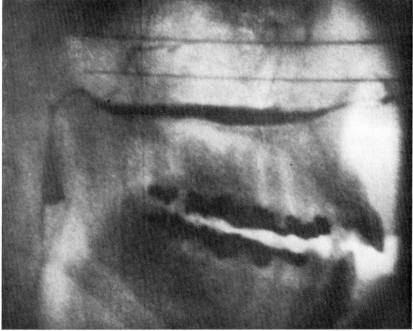

Fig. 58. Frames from a cinefluorograph showing a part of the supraglottic airway during singing. Left, top, the vowel "i" as in the German "mild"; right, bottom, during a quick inspiration between song phrases

upper E of my voice, and not even a thought was given to the possibility of higher tones. On Melamet's death I went with Pietro Minetti at the age of 19 years. At my second lesson with him Minetti opened the score of Verdi's "La Traviata" and turned to the aria "Di Provenza il Mar". I began singing it, but when I came to the high G in "Dio mi guido . . ." I stopped and explained Melamet's restrictions. He said to just go ahead and sing it. I easily produced as fine a G as I have ever done since. Minetti then said in his quiet voice, "Your high tones need not be practiced. They are like precious jewels which you only take out and show now and then."

One of the first questions I ask a patient who is in trouble with the voice is whether or not he practices his high tones. If he does so excessively this is very likely the source of trouble.

In addition to the simple scales, the use of exercise books such as Concone and Vaccai (Figs. 56 and 57) allow the student to develop some finesse in performance and add pleasure to the hard work of the scales and single tones. Another point of development, occurring with scales and simple exercises (such as in Concone and Vaccai) is the conservation of breath and control of subglottic pressure in going from one tone to another, learning the intervals, and in making the speech sounds which will have to come into play in song. Finally, as the voice matures, the student can begin song singing. I believe oratorio makes an excellent transition. The combination of recitative and aria, and the required complex vocalizations make not only beautiful music but marvelous vocal exercises.

An interesting vocal phenomenon, which is necessary in some singing but never quite mastered by some singers, is the "trill" (not to be confused with the execrable wobble which characterizes some of the worst singing). This consists of the rapid but clean variation of pitch by one semitone. From previous discussions of pitch control it should be clear that it is a complex maneuver. Exactly how this is accomplished is not clear. That it may be a simple rapid variation in vocal fold tension is possible.

The Fourth Formant

As training progresses more and more emphasis is placed on achieving optimal vocal resonance, not loudness but resonance. In essence this consists in the appropriate shaping of the supraglottic airway (28). One cannot simply decide to employ this or that muscle group to lower the tongue, change the position of the larynx in the neck, move the palate, lower the jaw, etc. Practice with the various simple vowel sounds will allow the student, with the teacher's guidance, to find the optimum shapes for each (Fig. 58). Some emphasis can be placed on lowering the entire mandible, not just opening the mouth in front. Keeping the larynx low in the neck (3, 6) lengthens the supraglottic airway. This is probably a key factor in adding to the three formants, usually present in vowel sounds, a fourth (19, 27). It is that fourth formant which appears to distinguish the fine full voice of the accomplished singer.

Lowering the larynx is not accomplished by a special muscle effort. Rather it probably results from singing with the neck muscles relatively relaxed. The quality of tone thus achieved is unmistakable. It can only result when the voice is produced effortlessly, without any sense of strain in the throat. In this connection the reader is referred to excellent papers by Bunch (3, 4) directed at the problem of defining the "covered" vs the "open" voice. She uses these terms in the sense that a degree of "covering" is recognized by singer and teacher alike as necessary for a proper tone especially in the higher register and that the "open" quality approaches a yell or scream and is highly undesirable. She was able to demonstrate that an enlargement of the pharyngeal cavity was a major factor in "covering" and comments, "This means that for good vocal production, the space must be achieved by a kind of spontaneous relaxation, not by an effort to physically manipulate the mouth, tongue and larynx" (5).

Resonance

In the effort to acquire the resonance needed for the voice to carry through a large hall even at low intensity, and at the same time minimize effort and avoid the "break" in the voice, a number of factors come into play (29). With optimum resonance the softest tone will carry. Indeed, one of my teachers used to say that when singing softly you should see people in the back rows looking up from their programs. The clear quiet voice is more likely to hold the audience's attention than is the loud voice. Resonance can be lost is passing from the quiet tones through mezza voce to a crescendo. It is helpful to think, not in terms of a "loud" voice, but a "big" voice. Only a moderate increase in abdominal muscle activity suffices to produce the added subglottic pressure. No change in the region of the neck is needed or should occur. A sense of strain there is a danger sign. Passages in the full voice or crescendo are far easier near the top of lung volume where relatively little abdominal muscle supplementation of elastic forces is required. As shown in Fig. 46, at 10 % V.C. the loud tone requires 40 cm H_2O pressure from the abdominal muscles compared to only 25 cm H_2O at 50 % V.C.

The term "covering" (7) is employed to emphasize the need for special expansion of the supraglottic airway in passing from the mid to the higher range of the voice. It is difficult to say of what this actually consists other than what has been written above. Probably, as Bunch suggests, it is accomplished by lowering the larynx, mandible, and tongue but the singer himself thinks of "darkening" the tone. It is a useful maneuver when there is difficulty avoiding the "break"; but, once the singer has mastered this transition from mid to high voice, the "darkening" and "covering" of tone may play a relatively minor role.

The curious student may wish to observe in himself some of the points made above. It is very easy to palpate one's own larynx (Fig. 59). The "Adam's apple" is readily identified in men and not too difficult in women. Move the

8*

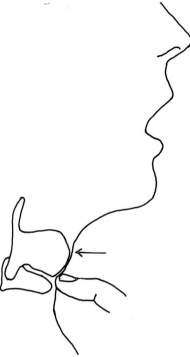

Fig. 59. The finger tip lies in the cricothyroid space. There it can note movements of the larynx up or down and changes in cricothyroid activity accompanying changes in pitch. The arrow indicates the "Adam's apple"

finger downward from the chin in the midline, pressing the skin inward. The hyoid bone is first encountered and just below it is the "Adam's apple", a small notch at the top of the thyroid cartilage. The finger then moves downward along the thyroid cartilage some two to three cm until a depression can be felt between its lower border and the readily palpable cricoid. With the finger held lightly in that space, movement of the larynx as a whole upward or downward can be noted, as well as any narrowing or widening in the cricothyroid space. Widening signifies relaxation of the cricothyroid muscle and shortening of the cords while narrowing signifies contraction of that muscle and lengthening of the cords. If one begins in the mid range of the voice and sings a scale going downward a clearly identifiable widening should be noted in the lowest tones. A marked narrowing should be noted as the scale goes upward to the highest tones. In my own voice during the lowest tones the cricoid is nearly at the level of the top of the sternum (breast bone).

After two or three years of hard work mastering breathing and tone production, attention must be divided between these facets of the voice and artistic interpretation. We have briefly referred to tone quality thus far. It is an almost indefinable quality but absolutely essential for a beautiful voice. Even two equally successful artists with similar voices will differ enough in tone quality to enable one to tell one from another by simply listening to a recording. With some the production of beautiful tone comes naturally. This is especially so of those whose native speech entails good tone, such as the Welsh and Italian. But what of the others? The optimum tone quality is a matter of the formants which make up the vowel sounds. The formants, or resonant sounds, are in turn a function of the natural shape and adjustments thereof of the supraglottic structures.

Sundberg (27) has pointed out (as McGinnis [19] before him) that trained singers exhibit the three formants found in most voices plus a fourth usually not found. He attributes this to their lengthening of the resonating airspaces. This formant is vital not only to the quality of sound produced but to the ability of the singer to make the voice clearly audible even when competing with the multiplicity of sounds emanating from a full symphony orchestra. How is it taught? Probably no two teachers approach this in the same way but all fine teachers recognize the product and its significance. Phrases such as "covering", "relaxing the throat", "keeping the larynx low", "lowering the jaw", "opening the mouth", "feeling the tone", etc. are all aimed at the same objective, appropriate adjustment of supraglottic airspaces for the sounding of any vowel with the most perfect clarity and beauty. In each of the exercises mentioned above constant attention is paid so that gradually the pairing of breathing and pressure with tone quality becomes instinctive.

Diction

Diction, especially when one is to sing in a number of different languages, is another matter. It requires conscious attention and conscientious work. The use of a tape recorder to allow the student to hear his own voice is of value here as well as in improving tone quality. Certain rules should be mastered. In contrast to ordinary speech, vowels must be clear and not slurred, but the quality of the vowel must be very close to that employed in speech if it is to achieve appropriate recognition by the listener. It is of interest and worthy of note here that, whereas some vowel sounds as in "far" can be sung with either good or poor tone quality, the vowel sound as in "moon" or the German "Ruhe" can only be sounded properly. It requires correct positioning of the supraglottic airspaces. Consonants must be pronounced more or less as in speech but, except for purposes of special emphasis, escape of air with some must be limited. A slight rolling of "Rs" and trilling of "Ls" not only adds to intelligibility but produces a pleasant sound. Of special importance is the occasional introduction of a vowel where none is ordinarily sounded, as in "der (a) Friede". One cannot do justice to the "r" at the end of "der" or the "F" at the beginning of "Friede" without the interposition of an almost imperceptible vowel. In the lines "Du bist die Ruh' der Friede mild, die Sehnsucht du und was sie stillt" (in Schubert's song "Du bist die Ruh'") an almost imperceptible vowel between "bist" and "die", "Sehnsucht" and "du", and "was" and "sie" are essential if one is to be clearly understood. The importance of a consonant sound must not drown out the essential vowel. The German word "ich" exemplifies this. Without care the "ch" will be heard and the "i" lost. At the same time the soft "ch" must be delivered with care not to lose excessive breath. Words beginning in "wh . . ." may be most clearly understood if the sound is "hoow . . .". Incidentally, disciplined diction will lead to clearer speech so that one's speaking voice will be understood more readily without resorting to undesirable loudness.

Performance and Pitfalls

In Shakespeare's "As You Like It" (Act V, Scene III) appears the following admonition:
"Touchstone: . . . Come, sit, sit, and a song.
First Page: Shall we clap into it roundly, without hawking or spitting or saying we are hoarse, which are the only prologues to a bad voice?"
    The teacher might well so advise the young student. Especially when nervous the beginner may hawk and clear his throat or start his song with a pessimistic view that the voice is a little hoarse today. No singer is always at his best. As a rule, within the first few minutes of a performance one knows how well the voice will meet the demand. When it is perfect the delivery of a fine performance is pure joy. When it is a little below par all of the art of the singer must be utilized and such thoughtful care will often be rewarded by resounding applause. Learning to deliver such a performance under imperfect circumstances is an important part of voice training.
    The professional singer never really stops studying, just as the serious scholar never limits himself to teaching but continues to learn. No matter how well the use of the voice has been learned it is possible to slip back into

Fig. 60. The beginnings of the first and second verses of F. Schubert's "Du bist die Ruh'"

bad habits which may have been initially discarded years before. But here let us consider the still young student who has devoted three to four years to learning the proper technique of voice production and is now ready to begin public performance.

Song Singing

Some appreciation of the necessity for the perfection of breath control may be derived from examining the events occurring in songs. In Figs. 60 and 61 we see as an example the song Schubert's "Du bist die Ruh'". First note that although the song was begun at a volume of 4 l (just about the top of the vital capacity) and although this song offers no remarkable problems in long phrasing, the third and fourth phrases end very near residual volume. Had the song been begun at a lower volume, had the breaths between phrases been less deep, had a little more air been leaked with such consonants as in "bist", "Sehnsucht", "was", or "stillt" either of the last two phrases might have had to be ended inappropriately because of lack of breath. Actually in singing this verse the lung volumes between 91 % and 0.7 % of V.C. were employed. Subglottic pressures ranged between four and fourteen cm H_2O.

"Zueignung" (R. Strauss) is a song in sharp contrast to the lovely "Du bist ..." (Figs. 62, 63, 64). In this dramatic song lung volumes between 93 and 0.5 % of V.C. were employed and subglottic pressure ranged from 5—38 cm H_2O (the latter on the first "Heilig"). To get full dramatic emotional emphasis more stress is placed on certain consonants. Note the

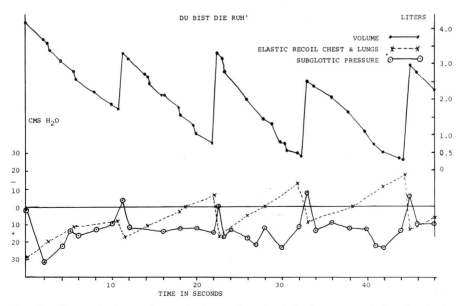

Fig. 61. Changes in lung volume, elastic recoil, and subglottic pressure during the singing of the first four phrases of F. Schubert "Du bist die Ruh'"

cost of such stress on "bis ich", "Heilig", and "Habe" (Figs. 63 and 64). Also note the nearly total vital capacity inspiration between "dir Sank" and the final "Habe Dank" (Fig. 64). Over a full second is available for that breath so it need not be excessively hurried, but the full lung volume is needed for the proper sustaining of the phrase and a clear "k" at the end. Other breaths between phrases had to be taken in times as short as $1/5$ sec.

Fig. 62. Phrase from R. Strauss "Zueignung"

It should be perfectly obvious that the artist in performance is directing most of his attention to what he is singing not how he is breathing. Basic proper breathing has been mastered and is now instinctive. Special versions of breath control are learned for each specific song in relation to the problem it offers, but learned thoroughly prior to performance.

This stage (age 19—22, third to sixth year of study) is an ideal time to perfect certain things which may be difficult later on in the face of a crowded schedule of performances. This is the time to acquire and master a fine repertoire of songs, to become thoroughly familiar with oratorio and other important choral pieces, to learn key operatic roles, to learn to sing in chorus, quartet, and duet, to listen to and observe accomplished artists. Public performance should be regular but infrequent and preferably before highly critical audiences. The good student is looking for criticism not acclaim.

An important part of the learning process at this stage is the use of audience feedback to modify performance. The true artist will rarely perform a single piece exactly the same way twice. In the first place he is constantly learning more and more about the various ways to approach any particular piece of music. In the second place he is learning that what pleases one audience at one time may be quite different from that which will win another audience at another time. This feedback process begins the moment one walks onto the stage. Look around the auditorium so that you have a feel of personal communication with individual listeners. Take a few quiet deep breaths and, at the first note, look in the back rows and see if heads are raised from programs to you. Utilize soft passages particularly to observe the degree of attentiveness in the corners of the hall. One quickly learns to "feel" whether or not the audience is literally hanging on your voice or merely giving it

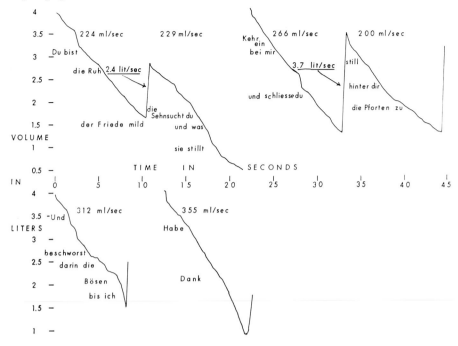

Fig. 63. Changes in lung volume, with flows and inspiratory volumes noted, during parts of "Du bist . . ." (above), and "Zueignung" (below). Note the loss of breath with "schließe", and "beschworst"

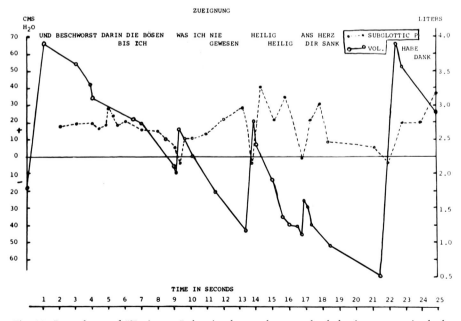

Fig. 64. Last phrase of "Zueignung" showing lung volumes and subglottic pressures in the last verse. Note the inspiration of nearly four liters before the final "habe Dank"

polite attention even when lights prevent your clearly seeing them. If the latter, you must do something to win their rapt attention, and that something is never singing more loudly. A subtle change in rhythm, more care in diction, spinning soft phrases are all fruitful. Correct performance is not enough. It has to be an inspired performance, inspiration arising both from the music itself and from the impact it makes upon the audience.

The experienced singer is familiar with the feeling of absolute control when the voice is exactly right. You know it will respond exactly and effortlessly to your every demand. Unfortunately none of us is perfect all the time. Every experienced singer is familiar with the sinking feeling which comes when unexpectedly the voice is found to be less than perfect. The soft tones lack their full resonance, the high tones are a little difficult, the easy flow of tone is just a little broken, the fine timbre of the voice is less lustrous than usual. It is on those occasions when the artist calls on every "trick" in his bag. Just a little more attention to diction, substituting here a soft voice dramatically emphasized for a passage ordinarily done near to full voice, beginning a crescendo passage very softly, all of these and more are used. Often, after such a performance, one is surprised to have people come up and say they never heard you in such perfect voice. So, having a few cards up one's sleeve is important for even the most talented and honest singer.

A number of "tricks" are especially valuable in this regard. The most important of these is the mastery of the pianissamo to the point at which you are sure of its carrying through the hall but where the audience is compelled to listen for it. On occasions when the voice is not perfect increased emphasis on diction can almost make up for it in the soft voice.

A second point is appropriate changes in tempo. To carry the listener's attention, abrupt changes in tempo are best avoided. Don't leave them behind or drag to the point where attention flags. Pauses can be very effective. Absolute silence, lasting just long enough, has a palpable effect.

A third point has to do with the full voice. Where crescendo is called for at the end of a phrase leave the swelling tone hanging in the air. Frazer Gange, my teacher during my last years of study admonished me, "Never give 100 per cent of your voice. If you do the audience knows it. If you give 95 per cent they are left with the impression that you have an infinite reserve left".

A passage typical of the last mentioned point is in R. Strauss' "Ruhe meine Seele". The song begins quietly and builds to a powerful crescendo in the phrase "... bringen Herz und Hirn in Not" (Fig. 65). The tone on "Not" swells but is stopped before full fortissimo without too sharp a sounding of the final "t". The sound appears to go on swelling into the ensuing silence. The pause must be just long enough for that to be fully appreciated before returning to the next "Ruhe, ruhe meine Seele". Gange was a master of song interpretation and filled his performances with fine nuances which kept his audiences spellbound and marked him as a true master. It is of incidental interest that his natural range was well under two octaves; but, with appropriate choice of repertoire and transposition of keys, no one would have guessed this limitation.

Fig. 65. Phrases from G. F. Handel "Where'er you walk" and R. Strauss "Ruhe meine Seele". See text for explanation. The rests occurring during the word "shade" (above) are brief silent pauses without breaths. The time for the rest after "Not" below is up to the discretion of the performer. It should be long enough to feel the full tone on the word "Not" hanging in the air

An example of the use of timing and pauses occurs in Handel's "Where'er You Walk" (Fig. 65). In the line ". . . shall crowd into a shade . . ." the pauses between the breaks in the last word are sung as indicated (without breath or sound during the brief rests). The effect is a clear denoting of the spread of the shade of the tree.

Acting

Another opportunity exists in this stage of training. The accomplished artist is as devoted to good acting as to singing itself. But most people find it impossible to act normally on stage without extensive coaching and experience. It seems impossible to observe oneself objectively. But in every hour of every day you do have the opportunity to observe others, not just look at them but observe minutiae of how they do things, sitting, standing, eating, drinking. Note what is awkward, what is graceful, what is appropriate to varying circumstances. With that background on stage you can fall back on what you have actually observed in life to guide your actions.

Singers seem especially prone to the use of meaningless gestures and exaggerated expressions. Experience in song singing in concert should instill in you confidence in your ability to convey a world of meaning through the voice alone without gestures, grimaces, props, or costumes. Once that has been mastered one finds it relatively easy to keep the actions to the minimum natural to the circumstances of the story when singing in dramatic roles.

Finally another word about the relative value of extreme ranges and power in the voice in contrast to delicate control. At the end of his excellent paper on voice production and the phenomenal voice Khambatta says, "Is there any real limit to that phenomenal instrument the human voice? Probably not" (see Ref. 19, Chap. 5). I concur in this tribute to the marvels of the human voice. But, as I have already mentioned, on one hand lies the temptation for the young talented singer to bowl his audience over with every performance, a course leading insidiously but almost certainly to undue strain on and permanent injury to the voice. On the other hand lies the acquisition and employment of the artistically delicately controlled voice mixed only rarely with more showy exhibitions of vocal capacity. This course leads not only to preservation of the singer's most valuable possession but to recognition as a true musical artist.

In summary the art of singing in its finest form cannot be learned from reading a book, nor can a respiratory physiologist or a laryngologist teach it. It must be taught by a gifted teacher of voice. The process of learning is of necessity a long one requiring years of study. Although anyone can be taught to improve vocal performance, only one gifted with the appropriate anatomy and possessed of a number of talents which might be grouped under the term "musical intelligence" has the potential of becoming a great artist. Certainly mastery of the use of the breathing mechanism is a sine qua non. Until that is accomplished to such a degree that control of the breath is instinctive it is useless to try to learn the multitude of other factors which combine to make the singer. Once it is learned so thoroughly that proper breathing is automatic, then the student can devote his attention to those other attributes which can lead to the transition from singer to artist.

References

1. Berlioz, H. (1862): A travers chants, études, musicales, adorations, boutades, et critiques. Paris: Michel Lévy.
2. Bouhuys, A., Mead, J., Proctor, D. F. (1968): Pressure-flow events during singing. Ann. N.Y. Acad. Sci. *155*, 165—176.
3. Bunch, M. A. (1976): A cephalometric study of structures of the head and neck during sustained phonation of covered and open qualities. Folia Phoniatr. *28*, 321—328.
4. Bunch, M. A. (1977): A survey of the research on covered and open voice qualities. N.A.T.S. Bull., February 11—18.
5. Bunch, M. A., Sonninen, A. (1977): Some further observations on covered and open voice qualities. N.A.T.S. Bull., October, 26—30.
6. Carroll, C. (1974): Longevity of vocal careers. Folia Phoniatr. *26*, 293—294.
7. Deinse, J. B., Frateur, L., Keizer, J. (1974): Problems of the singing voice. Folia Phoniatr. *26*, 428—434.
8. Duey, P. (1951): Bel Canto in Its Golden Age. New York: King's Crown Press.
9. Faaborg-Andersen, K., Yanagihara, N., Leden, H. v. (1967): Voice pitch and intensity regulation. Arch. Otolaryngol. *85*, 448—454.
10. Fields, V. A. (1947): Training the Singing Voice. New York: King's Crown Press.
11. Freud, E. D. (1955): Voice physiology and the emergence of new vocal styles. Arch. Otolaryngol. *62*, 50—58.
12. Gould, W. J. (1971): Effect of respiratory and postural mechanisms upon action of the vocal cords. Folia Phoniatr. *23*, 211—224.
13. Hirano, M., Koike, Y., Leden, H. v. (1967): The sternohyoid muscle during phonation. Acta Otolaryngol. *64*, 500—507.
14. Hirano, M., Ohala, J., Vennard, M. (1969): The function of laryngeal muscles in regulating fundamental frequency and intensity in phonation. J. Speech Hearing Res. *12*, 616—628.

15. Hirose, H., Gay, T. (1973): Laryngeal control in vocal attack. Folia Phoniatr. 25, 203 to 213.
16. Husson, R. (1962): Le chant. Vendomes: Presses Universitaires de France.
17. Large, J. (1972): Towards an integrated physiologic-acoustic theory of vocal registers. N.A.T.S. Bull., February-March, 18—36.
18. Large, J. (1973): Acoustic study of register equalization in singing. Folia Phoniatr. 25, 39—61.
19. McGinnis, C. S., Elnick, M., Kraichman, M. (1951): A study of the vowel formants of well-known male opera singers. J. Acoust. Soc. Amer. 23, 440—446.
20. McGlone, R. E. (1970): Air flow in the upper register. Folia Phoniatr. 22, 231—238.
21. Miller, F. E. (1910): The Voice. New York: G. Schirmer.
22. Pommez, J. (1962): Étude acoustique du vibrato de la voix chantée. Rev. Laryngol. 83, 249—264.
23. Proctor, D. F. (1968): The physiologic basis of voice training. Ann. N.Y. Acad. Sci. 155, 208—228.
24. Rubin, H. J., LeCover, M., Vennard, W. (1967): Vocal intensity, subglottic pressure and air flow relationships in singers. Folia Phoniatr. 19, 393—414.
25. Sonninen, A. (1954): Is the length of the vocal cords the same at all different levels of singing? Acta Otolaryngol. 118, 219—231.
26. Sonninen, A. (1968): The external frame function in the control of pitch in the human voice. Ann. N.Y. Acad. Sci. 155, 68—90.
27. Sundberg, J. (1977): The acoustics of the singing voice. Scientific American, March, 82—91.
28. Torp, I. M. (1954): X-rays for the voice instructor. Radiography 20, 210—213.
29. Van den Berg, J. (1968): Register problems. Ann. N.Y. Acad. Sci. 155, 129—134.
30. Vennard, W. (1964): Singing—the Mechanism and the Technic. Ann Arbor: Edwards Bros.
31. Vogelsanger, G. T. (1954): Experimentelle Prüfung der Stimmleistung beim Singen. Folia Phoniatr. 6, 193—227.
32. Zerffi, W. A. C. (1939): The search for a new vocal method. Bull. Hennepin Cty. Med. Soc. 10, 67—69.

9   Care of the Voice

Our ability to speak and sing are precious possessions and should be guarded from injury. Yet we usually take our voices for granted until serious vocal problems arise. When minor difficulties develop we have a tendency to simply hope they will go away. This chapter is devoted to a consideration of those factors which are of importance in protecting the voice (3, 7, 9, 13, 15, 17) and a brief consideration of the effects of pulmonary disease upon phonation. The problems of detecting the causes for vocal disabilities and correction of the underlying faults before irreversible injury has developed will be discussed in Chap. 10.

The factors involved in maintaining a healthy vocal mechanism fall into several categories. Among them are:
1. Negotiating the period from adolescence to the early twenties;
2. Avoidance of misuse of the mature voice;
3. General hygiene and the treatment of transitory illness;
4. Continued performance as one grows older; and
5. A few miscellaneous problems worthy of additional discussion.

All of these are epitomized in the singer; and, in general, what is good for the singing voice is equally desirable to the public speaker, actor, or salesman. Therefore, this discussion will be focused largely on the problems of the singing voice.

Early Development

When a child demonstrates musical talent, especially the boy soprano, considerable pressure may be brought to bear on parent and child to continue performing as long as possible (2). As the larynx begins its spurt of growth during adolescence, in spite of its rapidly changing anatomical characteristics the childlike singing voice can be continued for some time. If this is done the vocal cords are submitted to undue strain and may undergo changes which could preclude the successful pursuit of an adult vocal career. Since adolescence does not come on at any specific age the only safe rule should be that, at the slightest change in the speaking voice, serious singing should stop. This will ordinarily be at about the age of twelve years.

When can one safely resume singing? My own voice changed at a relatively early age and at 15 I was enthusiastically performing as the Captain of the Pinafore and singing "On the Road to Mandalay" at the drop of a hat. Fortunately just after I reached the age of 16 I was taken to David S. Melamet, an exceptionally fine singing teacher. After listening to me sing he advised me to either stop singing for two years or study with him. He accepted me as a pupil only on my assurance that I would neither drink alcohol nor smoke until my voice had fully matured. For the ensuing year I spent my time with him exclusively on exercises over a very limited range, about twelve tones from low G to D above middle C. In my second year he started me on a little oratorio (Handel's "Messiah" and "Judas Maccabeus"), and in my third year more oratorio and a few simple songs. No attempt was made to explore the extremes of my upper range and, in fact, high tones were strictly verboten.

These are the basic rules for the young singer. No smoking, no drinking of alcohol, place yourself under a careful and patient teacher, work on the control of the voice in your middle register, do not give public performances, do not test your high tones, and wait until you are 19 to 20 years of age to attempt serious performances. Obviously individuals vary and, whereas an occasional student will reach this stage at 18 years of age, others may not achieve reasonable maturity until 21 or 22. But, even then, the voice is growing and your knowledge of how to control it should be growing also. Don't ask too much of it, do not be tempted to start a professional career prematurely, and don't try to extend your range. The high tones which come effortlessly without being practiced should be the upper extent of your register. It is a common practice for the teacher or the choir director to try to make a tenor out of a high baritone or a coloratura from a lyric soprano. Don't try it. Finally both teacher and student must conscientiously refuse the temptation to seek for that glamorous but dangerous role of the child prodigy.

Vocal Misuse

When I was a young student at the Peabody Conservatory of Music in Baltimore there were a number of young students with such fine voices and excellent musical talent that their success seemed assured. Very few, in the long run, achieved that goal. In some instances it was clearly a case of deterioration rather than maturation of the voice. At the time I simply accepted the explanation generally given that the voice had not stood up to the strain of a professional career. Now, after forty years in the practice of otolaryngology, I know that these failures usually fell in one of three groups. One group had begun to suffer the effects of chronic misuse of the voice stemming from poor training but could be restored to normal again with proper care of upper respiratory disease and study with a skilled and understanding singing teacher. A small group may have had a vocal nodule ("singer's node"), a perfectly curable condition but also arising from vocal misuse. These two groups will be discussed in Chap. 10.

The third group consisted of those unfortunates in whom misuse of the voice had been continued long enough to result in permanent injury. A major objective of our discussions in this chapter is to consider the most important points involved in the avoidance of that tragic development. Sonninen and his colleagues have written important papers on this subject which have cast some useful light on this difficult problem (11, 12).

I have tried to stress in previous chapters that correct phonation (whether it be in conversation, public speaking, or the most difficult of operatic performances) is largely a matter of delicate control rather than application of great force. But, although phonatory airflows are low and subglottic pressures nowhere near those of which we are capable, phonation (especially professional singing) does involve certain special physical stresses. The first of these is the vibratory motion (necessary for sound production) imposed upon anatomical folds which developed phylogenetically purely for the purpose of tight closure as a valve. The second is the fact that this vibratory motion is continued for hours at a time, especially in certain concert, operatic, or even choral performances. The third, and more important, is related to the fact that for the high tones the vocal folds must be submitted to increased tension and elongation.

The vocal folds are covered with a thin delicate epithelium (Fig. 66) and beneath this lie the connective tissue, elastic elements, muscle fibers, and blood vessels. The stresses to which all of these structures are exposed in phonation

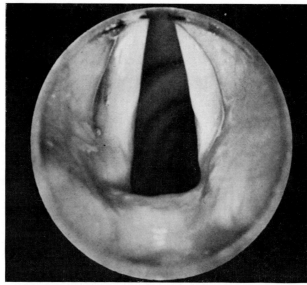

Fig. 66. Photographic view looking down upon the larynx. Note the vocal folds are almost pure white. This is the position of the folds during normal quiet breathing. The anterior commissure is not shown in this photograph

are very different from those associated with simple closure. With proper singing the vibratory motion itself is probably harmless as long as the voice has been allowed to mature sufficiently and slowly. But, even in the well trained voice, the elongation and tension necessary for the highest tones may be traumatic. What does this mean in terms of vocal hygiene?

It means that the singer who wishes to pursue a lifelong professional career must avoid the temptation of moving ahead too fast before the voice has matured or before the art of breathing and singing has been mastered. And, most importantly, it means that the highest tones must be used sparingly and with great care. Fortunately most good composers of vocal music are aware of these facts and seldom ask more of the voice than can be safely given. But the singer himself, with the guidance of a wise teacher, must limit his performance to songs and roles which fit his state of maturity and his natural voice. Otherwise, although there may be little immediate evidence of injury, gradually a thickened epithelium over the delicate vocal fold edges and scarring in the traumatized subepithelial tissues will inexorably take their toll. Such injury may be reversible in the earliest stages; but, after a year or two of vocal abuse, the vocal folds will be permanently damaged. This is the sort of injury which is usually totally undetectable on examination of the larynx. The damage is to the structures which make up the physiological components of the vocal mechanism and could only be surely identified by measurements which cannot be undertaken in the living larynx.

If the reader will refer back to Fig. 33 in Chap. 5 and consult similar diagrams in Ref. 12 we see that, whereas slight lengthening of the vocal folds (with moderately high tones) is achieved with little force, to produce maximum lengthening for the highest tones requires very great force indeed (Fig. 67), a force which can easily tear the tissues of which the vocal folds are composed. Please note in Figs. 33 and 67 the relatively small force necessary for moderate elongation. But there comes a point in this process when the length-tension curve bends sharply. That is to say that at that point a little more length is purchased at the expense of a great increase in force. This can only mean that the elastic structures within the vocal folds are reaching or passing their maximum stretch. This is a most important fact which deserves great emphasis.

Many singers who are easily able to produce the high tones expected of and natural to their voices find that, with sufficient effort on a good day they can proudly go still a little higher. That dramatic and unexpected extra range is impressive to the singer and audience alike, but highly dangerous. If injury, permanent injury, to the voice is to be avoided the singer must use his highest easily reached tones cautiously and sparingly, and the temptation to show off that additionally higher tone must be resisted. Remember that, although you may get away with it a certain number of times, each over-stretch will leave a minute but permanent injury. As they accumulate you may rather suddenly note that the fine quality of your voice is impaired; and, at that time, the change will almost certainly be irreversible.

Although some singers employ the falsetto voice without apparent harm, it is my feeling that the true falsetto also involves risk of injury. Some persons

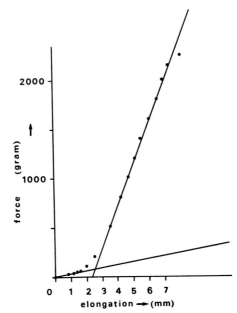

Fig. 67. From Sonninen (12). Compare to Fig. 33. Note the sudden break in the curve denoting the point at which further lengthening is accomplished only on expenditure of much greater force. (Used with the permission of the Editor, Acta Otolaryngologica)

speak of a special quality in the upper register as "falsetto". I use the term here to denote the mechanism already described which enables the singer to produce tones beyond the normal upper range of the voice. That is the close and tense approximation of the vocal fold edges so that only their mid portions participate in the vibration.

General Hygiene

During the period of early training, when no important singing engagements should be lurking on the horizon, is the ideal time for correction of physical problems which may handicap or impair the voice. If recurring respiratory infections, roughness, or hoarseness interfere with singing these early years offer the optimum opportunity for establishment of their cause and corrective action. More will be said of this in Chap. 10 but a few points deserve emphasis here.

If such problems develop the student should be referred to a competent laryngologist who has some special interest in and knowledge of the voice (10). That physician will be able to detect physical faults and advise as to their correction; or, if no such faults are found, offer some advice as to the possible erroneous phonatory behavior being indulged in by the student or the voice teacher. If nothing else, informing the teacher that there are no physical abnormalities to account for the problem will assist him in appreciating the need for an altered vocal approach. The skilled voice teacher soon learns which laryngologists he can trust in this regard (13).

The most common physical faults which may be uncovered are: chronic tonsillitis with frequently recurring acute infections, recurring or chronic sinusitis, allergic rhinitis, and grossly malformed nasal air passages. Not all sore throat is attributable to tonsillitis. If tonsillectomy is recommended a second opinion on its necessity might be wise. The young adult who suffers from two or more severe episodes of acute tonsillitis a year may well benefit from tonsillectomy, although appropriate conservative therapy should first be given a fair trial. Even when the tonsils have already been operated upon faulty surgical technique may have resulted in residual tonsillar remnants which can give rise to as much trouble as the tonsils did initially. If a tonsillectomy is decided upon, a time is selected when the student can spare at least two weeks from school. If the operation is to be performed with the use of an endotracheal tube a skilled anesthesiologist is of paramount importance. Tracheal intubation can be complicated by laryngeal granuloma, and the skill of the anesthesiologist is a major factor in the avoidance of that complication. Of course the surgeon must be skilled and avoid injury to the surrounding structures so vital to the voice while being certain of a complete removal of the tonsils. Properly performed tonsillectomy should produce no change in the voice (8, 16). The student may usually resume singing in about two to three weeks.

The common cold is often a mild disorder and the temptation may be to self-medicate with one of the various widely advertised over-the-counter remedies available at the neighborhood drugstore. Many of these remedies, although they may relieve symptoms, are more harmful than helpful in the long run. Even though the voice seems to be unaffected the wise singer will avoid any stress on it during the first two to three days of a cold. All of us are subject to the common cold and most of us to its occasional complications. Ordinarily this is a self limiting disease running its course to recovery in three to five days. Persistence of symptoms beyond that period generally means sinusitis and medical advice should be sought. At present there are no effective remedies for the cold itself. Rest, forcing fluids, aspirin, and antihistamines may reduce discomfort.

Sinusitis may offer a quite difficult problem. On one hand, symptoms may be very mild in an infection which nevertheless results in inflammation of the vocal cords. Therefore the possibility of this cause for difficulty with the voice should be considered especially in the face of a post nasal discharge and cough. More will be said of this in Chap. 10. Only a careful otolaryngologic study may uncover such an infection. On the other hand, problems thought to be attributable to sinusitis may have a totally different source. We have already discussed the normal drainage of mucus, downward from the nose and upward from the lungs (Fig. 25). One may become unduly aware of this normal mucus, and frequent attempts to clear it from the throat rather than letting it be swallowed can result in a hoarse voice. When sinusitis is uncovered its appropriate therapy should be followed by a careful check to be certain that the trouble is at an end. In some persons the common cold is regularly followed by sinusitis and some individuals in whom this occurs should have antibiotic therapy early in the course of a cold to prevent that complication.

Allergic rhinitis is characterized by sneezing, itching of the eyes and nose, a watery nasal discharge, and watering of the eyes. It may occur seasonally related to the prevalence of pollens, may come on suddenly for brief intervals related to exposure to specific allergens, or may produce chronic symptoms. It is readily recognized by the astute laryngologist; and, when the disease is suspected, a full allergy investigation and appropriate therapy are indicated.

As has already been stressed the nasal tract and the sinuses are important resonators for the voice (6). In addition a reasonably open nasal airway is essential to avoid chronic mouth breathing. When malformation of the nasal septum seriously impairs the nasal airway it should be corrected surgically. But beware the laryngologist who recommends such an operation if you are not having problems with the voice or with nasal breathing. A school of thought has become quite popular among otolaryngologists which attributes almost magical qualities to the shape of the nasal passage. Almost everyone has irregularities of the nasal septum and most of them produce no symptoms and have no effect upon the voice. If cosmetic surgery to the nose is contemplated try to obtain the advice of someone who understands nasal physiology. I have seen patients who had a beautiful cosmetic result from rhinoplasty but who never again had perfectly normal nasal function.

Such problems should certainly be considered during the early years of training. Unless the singer is completely free of upper respiratory problems contact with and confidence in a laryngologist should be established early. Assuming this period has been successfully passed we now come to the maintenance of a healthy voice in the mature singer.

The Mature Singer

It is now well recognized that no one should indulge in cigarette smoking. Its hazards to the general health are well established and it is certainly a major irritant to the voice. In the mature adult an occasional pipe or cigar is possibly harmless. The question of alcohol is another problem. Its consumption in moderation is probably harmless, but it certainly should not be indulged in prior to a performance. Sticking to mixed drinks or wine where the alcohol is well diluted is certainly desirable. But at least one very successful singer is said to have enjoyed a glass of akvavit after each performance (10). Decisions on this matter must be left to the individual's own experience and discretion. But cigarette smoking is never permissible.

For the free employment of the breathing mechanism tight clothing should be avoided. This includes girdles, belts, brassieres, and collars. All of these should be so loosely or flexibly fitted as to offer no significant impedence to the chest or abdomen, or neck. Posture is also important. An easy erect position is not only attractive but facilitates correct breathing. In concert performance, when the singer stands more or less quietly for prolonged periods, there should be a graceful stance where the weight can be shifted from one foot to the other imperceptibly. What to do with the hands may pose an awkward problem to the relatively inexperienced performer. Sometimes holding something, such as the program, produces an easier relaxed appearance.

The singer must remember that talking may be more traumatic to the vocal cords than singing. Conversation in noisy surroundings must especially be avoided (5). The crowded cocktail party in a smoke filled room is anathema to the singer and should be avoided if at all possible. This difference between the strain of talking and singing is commonly overlooked. At times the laryngologist advising voice rest may tell the patient that talking may be resumed after two weeks but not to sing for six weeks. This is the reverse of what is best for the voice. The trained singer knows how to use the singing voice. At the end of a period of voice rest the first use of the voice should be in brief periods of exercise of the middle register in the mezza voce. (The term mezza voce is used by me to describe the deliverance of a tone of low to moderate intensity, a clear tone, not a breathy tone.)

Today the professional singer may be forced to travel long distances by air between performances. As has been mentioned above, conversation should be minimized during flight. The singer has every right to insist on an appropriate number of hours to recover from "jet lag" prior to performance. If airotitis develops during landing the otolaryngologist should be consulted as to its avoidance in the future. If dulling of the hearing is noted on descent of the plane the nose should be closed and the ears cleared by blowing. This should be repeated as often as necessary. It is important not to be asleep during the plane's descent and no one should fly during a respiratory infection. Clear hearing is essential to effective singing. Prompt care of any problems involving the ears is almost as essential to the singer as care of the larynx.

The singer must beware of psychological problems which may interfere with the voice. A degree of nervousness and apprehension is normal. Most singers know that they must be a bit "on edge" to deliver their best. Incapacitating stage fright is an indication of the need for psychological help. The experienced performer knows that the voice requires rest before a long evening of singing. The temptation to keep trying the voice is to be resisted. It is possible to rehearse passages soundlessly. Clearing the throat should be minimized.

Except for singing with laryngitis the commonest source of injury to the voice (as described above) is undue strain. In addition to the cardinal errors listed above, this can arise from undertaking too arduous a schedule. It can also arise from attempting roles or songs which do not quite fit one's comfortable range. For the operatic singer protection from that strain can only come from appropriate choice of roles. For the lieder singer transposition from the original key may be the solution. One of my teachers, Frazer Gange, turned down an operatic career because he knew his range would not stand up to it. Those listening to his performance of Schubert, Strauss, Schumann, and Wolfe lieder in an appropriately transposed key never guessed that his full range was well under two octaves.

Especially early in one's career it is of paramount importance to avoid strain upon the voice. George London is said to have spoken the following wise words (14). Speaking of his voice as his "capital": "When I sing properly, I use only the interest on my voice and keep the capital intact. When I force my voice, I'm spending capital". In delivering a key crescendo at the end of a phrase (as already discussed in previous chapters) the tone should swell effortlessly and end so as to leave the impression that the tone goes on swelling through the hall. Maximum crescendos are expenditure of "capital".

The Older Singer

I am occasionally consulted by the singer who fears that his career may come to an end because of aging of the voice. Although it is true that some persons suffer a weakening of the voice with advancing years, the properly trained singer who has cared for the voice conscientiously may continue professional performance well beyond the age of 60. I myself am 65 and have not treated my voice with sufficient care. Still, if I take the time to practice for a few weeks, I am able to give a creditable performance. My old teacher David Melamet once told me a pertinent story. In his student days at the Royal Conservatory of Music in Berlin he went with other students to occupy the box reserved for students in the composer's class at an important performance of Handel's "Messiah". An old, retired, but formerly great singer was to do the difficult aria "The Trumpet Shall Sound" and they were all prepared to jeer. His performance was not only impeccable, it was thrilling. While the audience roared their enthusiastic approval the old man simply walked over to the composer's students box and scornfully tossed the score in to them.

In singing, as with all other physical activities, one passes the prime of life and reaches the time when there is a tendency to tire more easily. Some of the caution advised for the young maturing voice is applicable to the voice of the older singer. Avoid arduous schedules and do not undertake roles and songs which try the more difficult parts of one's range. If troubles develop with increasing age in spite of such exercise of discretion consult a laryngologist. If his findings are negative ask yourself if you have fallen into bad vocal habits.

Other Problems, Acute Laryngitis

Ordinary simple laryngitis offers a real threat to the maintenance of a healthy voice. It often impairs the voice so little that the singer is tempted to take some homemade remedy and go on with the performance. In that course lies danger. Laryngitis may be the result of a simple acute viral infection (as with the common cold or influenza), may be secondary to either an upper or lower respiratory infection, may result from trauma (yelling, screaming), or may even be the first sign of laryngeal cancer. Certainly, except for the brief viral illness during which voice rest is feasible, laryngitis is a good reason for consulting the laryngologist.

The first step for the laryngologist in management of the patient with laryngitis is certainly a careful history and examination. Not all acute episodes of hoarseness are simple cases of laryngitis. Only by determining that the symptoms came on acutely and recently, were not precipitated by vocal misuse (such as yelling at a football game), are not accompanied by an acute infection in the tonsils, chest, or sinuses, and are not the result of a vocal cord paralysis or even early laryngeal cancer, only by considering all of these and more can one be satisfied with a diagnosis of simple acute laryngitis. If that is the diagnosis there may be remarkably little to see on examination of the larynx. Even in the patient exhibiting an obviously hoarse voice there may be barely perceptible edema and reddening of the vocal folds. Very little thickening of those delicate structures is necessary to produce a gross change in voice quality, especially in singing. Acute laryngitis is most commonly the result of a simple viral infection and commonly accompanies the ordinary head cold or influenza.

Once one is satisfied that the problem is simple acute laryngitis therapy will depend on a variety of factors. If the patient is willing to go on complete voice rest for 48 hours and if the voice returns to normal in that time, consultation with the laryngologist is not necessary. But if there is an impending speaking or singing engagement, or if hoarseness persists after 48 hours, his advice should be sought. To my mind, in any event, there can be no question but that primary optimum therapy consists of voice rest. It is necessary to carefully explain that this means no singing, talking or whispering. Communication must be limited to pencil and paper. Such rest should be for a minimum of 48 hours and resumption of use of the voice should be preceded by a re-examination to be certain all evidence of vocal cord inflammation has disappeared. During the ensuing week talking should be kept to a minimum and singing limited to the simplest of exercises with the mezza voce, only in the middle register, five minutes or less two to three times a day. Full resumption of voice use can then be determined by the patient's reaction to these brief exercises.

But what of the part time singer who has a regular job requiring talking, or the singer who is scheduled for an important performance in the near future? For the former it should be made clear that he should remain at home, or go to work only if that work can be transacted without use of the voice. The decision for the latter is more difficult. If the laryngitis is mild with a nearly normal appearance of the vocal folds it is conceivable that a return to normal may take place in 48 hours or even 24. I advise the patient to return to see me the next day or 24 hours prior to any scheduled performance. It must be emphasized that singing within 48 to 72 hours of any acute laryngitis carries some risk to the voice. If the patient elects to take the risk I urge persistence in full voice rest right up to the actual performance. The temptation to "try" the voice a little should be resisted. The lack of any vocalization for 48 hours or more will not interfere with creditable performance by the well trained singer.

What about medicinal therapy? Many laryngologists pride themselves on their very own therapeutic regime which will rapidly restore the voice in a few hours even in the face of severe laryngitis. Certainly the inflammation of the vocal folds can be reduced by a number of topical or systemic medications. Among them are steroids, vasoconstrictors (decongestants), and antihistamines. The effects of such drugs may enable the singer to perform through an entire concert or opera. But the infectious process in the larynx is not so quickly cured. The risk of injury to the infected tissues, in which their inflammatory response has been pharmacologically reduced, is real. The long term preservation of the voice must take precedence over the importance of keeping any single engagement. Even though the singer escapes one such experience apparently unscathed, repetition of this approach with subsequent infections may lead to gradually increasing injury to the tissues of the vocal folds. Sometimes the professional who attributes his weakening voice to age may actually be suffering the results of such hazardous management of episodes of acute laryngitis over the years.

Steam inhalations from water treated with benzoin or other medicaments were at one time quite popular. They certainly do no harm and I never object to them but I doubt if they significantly alter the course of the disease. A long hot shower in a steamy bathroom may have a salubrious effect. Antibiotics have no use in the treatment of a viral infection; but, if there is evidence on the examination suggesting bacterial infection, one should be tried. I will say more of this below in discussing pharmacological agents in Chap. 10. Since a mild laryngitis (often without evident hoarseness) so often accompanies a common cold, my advice regarding the voice is similar for that condition.

If you have been properly advised as to treatment for laryngitis, with the consent of the laryngologist, you may usually plan on singing within a few days. But voice rest should be continued until the vocal cords are normal.

Respiratory infections may be readily spread from one infected person to another in a group singing together. Do not sing during a cold and do not sing in a group with a person who has a respiratory infection (1).

Mucous Membranes

The respiratory tract which we have discussed in previous chapters is lined with respiratory mucous membrane, and it is essential that that membrane be healthy if the voice is to be unimpaired. Respiratory mucous membrane, especially that of the nose and throat, is of necessity continually exposed to the ambient air which passes over it with every breath we take. It is affected by a wide variety of commonly employed medications. It responds to changes in weather and climate, both those which occur naturally and the artificial changes imposed by indoor heating, cooling, humidifying and ventilating. It is affected by emotional stress. Finally no two individuals respond in exactly the same manner to these various influences. In addition, of course, nearly everyone suffers from periodic respiratory infections especially the common cold and influenza.

If the professional singer is to fulfill most of his engagements he must be aware of all these influences and his own individual reactions to them. Such an awareness can become excessive and lead to a neurotic fear of a wide variety of factors which may impair the voice. I have had many patients who had become slaves to their desires to protect themselves from threats to their respiratory health. Some fear drafts, others dampness, others dry air, and others still going without a hat. The list could be endless. Although the intelligent person may pick up a few environmental influences which actually affect his health and use the information to his benefit, by far the majority of such fears are groundless. For the individual to fail to enjoy the ordinary pleasures of life because of false fears about health is a tragedy. In general ignore folklore and the advice of well meaning friends and seek the advice of your physician.

Some singers fall into the trap of becoming addicted to various medications or regimes some of which may be more harmful than helpful. In general self-medication is to be avoided. Drugs should be taken only on the advice of a physician who is cognizant of the problems of the singing voice. Exceptions to this rule are the use of aspirin for relief of minor discomfort, and the employment of certain mild troches the use of which may allay throat driness which seems to plague some singers.

Efforts should be made to avoid severe and sudden changes in climate, indoor and outdoor, as far as possible. When possible avoid indoor temperatures in excess of 23 °C (73 °F); and smoke filled noisy rooms should be considered off limits. It is sometimes difficult to determine which problems are related to emotional stress and which to organic disease. One should at least be aware of the possibility of the former, but laryngological consultation may be necessary to reach a clear decision.

Pulmonary Disease

An obvious factor in the care and preservation of the voice is the prevention of lung disease or its optimal treatment if it develops. Singers, actors, and public speakers probably have a susceptibility to respiratory disease similar to that found in those not pursuing vocal careers. But termination of such a career due to the development of such problems seems to be a relatively rare occurrence. The more obvious necessity, for those whose livelihoods depend upon the quality of their voices, to avoid cigarette smoking, heavy alcohol consumption, and frequent or severe respiratory infections must have some beneficial effect in reducing such susceptibility. The early development of the more severe forms of lung disease will either preclude the entrance into a vocal career or bring it to a premature conclusion. Still, a certain percentage of singers and speakers will inevitably develop pulmonary problems. Those problems may be so mild as to result in a handicap only apparent to the

individual because of his mastery of the use of the breath which enables him
to adjust to the interference with optimal function. But, when such interference
goes beyond a certain point, the impaired function will be apparent to the
expert critic and finally to the ordinary member of the audience. The teacher
of voice and the singer or speaker should be aware of the ways in which lung
disease may significantly affect performance. Such an awareness can lead
to early recognition of the nature of a problem; and, in some instances, it
may permit adjustment of the method of breath control to adapt the voice to
the limitation resulting from disease.

From the point of view of the chest physician one definition of a number
of lung diseases is the development of "inability to blow air rapidly from the
lung". That definition is especially useful to the physician since such an abnormality is readily detectable through common lung function tests such as the
forced expiratory vital capacity. If you have followed what has been written
in preceding chapters it will be readily apparent that such a definition is not
applicable to the determination of the effect of lung disease on voice production. Phonation never requires rapid expiratory airflow. But, since limitation
of expiratory airflow is often a sign of pathological conditions limiting other
facets of breath control, it may also signify the early stages of disease which
can affect voice production. Such abnormalities can be considered under several
headings including a reduction in useful lung volume, inability to breathe in
rapidly, inability to sustain prolonged expiration, and impairment of the fine
control of airflow. Parenthetically we may point out here that the chest
physician is aware of the fact that one manifestation of deterioration in lung
function is the inability of the patient to continue talking while walking.

We have already stated that the vital capacity per se is not a major factor
in voice production. A small woman with a vital capacity under 4 l can sing as
well as a large man whose vital capacity may be 6 l or more. Rarely do
passages in singing require the expenditure of more than 3.5 l of air. Because
of this the loss of lung volume through surgical excision of one or more of the
five lung lobes, or permanent damage of a portion of lung through pulmonary
infection is unlikely in itself to terminate the singer's career. Some adjustment
in the use of the air which the remaining lungs can hold may be necessary. But,
when the vital capacity is reduced much below 4 l the ability to sing will be
proportionately impaired.

There are other causes for the loss of useful lung volume such as injury
leading to fixation of a portion of the thoracic cage. Since this may also
affect the ready use of the intercostal muscles such injury can have a profound
effect upon the voice. A more important factor impairing the voice is the development of pulmonary emphysema. This unfortunate malady results in two
deficits. First there is an increase in residual volume, the volume of air in the
lungs which cannot be expelled in expiration. Thus, although total lung
capacity for air may be increased, vital capacity is reduced. Second there is a
loss of lung elasticity. The latter affects the voice in two ways. A lack of lung
elastic recoil, which normally brings the resting diaphragm high in the chest
ready for its forceful descent in inspiration, results in a relatively flat, low
contour of this muscle. From such a position the diaphragm can do little to

augment inspiratory airflow. More will be said of this below. In addition the loss of lung elasticity limits the degree to which this important force can be employed in generating subglottic pressure at high lung volumes. As a result muscular force is required at all lung volumes for the production of voice.

Whereas rapid expiratory airflow is not employed in phonation, relatively rapid inspirations are a sine qua non in singing and of importance to normal speech. Ordinarily the singer employs no more than a quarter of the capacity for rapid inspiration. In our studies we found only occasional breaths in the range of 3—4 l/sec, rarely as high as 5. But it is important for the singer to avoid the awkward appearance of making a maximum gasp for breath. Thus a reduction in the ability to breathe in as fast as 4—5 l/sec is awkward and a reduction much below that level will limit the performance of the singer or even the public speaker.

Impairment of inspiratory airflow can result from either increased resistance of the airways to airflow or a fall in lung compliance. The latter term "compliance" signifies the pressure across the lungs required to bring them to a given volume (cm H_2O/l). Among the conditions increasing airflow resistance is bronchial asthma, a disease associated with contraction of the bronchial smooth muscle narrowing the airways. Thus bronchial asthma may severely handicap the singer or the speaker. Although medications are available for the modification of such airway constriction they may have side effects injurious to the voice.

Reduction in lung compliance, which may be thought of as a "stiffening" of the structures involved in breathing, can result from a variety of disease processes. We need not list them here but merely note that they result in impeding motion in the normally well oiled machinery of breathing.

In addition to the accomplishment of quick inspirations the sustaining of relatively long expirations is necessary for singing and even ordinary speech. As has been mentioned the singer uses a breathing pattern which avoids a reduction in blood oxygen or a rise in blood carbon dioxide. But, if pulmonary disease has impaired the normal capacity for blood gas homeostasis, dyspnea (the feeling of shortness of breath) may develop with even mild demands for increased pulmonary ventilation. In such abnormal conditions the expenditure of the vital capacity may no longer be the factor limiting vocal phrasing. The termination of a phrase may be determined by an irresistable desire for a breath in. Such a sensation may also result from fear. Thus, in the public performer, breathlessness interfering with proper phonation is an indication for careful pulmonary function testing to determine whether it is based on lung disease or stage fright.

When neuromuscular disease affects the muscles of breathing phonation will of course be affected. Such diseases can produce their effects through muscle paralysis as in poliomyelitis or injury to the phrenic nerve by intrathoracic neoplasm with diaphragmatic dysfunction. But they may have more subtle effects impairing the fine control requisite to phonation, effects which may be uncovered only on careful neurological study.

Any pulmonary disease which results in chronic cough is especially damaging to the voice. The trauma of cough to the vocal cords is significant even during a transitory illness such as a cold or influenza. But the chronic cough characteristic of chronic bronchitis is very likely to permanently injure the voice.

The simple process of aging will affect the voice. It has already been stated that aging per se need not preclude the continuance of a successful career. But, without question, there is a loss of vital capacity with age, some reduction in lung elastic recoil, and a tendency toward drying of mucous membrane surfaces. The well trained singer or public speaker will gradually adjust to these insidious deleterious changes, but some adjustment is necessary in almost all who live beyond the age of 60 years.

Finally let us return to the problem of pulmonary emphysema. Not only can the well trained singer continue to perform during the milder stages of this disease but his performance may alleviate some of its symptoms. As stated above the loss of lung elasticity results in a fall of the diaphragm to a point from which it cannot effectively contract in inspiration. Respiratory therapists have long recognized that this can be partially alleviated by contraction of the abdominal muscles producing compression of the abdominal contents thus pushing the diaphragm upward. Thus the force of those muscles in part replaces the normal pull of lung elasticity. The singer is well trained in using his abdominal muscles to accomplish just this.

In view of these considerations the teacher and student of voice should consider the need for pulmonary function testing when breathing problems develop and cannot be otherwise explained.

References

1. Bates, J. H., Potts, W. E., Lewis, M. (1965): Epidemiology of primary tuberculosis in an industrial school. New England J. Med. *272*, 714—717.
2. Greene, J. S. (1942): Atypical laryngeal and vocal changes in adolescence. J.A.M.A. *120*, 1193—1197.
3. Greene, M. C. L. (1968): Vocal disabilities of singers. Proc. Roy. Soc. Med. *61*, 1150 to 1152.
4. Habermann, G. (1976): Sänger und Schauspieler in der Sprechstunde des HNO-Arztes. Laryngol. Rhinol. Otol. (Stuttg.) *55*, 433—446.
5. Klingholtz, F., Maerz, H., Siegert, C. (1976): Die Belastung des Stimmorgans bei Phonation im Lärm. Z. Gesamte Hyg. *22*, 812—815.
6. Lindqvist-Gauffin, J., Sundberg, J. (1976): Acoustic properties of the nasal tract. Phonetica *33*, 161—168.
7. Meurman, O. H. (1970): Should phoniatry be an independent specialty or a sub-specialty? Acta Otolaryngol. Suppl. *263*, 135—136.
8. Pfau, W. (1954): Tonsillektomie und Stimme. Z. Laryngol. Rhinol. Otol. *33*, 39—47.
9. Punt, N. A. (1968): Applied laryngology—singers and actors. Proc. Roy. Soc. Med. *61*, 1152—1156.
10. Sargeant, W. (1966): Profiles—Birgit Nilsson. New Yorker, October 29, 66—92.
11. Sonninen, A., Damsté, P. H., Jol, J., Fokkens, J. (1972): On vocal strain. Folia Phoniatr. *24*, 321—336.
12. Sonninen, A., Damsté, P. H., Jol, J., Fokkens, J., Roelofs, J. (1974): Microdynamics in vocal fold vibration. Acta Otolaryngol. *78*, 129—134.
13. Takahashi, H., Koike, Y. (1976): Some perceptual dimensions and acoustical correlates of pathologic voices. Acta Otolaryngol. Suppl. *338*, 1—24.

14. Wechsberg, J. (1957): Profile—George London—The vocal mission, I and II. The New Yorker, October 26, 49—84, November 2, 47—75.
15. Zerffi, W. A. C. (1939): Functional vocal disabilities. Laryngoscope *49*, 1143—1147.
16. Zerffi, W. A.C. (1942): Tonsillectomy and its effect on the singing voice. Arch. Otolaryngol. *35*, 915—917.
17. Zilstorff, K. (1968): Vocal disabilities of singers. Proc. Roy. Soc. Med. *61*, 1147—1150.

10 Detection and Correction of Faults

In contrast to the problems which we have just discussed the question of the voice in trouble in spite of reasonable attention to vocal hygiene may offer a knotty problem indeed. This chapter is directed at the voice in trouble and the multiple considerations necessary for detection of the cause as well as, whenever possible, restoration of normal function. Prompt and proper attention to these individuals is particularly urgent for two reasons. First, from the vocal point of view these persons are at least partially incapacitated. Second, the longer the voice problem persists the greater the likelihood or irreversible damage to the vocal folds. Obviously much of what is said in this last chapter must be directed to those on whom the responsibility falls for detection and correction of faults in the phonatory mechanisms; but the wise voice student, mature singer, or professional speaker should know enough to at least recognize the individual who pursues a reasonable course in diagnosis and therapy (8, 12, 16, 17, 18).

To Whom to Turn

When the voice is in trouble to whom should one turn for help? Primary consideration should be given to the laryngologist. Early detection of physical faults is the best possible path toward reversal of difficulties prior to permanent injury. If no physical fault is found the physician may then advise as to the need for the added help of the phoniatrist or singing teacher. The phoniatrist will suffice in most problems of the speaking voice, but the singing teacher will usually have first hand knowledge of the singing process through being, or at least having been, a singer. Most important of all the laryngologist should be able to work with the patient and whatever other voice professional is involved to decide upon the time course to be followed toward a quick and full recovery of function.

In the case of the young voice student perhaps the most difficult problem involved in the physician student patient relationship is to reach a decision as to whether or not a change in voice teacher is desirable. The fact that the student is in trouble is not in itself sufficient evidence for the need for such a move. It may be that other unsuspected respiratory disease has caused the problem, or it may be that the student has simply not been successful in following even a good teacher's instructions. In the latter case a thoughtful laryngologist may be able, through simple explanations of laryngeal function and the mechanism of breathing, to reestablish the necessary rapport and mutual understanding between teacher and pupil.

But, when questioning uncovers some of the cardinal errors in teaching methodology discussed in previous chapters, advice to change teachers is clearly indicated. The fact that a teacher may have played a part in the development of a number of successful or even famous singers is not proof that, in a specific instance, he is capable of solving the problem. Even extremely talented teachers may meet a seemingly insuperable problem in an occasional student, a problem which another teacher may solve. Chief among the teaching faults which I look for are: insufficient attention to breathing problems or evidence of mistaken beliefs about control of the breath, attempts to overextend the natural range of the voice, urging the student to tackle singing tasks which are too advanced for the young voice, undue practicing of high tones, excessive dwelling on the use of the full intensity voice, failure to concentrate on the mezza voce in the middle range of the voice, and most importantly failure to use appropriate simple exercises to develop that correct use of the breath and breathing mechanism so absolutely essential to effective talking or singing. In borderline instances the laryngologist may drop a few hints to the teacher which may be appreciated or resented. But a word to the wise is sufficient and may serve to reverse an unfavorable tide in the learning process. Only rarely have I found it necessary to recommend a change in teacher although I have suggested modifications in teaching method.

I have recently seen a young woman twenty years of age who epitomizes this problem. She came to me with the complaint of having lost her top tones. She had been told by her teacher that she must have vocal nodules and was convinced that her voice was gone for good. She had studied two years with one teacher and one year with another, and in spite of her youth had already tried her hand at opera. Examination showed a mild chronic laryngitis with no nodules and questioning revealed that she had not been even introduced to the simplest fundamentals of correct breathing with singing. I have instructed her as to some of the exercises which can help her to get started on that process and advised her to enroll with a first rate singing teacher. No permanent damage has been done to her voice as yet and she should rapidly return to her previous range.

From the teacher's point of view, when troubles develop which do not rather promptly respond to the teacher's best efforts, consultation with a competent laryngologist should be urged before permanent injury to the voice has taken place.

From the laryngologist's point of view the non-singing patient with a speaking voice problem who has no physical disease of the involved organs may be helped by a competent phoniatrist.

Since it is in singing rather than speaking where optimum control of the breath is so absolutely essential, when the major problem centers about breath control it is my preference to have the patient under the care of the singing teacher. Sometimes, even though the difficulty is with the speaking voice, the singing teacher interested in such problems may offer the best answer.

The Laryngologist's Role

We have already discussed at some length the diagnosis and treatment of a variety of physical problems which must be managed skillfully to preserve a healthy voice. In the case of the person in whom voice difficulties have already developed we have a different question. The singer (or speaker), the teacher, and the laryngologist must all be aware of the possibility that what appears to be merely a fault related to improper use of the voice may actually have its origin in totally unsuspected disease.

When I am consulted by a patient with a voice problem my first effort is to discover the exact history of events leading up to its onset. While, in the patient's mind, the key fact may be that only recently normal use of the voice has proven impossible close questioning may reveal that some months ago he had an unusually severe cold, or indulged in some indiscrete misuse of the voice. Not only will the correct history help in establishing the true diagnosis and therefore the correct therapy, but it is the best hope for understanding what must be done to avoid repetition. Often this story alone yields the most important clues as to the nature of the problem and its causes. In addition to the usual medical history I devote some time to learning as much as possible about the usual use of the voice and, if this is a student of singing, the manner in which the voice is being trained. When the difficulty was preceded by symptoms of respiratory infection or laryngitis, in addition to curing the patient of this episode, advice should be offered as to the avoidance of similar problems in the future.

If the patient smokes cigarettes they must be forbidden. The patient is unlikely to volunteer the information that he is a smoker. He must be explicitly asked. Forbidding their use is not enough. The habitual smoker finds the addiction very difficult to break. Careful explanation that their effect is not only on the vocal cords themselves and the efficiency of the breathing apparatus but also an increase of the chances of later development of lung or laryngeal cancer, pulmonary emphysema, chronic bronchitis, heart disease, and other serious and life threatening illnesses. Certainly the possible role of cigarettes in voice difficulties must not be overlooked.

When the vocal disability came on in circumstances where the subject was forced to talk or sing in noisy surroundings or under other adverse conditions such as overheated, cold, or smoke filled rooms there may be little one can do to prevent recurrences unless the patient is willing and able to forego such circumstances in the future. But often some help can be provided for those who are forced to perform in such unfortunate environments. Even the "pop" singer working in a night club who is unwilling to give up that way of life may be helped by advice on breathing and use of the voice. Indeed such persons may be in special need of such advice since they seldom have enjoyed the benefits of prolonged formal voice training. This careful history is a most important factor in obtaining long term good results. The patient must understand the significance of the factors resulting in, or at least contributing to, his difficulty. Even if the fault is found to consist of a simple physical abnormality, such as a vocal nodule, to prevent a recurrence both physician and patient must have an understanding of the most likely causative factors. More will be said of this later.

When a simple acute respiratory infection is the occasion for the patient's visit the conventional methods of treatment of such infection are only half the story. It is also necessary to advise about resting the voice and resumption of phonation. In addition examination after the infection has subsided (especially in those with unusual susceptibility to respiratory infections) may yield clues as to future prevention. On one hand chronic upper respiratory infection may exist without any symptoms other than the voice problem. In that case it will be uncovered only by careful examination. On the other hand, symptoms thought to be related to sinusitis may be purely functional in origin. Stress alone can result in headache, nasal congestion, postnasal discharge, and even sore throat. "Sore throat" may be wholly attributable to voice strain.

Paralysis of the vocal cord is readily detected if looked for, but this possibility may be overlooked entirely if the hoarseness is mild as is often the case. Malfunction of the superior laryngeal nerve is usually quite difficult to detect (22). When high tones are lost without any alternative explanation this diagnosis should be considered. Not only does this nerve supply the cricothyroid muscle (essential to lengthening the cords for high tones), but it is also the carrier of sensory fibers which play an important role in the neural feedback necessary for fine control of the muscles of phonation. If there has been permanent injury to that nerve (especially if bilateral) return to normal voice is probably impossible. Work with a phoniatrist may result in an improved voice. A tendency to choke and cough on swallowing is another symptom with suggests loss of function in the superior laryngeal nerve. Injury to strap muscles of the neck, as in thyroid surgery, may also eliminate high tones. A singer about to undergo thyroid or other neck surgery should so advise the surgeon who may be able to then take special care to preserve the full function of these muscles.

Although vocal cord paralysis may leave a person with remarkably little hoarseness, sometimes a very weak, breathy voice is the result. This comes from the fact that the paralyzed cord, although lying near the midline where it can be met by the normally moving cord of the opposite side, may atrophy and leave a gap for escape of air during phonation. In such patients injection of teflon into the involved cord will often restore a nearly normal contour of the paralyzed cord and resumption of a quite satisfactory speaking voice.

Collaboration between singing teacher, singer, physiologist, and laryngologist can be the basis for important research on the physiology of the voice, and also for investigations leading to the proper diagnosis of vocal disabilities and their rehabilitation (7). Such studies have often involved electromyography, high speed cinematography, and cinefluorography, as well as studies of breathing mechanics (6, 9, 13, 15). Most singers and their teachers will not have the time or inclination to indulge in these time consuming researches. If the simplest of them (such as measurement of phonation time, and spirometric evaluation) were available at conservatories of music they would probably prove valuable, but only if the appropriately trained personnel were available to conduct and interpret them.

The experienced singer will quickly recognize the competent laryngologist who has an intelligent interest in the voice. But beware of the physician, no matter what his reputation is in these regards, who takes a quick look at the vocal cords and prescribes his favorite "secret" medications. Unless the examination includes the ears, nasal passages, the mouth and throat, as well as the larynx the true cause for the problem may have been overlooked. Even if the medications did provide at least temporary restoration of the voice, recurrent difficulties suggest the possibility that their cause has been missed.

The initial consultation with the patient should include careful inquiry as to understanding of the breathing mechanism. Misconceptions should be corrected with simple but clear explanations. At the very least stress should be laid on vocal exercises which are directed toward the ability to fully employ nearly all of the vital capacity. The importance of the low intensity tone attack at full lung volume should be discussed and explained. Discussion of these questions will assist the physician to arrive at an evaluation of the adequacy of the singing teacher. Perhaps he will be able to make clear to the patient what the teacher has been driving at but not getting across. Or perhaps it may be evident that the teacher is simply misguiding the student in which case a change of teacher may be necessary. The physician cannot hope in one visit to substitute for the hours and hours spent in singing lessons; but the introduction of even a little understanding may be the catalyst necessary for an improved appreciation of the nature of the teacher's problem. I especially emphasize the use of the single tone and simple scales about the "break" described in Chap. 8, stressing the mastery of the clear tone in the mezza voce in mid voice range, the pianissimo attack, and the gentle crescendo and diminuendo. It is gratifying to see how much information is forthcoming in response to a few key questions and how much appreciation of the role of proper breathing in singing can result from such simple explanations.

In discussing these breathing problems with the singer the fact often emerges that the teacher is indeed aware of the importance of correct use of the breathing mechanism but is resorting to complex manipulations to try to convey the requisite information. Proper control of the breath does not result from the employment of special artificial maneuvers not natural to singing itself. Rather one shows through the product (smooth attack, clear tone, ability to sustain tone for the longest possible time) that breath control is being mastered.

Specific Problems

Now let us turn to certain typical and common problems and their management. It is surprising how much disagreement exists among experienced laryngologists as to specific therapy. To my mind such disagreement is usually an index of the fact that the ideal therapy has not yet been clearly established. Indeed the multiplicity of pharmacological agents employed today in otolaryngology makes it very difficult to accumulate sufficient data on any one to demonstrate a clear case pro or con. Here I shall present my own opinions derived from management of these problems through four decades, admitting that my own views change from time to time as fresh evidence appears on the scene.

Chronic Laryngitis

In Chap. 9 we have discussed the management of acute laryngitis. By chronic laryngitis I mean one of two conditions. An example of the first is the person with a chronically hoarse voice who on examination is found to have a gross change in the vocal folds which may range from diffuse thickening and inflammation to a simple large vocal cord polyp or node. These are all problems commonly faced by the laryngologist and details of differential diagnosis and treatment are not pertinent to our subject. It is only necessary to note here that restoration of the normal laryngeal contours must be accompanied or followed by work with a voice teacher to restore good use of the voice.

The second condition is one in which the voice is grossly normal but tires or roughens on prolonged use. If a small vocal nodule or polyp is discovered its removal must be followed by voice training to eliminate the misuse which led to it. This will be discussed in detail below. More commonly the larynx will be found to have an entirely normal appearance. The fault arises from repeated or chronic strain of the tissues of the vocal folds. Excessively high subglottic pressures, poor use of resonance chambers, inappropriate application of the breath during phonation are among the common causes. The early stages of such injury will not produce visible changes in the larynx. In these individuals relief from the problem must come from the voice teacher.

Nasal Problems–Allergies

A complaint of nasal congestion or discharge, or postnasal discharge may be on a purely functional basis, commonly related to emotional stress. Sometimes these symptoms may be relieved by judicious use of antihistamines. Diagnosis of a functional disorder can only be safely made in such patients after a meticulous search for a low grade sinusitis, allergic reactions, or other respiratory disease. Appropriate treatment in such patients can only be determined on an individual basis. But the use of the voice should be restricted until the disease process is brought under control. When signs and symptoms point to possible allergy but little evidence of a specific allergy can be found, sometimes the use of a dust free bedroom may be of benefit. The patient should be carefully instructed as to the elimination from the bedroom of dust catchers such as rugs, complex draperies or venetian blinds, etc. Books and papers should be kept in another room. Blankets and pillows should be non-allergenic or carefully covered. Common sense can dictate what other measures can be useful in freeing this room, in which one third of each twenty four hours is passed, of dust. The advice of a specialist in allergy should be sought.

If specific allergies are demonstrated the material to which the individual is allergic may be removed from the environment. In the case of seasonal pollen allergies, such as hay fever, desensitization may be helpful but only over a period of years. The symptoms of acute allergic rhinitis may respond to antihistamines. The reaction of the individual to this group of drugs is highly variable. Whereas one may induce drowsiness or unpleasant driness of mucosal surfaces, another may reduce or fully alleviate symptoms without such undesirable side effects.

Cough–Dry Throat

Cough is sometimes the only manifestation of sinusitis. Although the possibility of disease in the chest must be given full consideration, when no evidence of this is found a search for sinusitis should not be overlooked. Especially when cough follows a severe cold or influenza sinusitis is a likely diagnosis. Cough is peculiarly traumatic to the vocal folds which close tightly just prior to the cough and then open abruptly to permit the explosive air blast. Here again use of the voice should be restricted until this symptom has been relieved.

A common complaint of the singer is of a dry throat. This may be a result of nervousness. Fear will effectively dry up airway secretions in many persons. If this is the result of recurring stage fright only time and experience may partially alleviate it. In some instances the use of almost any highly flavored, non-antibiotic troche will sufficiently stimulate salivary secretions to give temporary relief.

Vocal Misuse–Granuloma–Nodule

Chronic hoarseness or roughening of the voice on prolonged talking or singing should suggest the possibility first of vocal strain, and second of vocal nodule or granuloma. The diagnosis of vocal strain or misuse can be safely arrived at only after making certain there is no respiratory disease and identifying the fault in voice usage. Abuse of the voice may consist of episodic trauma such as yelling or screaming, being forced to talk or sing in noisy surroundings, or chronic faulty vocal technique. It seems clear today that one of these forms of misuse of the voice underlies most instances of vocal nodule (14). This makes it imperative to identify problems and correct them before such an eventuality has occurred whenever possible. We'll return to the vocal nodule problem in a moment.

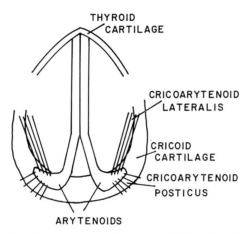

Fig. 68. Possible mechanism of contact granuloma (ulcer) formation. In this configuration the anterior tips of the vocal processes of the arytenoids collide with each phonatory effort. Compare to Fig. 32

Laryngeal granuloma usually results from endotracheal intubation (as with general anesthesia) or the sort of injury resulting from an inappropriate configuration of the vocal cords with talking (5). The reader is referred back to Fig. 32 and the accompanying text in Chap. 5. The mechanism involved is also diagrammed in Fig. 68 and the lesion is shown in Fig. 69. This condition (sometimes referred to as contact ulcer) usually occurs in a teacher or one working in some other field requiring frequent and prolonged talking. It should be suspected in the patient complaining of pain or hoarseness after prolonged talking. I have never seen it in a trained singer. In my experience it is best treated by referring the patient to an understanding teacher of singing. A typical patient is described below.

If the granuloma follows endotracheal intubation the patient may complain little of hoarseness but state he has a peculiar feeling in the throat difficult to describe. Such a complaint in one who has recently been subjected to anesthesia and surgery should suggest the diagnosis. This granuloma invariably is largely confined to the posterior larynx and is readily seen on mirror examination. Complete relief of symptoms will follow removal of the lesion at direct laryngoscopy.

The vocal nodule (vocal polyp or singer's node) is an entirely different matter (20, 23). The overwhelming majority of patients whom I have seen

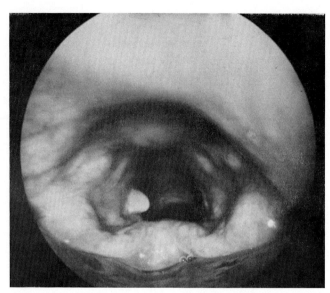

Fig. 69. Granuloma on posterior left vocal cord. In this location only slight hoarseness resulted. (Photograph used with the kind permission of Dr. Haskins Kashima, the Johns Hopkins Hospital)

with vocal cord polyp or nodule are not trained singers. The correctly trained singer has learned to avoid the type of misuse of the voice which leads to such injury. When I do see such a lesion in a singer that individual usually clearly recalls the occasion on which the ground rules of proper voice usage were broken. For this reason I generally recommend singing lessons for rehabilitation of the voice (if such is necessary) after removal of the lesion.

The patient with a vocal nodule may complain of gross and constant hoarseness or of no hoarseness at all but only of some ill defined difficulty in speaking or singing. Since a nodule the size of a pinhead on the edge of the anterior vocal cord may produce those symptoms it can be quite difficult to diagnose. In some persons the anterior vocal fold is nearly impossible to see with the laryngeal mirror. When in doubt, the patient deserves the benefit of a direct laryngoscopy. Treatment of this condition offers one of the most controversial points in the management of voice problems. Some physicians recommend prolonged voice rest (three to six months) while others suggest modified voice rest combined with cautious voice training. Many laryngologists seem to be influenced in their advice by fear of permanently injuring the voice in an attempt to remove the nodule surgically, and thereby laying themselves open to malpractice suit. Indeed this fear is well based since removal of even the most minute portion of the anterior vocal cord may result in permanent hoarseness for which there is no satisfactory therapy. Nonetheless my advice is the following and for the following reasons.

Direct laryngoscopy should invariably be done. This is the only way in many instances to be certain of the diagnosis, and, indeed, to rule out very early laryngeal cancer (although that disease is extremely rare except in the cigarette smoker). This procedure should be carried out in an appropriately equipped hospital under general anesthesia. The suspension laryngoscope should be used if possible and the larynx is examined with the operating microscope. Once this has been done it is only a matter of an additional minute or two to remove the nodule if one has been found. An appropriate size forceps is used to seize the lesion, being cautious to stay outside the normal

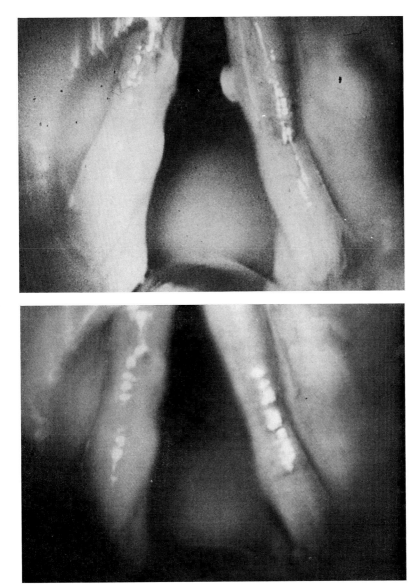

Fig. 70. Photographs taken in the operating room through the operating microscope. Above, rather large nodule on right vocal cord associated with severe hoarseness. A nodule far smaller than this may produce little hoarseness but interfere with singing. Below, the same larynx immediately after excision of the nodule

line of the fold itself. If the nodule is properly grasped it can be removed with only the slightest pull. If there is a "tug" on pulling on the forceps the grasp has been too deep. The lesion should then be released and a new more superficial hold taken. Err on the side of removing too little tissue, not too much. If necessary one can always return a second time to complete the job. With the use of the operating microscope this has been very rarely necessary in my experience except in the case of multiple or very large polyps almost never found in the trained singer (Fig. 70). If there is a nodule on both cords (again rare in the singer) I remove both at the same sitting unless the anterior commissure itself is involved. The tissue removed is invariably sent for examination by the surgical pathologist.

Why do I feel so strongly as to this course of therapy, especially since voice rest and training will end in resolution of the lesion in some patients? First, because the patient is ordinarily restored to talking or singing much more rapidly (within two to six weeks). Second, because it enables one to be certain of the diagnosis. Mirror examination of the larynx yields valuable information but cannot wholly substitute for direct laryngoscopy and visualization of the region with the microscope. It is important to explain to the patient that the nodule resulted from vocal abuse, identify its nature, and see that it is corrected. After removal of the nodule some recommend no resumption of singing for six to ten months. My instructions are for two weeks only of absolute voice rest. In the public speaker I suggest gradual resumption of talking after that time. In the singer I suggest very brief periods of vocal exercise (mezza voce, middle register) during the third week, cautious but steady increase in the number and duration of exercises during the fourth week, and resumption of full singing about the fifth to sixth week.

The Speaking Voice

It is not uncommon for the singer, even one who can carry through a full evening's concert or opera without trouble, to find that prolonged talking tires and roughens the voice. If such a singer participates in a musical show involving both talking and singing special attention must be paid to employing the talking voice with the same attention to breathing, diction, and resonance as in singing. A more pleasant and intelligible speaking voice will result in addition to a reduction in vocal trauma.

In the management of speaking voice problems a difficult question often arises as to whether first consideration must be given to treatment of a physical abnormality or to correctional voice training, and whether through a singing teacher or a phoniatrist. One example of this is the child with a hoarse voice found to have a small vocal nodule. Although it is common practice to ignore the nodule hoping it may go away and to ask the phoniatrist to manage the problem, it is my belief that if the hoarseness is sufficient to interfere with the child's participation in normal school life the nodule should be removed. This should be followed by careful instructions to the parents and the child as to the avoidance of excessive screaming and yelling. It is usually possible to convey to the child the fact that a voice can carry through even a crowded noisy gymnasium or on a playing field without the forced screaming quality.

When the voice problem results from a contact granuloma, or when there is a story of recurrent vocal nodule or polyp, work with a good singing teacher may be more productive than with a phoniatrist. But for certain problems a good phoniatrist may be the most effective person to whom to turn. Among these fall the patient with hysterical aphonia and the patient in whom the voice problem is related to a hearing deficiency. The phoniatrist can also work well with speakers with chronic laryngitis and with those who are undergoing removal of extensive hyperkeratosis or polypoid lesions of the larynx. What can the phoniatrist do?

Generally his task is made easier if his own efforts are integrated with those of the physician. A first step is to look into personal habits including smoking, alcohol consumption, habitual use of the voice, and home and work environment. A second step is to consider the possible role of emotional stress. Correction of problems related to those factors alone will often have a remarkably beneficial effect on the voice. In correcting the use of the voice the primary consideration must be given to breathing. Faults in the use of the breath will range from failure to inspire sufficiently prior to talking, through the unnecessary leakage of air yielding a weak breathy tone, to a few persons who will be found trying to phonate on inspiration rather than expiration. The patient has often not even thought of speech as use of the breath and simple explanations and exercises may be all that is needed for solution of the problem. When breathing faults have been corrected attention can be devoted to diction, resonance, and rhythm. In general the phoniatrist tends to overlook the potential value of simple singing in connection with improvement in the spoken voice. A high fidelity tape recorder is an immense asset in working with these patients.

Prolongation of phonation time is an important goal in restoring normal voice usage. The degree to which it is accomplished is also a useful measure of effectiveness of therapy. As far as I can discover few phoniatrists make use of two simple exercises aimed at this objective. One of these is instructing the patient to take in a deep breath and sing a simple vowel on a tone in the comfortable middle register of the voice. The duration of that tone is timed with a second hand. Another is, again after a deep breath in, having the patient read aloud from an appropriate text trying to go as far as he can without stopping to breathe. The duration of this is likewise timed. Demonstration that, in both, the patient is able to gradually increase phonation time is a source of encouragement to teacher and pupil alike. The patient will also note that, as he learns control of the breath and acquires the habit of starting after a deep breath, his voice comes more easily and has more carrying power. The second portion of the exercise combines a test of the use of the breath with an effort to diminish excessive airflow associated with the correct utterance of certain consonants. Both of these exercises are best performed in the standing position as this somewhat facilitates the prephonation deep inspiration.

Evidently in an effort to achieve louder sound for a weak voice and eliminate breathiness in the attack, at the onset of phonation some speech therapists are fond of a maneuver known under the term "coup de glotte". To my mind this is an unfortunate phrase. For either the teacher or the patient to think in terms of sound beginning as a blow (coup) on the glottis can lead to exactly the wrong result. While a louder sound and a cleaner attack may result, the harm which may ensue from learning to apply excessive subglottic pressure may far outweigh that gain. As I have repeatedly stated, assaulting the vocal folds with a high subglottic pressure is not only unnecessary but highly undesirable. The word "attack" could have the same unfortunate connotation. But, if it is stressed that after a moderately deep inspiration an appropriate "attack" can occur effortlessly we are approaching the right idea. If the speech therapist can convey to the patient the conception that (with moderately full lungs) mere relaxation at the onset of phonation provides all the force necessary, then attention can be properly focused on control of airflow (avoidance of breathiness) and good resonance, and diction.

Examples from Patients

1. A nineteen year old student of voice at the Peabody Conservatory of music consulted me because of acute laryngitis. She was scheduled for an important and difficult exhibition concert five days away. The voice was hoarse and she found singing impossible. My examination revealed a relatively mild inflammation of the larynx but a severe sinusitis and pharyngitis. I placed her on strict voice rest, told her to stay at home and rest, and began penicillin, nose drops, and an antihistamine. At examination 48 hours later the larynx was entirely normal in appearance and all signs of infection in the sinuses and throat had subsided. Voice rest was continued right up to her entering the stage for the concert. Her performance was excellent and no injury resulted. The antibiotic therapy was continued for a full two weeks. I examined her at the end of that period to be sure that all infection had cleared and there was no need for further consideration from the point of view of prevention of recurrent difficulties.

2. A young ophthalmologist consulted me late one afternoon, so hoarse his voice could barely be heard from two feet distance. The problem had come on acutely the night before. Examination showed a severe acute laryngitis without other evidence of disease. He was scheduled to deliver a brief (ten minute) but important paper at a scientific meeting the following day (18 hours later). I told him I could make no promises and explained that there would be some risk of vocal cord injury. He was instructed to completely rest his voice, take an antihistamine that night and again the next morning (along with 2.5 mg dexedrine to allay the sleepiness often accompanying the antihistamine). He delivered his talk without trouble and the laryngitis cleared spontaneously during the next few days. I also reminded this young doctor that careful attention to diction could substitute for loudness in making the voice intelligible.

3. A student of voice, 30 years of age, consulted me with the following story. She had studied voice between the ages of 20 and 25, had a fine voice and took part in amateur performances. At 25 she had given up study. Some three years later she found she was having some difficulties with the voice and started study again, this time with a different teacher. This teacher followed a method entirely different from that on which the patient had been started. She used complex and artificial maneuvers in instructing about breathing, instructed her in various exercises which could not possibly result in proper use of the breathing mechanism, and urged her to practice her fortissimo voice in her highest tones. Under this teaching her voice steadily deteriorated. When I found no physical abnormality to account for her problem I explained how her current teaching was wrong, what should be done, and referred her to another teacher. Within three months she was delighted to find she was back to her normal voice.

4. A teacher in our school of public health who had a heavy lecture schedule consulted me because he found he could no longer lecture for more than half an hour without intolerable pain and hoarseness. He had been under the care of another laryngologist who had little special knowledge of the voice. Both vocal cords were brilliantly inflamed and thickened. I performed a direct laryngoscopy which revealed tiny granulomas bilaterally at the junction of the posterior and middle thirds of the cords (see Fig. 68). I referred him to an understanding singing teacher. Within weeks his larynx had returned to normal and he was able to resume his regular teaching schedule without further difficulty.

5. A forty year old man consulted me because of hoarseness of increasing severity of three months duration. He was a head waiter in a busy restaurant and of necessity engaged in a great deal of talking nightly. The problem began after he went to work one night with a bad cold and laryngitis. Examination showed a moderately large polyp on one vocal cord. Its removal at laryngoscopy followed by two weeks voice rest resulted in a complete return to normal voice. The importance of avoiding any subsequent similar vocal trauma was explained to him.

6. A young woman of 22 years came to me because of rather marked weakness of voice, with an incidental complaint that her singing voice had disappeared. Some eight weeks prior to her visit to me she had undergone an operation under endotracheal anesthesia. During the immediate postoperative period she noted nothing remarkable about her voice; but, within two weeks she noted first that something was wrong with her voice when singing and a few days later her speaking voice was definitely hoarse and weak. Examination confirmed the diagnosis of laryngeal granuloma. Its laryngoscopic removal and voice rest was followed by complete return to normal voice.

7. Morris Mechanic, the late manager of a Baltimore theater, called me one evening to say that the feminine lead in a new musical show, opening the following night, had laryngitis. When I examined her there was ample evidence of a severe laryngitis and sinusitis. I advised her that her understudy must take over and that she herself should not plan on returning to the show for a minimum of two weeks. Penicillin was begun along with strict voice rest

and at the end of two weeks she was able to resume her role. It turned out at a later examination that this young lady had vocal cords which normally gave the appearance of laryngitis, that is were somewhat redenned and slightly thick, a fact which accounted for the attractive warmth and depth of her speaking voice. Nonetheless acute infection had produced changes which made it impossible for her to sing until her own "normal" state had returned.

8. A 35 year old opera singer consulted me because of troubles with his singing voice which had developed over a two year period. He had no obvious hoarseness. For some 15 years he had pursued a busy and successful career as concert singer and operatic baritone. Two years previously he had sung Rigoletto in the face of mild acute laryngitis. (A well trained singer can do a remarkable job even under such circumstances, but may pay the price.) Since that time his voice had been below par and he had reached the point where he could only sing once or twice a week and then with difficulty. Examination revealed a tiny vocal nodule and a mild chronic laryngitis resulting from his attempts to sing in spite of the nodule. On August 17 I removed this nodule at laryngoscopy. He rested his voice completely for two weeks and followed my schedule of gradual resumption of singing after that. On September 21 he was scheduled to perform in Rigoletto in Baltimore and he sent tickets for myself and wife to attend. To the relief of both of us his performance was flawless. He was able to resume his full career and fifteen years later was playing the lead in the musical show "Most Happy Fella", a difficult and demanding role. Shortly afterward he developed some mild vocal difficulties and was fearful that the nodule had recurred. I found a simple sinusitis and, on its successful treatment, the voice returned again to normal and remained so until his death some years later.

Medications

The singer is often advised to take one or more of a wide variety of over-the-counter or prescribed medications and a word on them may be useful here. It is wise to bear in mind that faulty vocal technique or breathing control will not be remedied by medications. Too often the laryngologist fails to recognize the signs of such faults and attempts to restore the voice with drugs.

The singer, like others, is often tempted to self medicate with one or another of the over-the-counter preparations available at the neighborhood pharmacy. Many of these contain combinations of drugs. Combining two or more drugs in a single pill or solution is usually unwise since a relative overdose of one ingredient is likely. In addition, many of these, especially nose drops and sprays, may yield temporary relief from symptoms but in the long run be harmful. No nose drops or sprays should be used frequently or regularly. Their employment to relieve symptoms of nasal congestion during an acute infection may be justifiable. In my opinion and experience the most useful and least harmful is xylometazoline (Otrivin®) 0.05 % solution. When chronic nasal congestion develops with the use of nose sprays or drops it may be entirely attributable to that source. Complete cessation of the medication for 48 hours will result in a return to normal breathing if such was the cause. Antihistamines are quite useful in some allergic patients and in the relief of nasal symptoms in some patients without clear evidence of allergy. Some of these patients will also respond quite satisfactorily to a spray of one of the steroids (Turbinaire Decadron®). The antihistamines bring about highly unpredictable effects in different individuals. Annoying or even dangerous drowsiness may occur. In some persons they induce an unpleasant drying of the mucus. When they are indicated I have found tripelennamine (Pyribenz-amine®) or chlorpheniramine (Chlortrimeton®) most frequently helpful and free of side effects.

Decongestants, frequently combined with antihistamines, taken by mouth are in my experiance more frequently harmful than helpful. They too may induce an unpleasantly dry mucosa.

Today steroids, systemically or topically, are very commonly used. They are dangerous drugs and should be taken only when prescribed by, and under the care of, a physician. With the exception of the nasal spray mentioned above it is my belief that they should play no role in the management of problems related to the voice per se.

Antibiotics may be essential in the control of some bacterial infections, although it is well to remember that before their discovery most people recovered from such infections. The proper drug must be employed in the proper dosage over a sufficient time. It is most important to remember that 10 to 14 days is the minimum duration required to bring an infection under control (even though symptoms may disappear well before that). Most commonly I prescribe erythromycin, tetracycline, or penicillin, one gram a day for 14 days. The pruritis ani or vaginal irritation which sometimes follows broad spectrum antibiotic therapy may be prevented by taking two lactinex tablets with each dose.

Mood modifying drugs have achieved great popularity today. They serve a useful role in the management of certain minor and major psychiatric problems. The natural "mood" of the artist is a major factor in performance. Its pharmacological modification is more likely to affect that performance in a detrimental manner than otherwise.

The professional singer with a heavy schedule may be tempted to fight exhaustion by the use of one of the amphetamine type agents. This is not justifiable. Exhaustion is the way the body has of telling us that we need rest. Use of a drug to obscure that need can only lead to an increase in exhaustion in the long run. The temptation may be to use such a drug "just this once"; but the euphoria which may follow even a single use may insidiously lead to drug abuse.

In a sense the employment of sleep inducing drugs may carry a similar risk. The frustrating inability to sleep, especially after crossing several time zones in air travel, can lead to a desperate desire to get to sleep and thus rest before an impending performance. Here again the relief which can come from such a medication induced sleep may lead to subsequent dependence upon and abuse of this class of pharmacological agents. Whereas the amphetamine class of drugs should almost never be resorted to, nocturnal sedation may be used on the advice of a physician on special occasions. But the real answer is a readjustment of one's schedule to permit natural sleep to suffice.

For the singer or actor who suffers from emotional stress "tranquilizers" may be suggested. Whereas there may be adequate reason medically for prescription of this group of drugs, a degree of emotional tension is essential for a fine performance. They should be avoided if at all possible.

A good general rule is that any pharmacological agent should be used only on the advice of and under the care of a physician. The patient should inform the doctor that he is a singer or otherwise dependent on the voice for a living.

Finally we should mention the fact that certain drugs used in the treatment of a variety of disorders may affect the voice. Some medications used for the treatment of hypertension (especially the rauwolfia compounds) will produce nasal congestion. This can occasionally also occur with the use of oral contraceptives, at times accompanied by headache. A variety of disturbances of the endocrine system or hormonal medications may affect the voice (1, 2, 3, 10, 11, 21). Hypothyroidism may be associated with nasal congestion and, in some patients, hoarseness may be an early symptom (4, 19). Pilocarpine eye drops, used in the treatment of glaucoma, may be followed by an annoying watery nasal discharge lasting 10 to 30 minutes. The astute laryngologist will be on the lookout for all of these possibilities in dealing with the patient with voice disorders.

Conclusion

Speech and song are special by-products of breathing. A clear understanding of the simpler aspects of breathing mechanics and their modification for phonation is a sine qua non for teaching or learning optimum use of the voice.

The management and correction of voice problems sometimes involves collaboration between student or patient, voice teacher, and laryngologist. Communication between them is essential for the best results. It is important for the teacher and student to know when to turn to the laryngologist for help and equally important for the laryngologist to understand the voice and appreciate the role of the voice teacher.

Finally, optimum performance in speech and song results from delicate control of the breathing and vocal mechanisms, not from the expenditure of great force.

References

1. Amado, J. H. (1954): Modifications des caractéristiques phonatoires sous l'influence de divers états endocriens. Rev. Laryngol. Suppl. *75*, 235—250.
2. Amado, J. H. (1955): Glandes endocrines et phonation l'endocrino-phoniatrie. Conférence du Palais de la Découverte, Série A, *211*, 1—48.
3. Bauer, H. (1967): Der Einfluß endokriner Störungen auf die Stimme. Wien. klin. Wschr. *79*, 850—853.
4. Bicknell, P. G. (1973): Mild hypothyroidism and its effects on the larynx. J. Laryngol. *87*, 123—127.
5. Bloch, C. S., Gould, W. J. (1974): Vocal therapy in lieu of surgery for contact granuloma: A case report. J. Speech Hearing Dis. *39*, 478—485.
6. Brewer, D. W., Briess, F. B., Faaborg-Andersen, K. (1960): Phonation, Clinical testing versus electromyography. Ann. Otol. *69*, 781—804.
7. Brodnitz, F. S. (1963): Goals, results and limitations of vocal rehabilitation. Arch. Otolaryngol. *77*, 148—156.
8. Brodnitz, F. S. (1960): Actor and singer as patients of the otolaryngologist. Trans. Amer. Acad. Ophth., Instruction Section, Course 414.
9. Ferguson, G. B. (1977): Speech and voice changes that aid in diagnosis. Trans. Amer. Acad. Ophth. *84*, 90—91.
10. Frable, M. A. (1962): Hoarseness, a symptom of pre-menstrual tension. Arch. Otolaryngol. *75*, 66—68.
11. Goldman, J. L., Salmon, V. J. (1942): Effect of androgen therapy on voice and vocal cords of adult women. Ann. Otol. *51*, 961—994.
12. Greene, M. C. L. (1964): The Voice and its Disorders. Philadelphia: J. B. Lippincott.
13. Haglund, S. (1973): Electromyography in the Diagnosis of Laryngeal Motor Disorders. Stockholm.
14. Härmä, R., Sonninen, A., Vartiainen, E., Haveri., P., Väisänen, A. (1975): Vocal polyps and nodules. Folia Phoniatr. *27*, 19—25.
15. Hirano, M., Koike, Y., Leden, H. v. (1968): Maximum phonation time and air usage during phonation. Clinical study. Folia Phoniatr. *20*, 185—201.
16. Macfie, D. D. (1966): Asymptomatic laryngoceles in wind-instrument bandsmen. Arch. Otolaryngol. *83*, 270—275.
17. Moore, G. P. (1976): Observations on laryngeal disease, laryngeal behavior and voice. Ann. Otol. *85*, 553—564.
18. Moses, P. J. (1963): Der Laryngologe und die neueren Probleme des Singens. Z. Laryngol. Rhinol. Otol. *42*, 445—452.
19. Proetz, A. W. (1950): Further observations of the effects of thyroid insufficiency on the nasal mucosa. Laryngoscope *60*, 627—633.
20. Sander, E. K. (letter) (1975): Reply to Bloch and Gould's "Vocal therapy". J. Speech Hearing Dis. *40*, 544.
21. Sonninen, A. (1970): La voz en el mongolismo y en el hipotiroidismo. Fonoaudiologica *16*, 357—370.
22. Ward, P. H., Berci, G., Calcaterra, T. C. (1977): Superior laryngeal nerve paralysis. Trans. Amer. Acad. Ophth. *84*, 78—89.
23. Zerffi, W. A. C. (1935): Vocal nodules and crossed arytenoids. Laryngoscope *45*, 532 to 534.

Index of Names

Adams, C. 93, 101
Adams, M. R. 101
Agostoni, E. 42
Amado, J. H. 159
Ancilla, C. 13
Andersen, I. 48, 50, 51
Andrew, B. L. 42
Ardran, G. M. 64
Arkebauer, H. J. 101
Arnold, G. E. 102
Aubry, C. 11, 13

Barbara, D. A. 101
Bartlett, D., jr. 86
Bates, J. H. 140
Batson, O. V. 32
Bauer, H. 159
Bell, A. G. 11, 13
Berard, J. A. 13
Berci, G. 159
Berg, J. v. d., see Van den Berg
Berger, K. W. 13, 87
Berlioz, H. 103, 124
Bicknell, P. G. 159
Biondi, S. 32
Biondi-Zappala, M. 32
Bishop, B. 42, 74
Bloch, C. S. 159
Bogert, B. P. 101
Bole, C. T., II 101
Bosma, J. F. 32, 65, 66
Bouhuys, A. 12, 13, 65, 76, 86, 94, 103, 104, 124
Bowden, R. E. M. 32
Bradley, M. 87
Braidwood, T. 11

Brain, J. D. 50
Brewer, D. W. 159
Bridger, G. P. 43
Briess, F. B. 159
Brodnitz, F. S. 5, 13, 101, 159
Broschi, C. (Farinelli) 6
Brown, W. S., jr. 101
Browne, L. 13
Bunch, M. A. 115, 124
Bunn, J. C. 68, 86, 87
Burton, R. 11, 13
Byrd, W. 8, 14

Caccini, G. 5
Calcaterra, T. C. 159
Calnan, J. 97, 101
Calnan, M. 101
Campanelli, P. A. 101
Campbell, E. J. M. 32, 43
Camporesi, E. M. 64
Carrasco, H. de P., see Portillo Carrasco
Carroll, C. 103, 124
Casserius, J. 4, 5, 14
Casson, H. 13
Cavagna, G. 64, 65, 69, 102
Chadwick, L. E. 43, 55
Cherry, J. 43
Chopin, F. 11
Christiansen, R. L. 65
Clark, R. G. 87
Clausen, C. 3
Clerf, L. H. 14
Cole, P. 50
Concone 109, 114
Cooke, J. P. 64
Cramer, L. M. 102

Critchley, M. 14, 65
Critchlow, V. 43

Damsté, P. H. 140
Danon, J. 43
Darwin, C. 2
Davis, J. N. 43
Deinse, J. B. 124
Delahunty, J. E. 43
Desvernines, C. M. 14
Devine, K. D. 33
Dodds, G. 14
Dogiel, I. M. 9, 11, 14
Doornenbal, P., jr. 66
Draper, M. H. 12, 14, 86, 101, 107
Druz, W. S. 43
Duey, P. 124
Dunbar, J. Y. 65

Elnick, M. 125
Euler, C. v. 43

Faaborg-Andersen, K. 64, 124, 159
Fabricius, H. 11, 14
Falck, F. J. 101
Falck, V. T. 101
Farinelli, see Broschi
Faulkner, M. 14
Fellowes, E. H. 14
Fenn, W. O. 12, 43, 55, 66, 88, 101
Ferguson, G. B. 159
Fields, V. A. 124
Fink, B. R. 27, 33
Finney, G. 7, 8, 14
Flanagan, J. L. 101
Floyd, W. F. 65
Fogle, J. L. 65
Fokkens, J. 140
Frable, M. A. 159
Frateur, L. 124
Freedman, L. M. 64
French, T. R. 14
Freud, E. D. 124

Galen 8, 14
Gange, F. 122, 133
Garcia, M. 6, 14
Gautheron, B. 102
Gautier, H. 15, 86
Gay, T. 101, 125
Gilson, J. C. 43
Goldberg, N. B. 43
Goldman, J. L. 159
Goldman, M. D. 86, 87
Gordon, M. T. 102
Gould, W. J. 64, 66, 84, 86, 124, 159
Grant, J. D. 13

Gray, G. W. 101
Greene, J. S. 140
Greene, M. C. L. 140, 159
Grim, M. 33
Guthrie, D. 15
Guttman, O. 14
Gutzmann, H. 101

Habermann, G. 140
Haglund, S. 159
Handel, G. F. 5, 73, 123, 127, 134
Hardy, J. C. 101
Harless, E. 58, 64
Härma, R. 159
Harnad, S. R. 14
Harrer, G. 10, 11, 14
Harrer, H. 14
Harrison, D. 43
Hast, M. H. 5, 58, 64, 65
Haveri, P. 159
Healey, E. C. 101
Heitlinger, L. W. 65
Heller, S. S. 86
Hemming, S. M. 14
Henner, R. 101
Henson, R. A. 14, 65
Hicks, W. R. 86
Hinchcliffe, R. 43
Hirano, M. 65, 87, 124, 159
Hirose, H. 65, 95, 101, 125
Hixon, T. J. 75, 86, 87, 101
Holtsmark, E. B. 14
Homer 2
Hoshiko, M. S. 69, 86, 92
House, A. S. 65
Hugh-Jones, P. 43
Huizinga, E. 14
Husson, R. 65, 125
Hutchinson, J. M. 100, 101

Ingalls, T. H. 14
Ingelstedt, S. 50
Isshiki, N. 65, 71, 87

Jaeger, M. J. 43
Jain, C. K. 101
Jensen, P. L. 48, 50
Jol, J. 140
Judiesch, M. 101
Judson, L. S. V. 87

Kanthack, A. A. 33
Kaplan, H. M. 102
Kashima, H. 150
Kay, R. H. 65
Keizer, J. 124
Kelemen, G. 43, 102

Kelman, A. W. 102
Kemp, F. H. 64
Kenyon, E. L. 102
Khambata, A. S. 65, 123
Kirchner, J. A. 33, 43, 60, 65, 87
Kishore, B. 101
Kitajima, K. 66
Klatt, D. H. 14, 66, 102
Klingholtz, F. 140
Knudson, R. 102
Koike, Y. 65, 87, 124, 140, 159
Konno, K. 43
Kraichman, M. 125

Labarraque, L. 14
Ladefoged, P. 12, 14, 65, 79, 80, 86, 87, 101,
    102
Laget, P. 65
Lambiase, A. 66
Lamm, H. 65
Lamperti, F. 14
Lancaster, J. 14
Large, J. 125
Lawson, F. D. 102
LeBel, C. J. 65
LeCover, M. 125
Leden, H. v. 65, 66, 87, 124, 159
Leith, D. E. 84, 87
Leonardo da Vinci 99
Lessler, M. A. 101
Lewis, M. 140
Lickley, J. D. 14
Lieberman, P. 65, 102
Lilly, J. C. 14
Lind, J. 65
Lindqvist-Gauffin, J. 50, 140
London, G. 134
Lubker, J. F. 102
Luchsinger, R. 102
Lundqvist, G. R. 48, 50, 51

Macfie, D. D. 159
Mackenzie, M. 6, 14
Macmillan, A. S. 102
Maerz, H. 140
Malcolm, J. E. 65
Mallard, A. R., III 101
Malmberg, B. 102
Manchanda, S. S. 101
Mancini, G. 14
Margaria, R. 64, 65, 102
Martensson, A. 65
Matthys, H. 43
Mayow, J. 11, 14
McCormack, R. M. 102
McDonald, J. R. 33
McGinnis, C. S. 117, 125

McGlone, R. E. 65, 101, 125
Mead, J. 42, 43, 65, 68, 74, 75, 76, 86, 87,
    94, 102, 103, 104, 105, 124
Mechanic, M. 155
Melamet, D. S. 108, 111, 127, 134
Meurman, O. H. 140
Michaels, S. B. 66
Miller, A. M. 14
Miller, F. E. 125
Minetti, P. 114
Moll, K. L. 102
Montagu, A. 14
Monteverdi, C. 5
Moore, G. P. 159
Moore, P. 65, 66
Moreschi 6
Morimoto, M. 87
Morton, F. M. 102
Moses, P. J. 159
Munro, R. R. 101
Murry, T. 87

Nassar, V. H. 43
Negus, V. E. 33, 65
Neil, E. 65
Nicolini 6
Nilsson, B. 140

Ohala, J. 124
Okamura, H. 86, 87
Otis, A. B. 12, 43, 55, 87

Pandolfini, F. 14
Pepys, S. 6, 15
Peri, J. 5
Perkell, J. S. 102
Perkins, W. H. 65
Pfau, W. v. 140
Philips, D. 101
Pick, H. L., jr. 66
Pollack, F. J. 101
Pommez, J. 87, 125
Portillo Carrasco, H. del 42
Portmann, G. 65
Potts, W. E. 140
Pressman, J. 43
Proctor, D. F. 50, 51, 65, 86, 87, 94, 124,
    125
Proetz, A. W. 159
Proffit, W. R. 65
Punt, N. A. 43, 140

Rahn, H. 12, 42, 43, 55, 66
Ramazzini, B. 11, 15
Reid, L. 50
Remmers, J. E. 15, 86
Richardson, K. 101

Richmond, W. H. 65
Robin, J. L. 65
Roelofs, J. 140
Roger, J.-L. 15
Rohrer, F. 12, 15
Root, W. S. 86
Rosenblum, R. M. 102
Rothenberg, M. 102
Rubin, H. J. 125
Runyon, J. C. 102
Ryan, R. F. 33

Sakuda, M. 102
Salmon, V. J. 159
Sander, E. K. 159
Sant' Ambrogio, G. 42
Sargeant, W. 140
Schaffrath, H. 65
Schiratzki, H. 43
Schmitke, L. K. 87
Schön, M. A. 15
Schubert, F. 117, 118, 119, 133
Sears, T. A. 43, 67, 87
Seiler, C. 15
Sergeant, R. L. 65
Sewall, H. 15, 87
Shakespeare, W. 91, 118
Sharp, J. T. 43
Sharpey-Schafer, E. P. 14
Shaw, G. B. 95
Sheets, B. V. 66
Sheil, R. F. 43
Shelton, R. L. 66
Siegel, G. M. 66
Siegert, C. 87, 140
Simpson, I. C. 102
Singer, K. 11, 15
Smith, W. 15
Smith, W. R. 102
Sokolowsky, R. R. 66
Sonninen, A. A. 57, 66, 124, 125, 128, 130, 140, 159
Stead, J. 33
Stefanski, R. A. 14
Steklis, H. D. 14
Stevens, K. N. 65, 66, 102
Stevenson, R. S. 15
Stockhausen 11
Strauss, R. 119, 120, 122, 123
Strenger, F. 66
Subtelny, J. D. 102

Sundberg, J. 50, 85, 117, 125, 140
Suzuki, M. 33, 87
Swift, D. L. 50

Tait, J. 15
Takahashi, H. 140
Tanabe, M. 64, 66
Thornton, W. 11
Timcke, R. 65, 66
Titze, I. R. 66
Torp, I. M. 125
Tosi, P. F. 6, 15
Travis, L. E. 102
Tucker, G. F., jr. 33
Tucker, J. A. 33

Vaccai 110, 114
Väisänen, A. 159
Vallancier, B. 102
Van den Berg, J. 66, 125
Vartiainen, E. 159
Vennard, M. 124, 125
Verdi, G. 114
Vidic, B. 33
Vogelsanger, G. T. 125
von Euler, C., see Euler, C. v.

Ward, P. H. 159
Warren, D. W. 87
Wather-Dunn, W. 66
Weaver, A. T. 87
Wechsberg, J. 141
Wheatley, H. B. 15
Whitteridge, D. 12, 14, 86, 101
Widdicombe, J. G. 43
Wieck, H. H. 66
Wingate, M. 102
Wise, M. 101
Wood, M. T. 87
Woods, R. H. 15
Worth, J. H. 102
Wustrow, F. 66
Wyke, B. 12, 15, 43, 65, 102
Wyndham, C. H. 102

Yanagihara, N. 87, 124

Zantema, J. T. 66
Zerffi, W. A. C. 125, 141, 159
Zilstorff, K. 141

Subject Index

Aarhus, Denmark, studies in 48
Abdominal
    contents, weight of 25, 35
    girth, changes with breathing and sing-
        ing 83, 84, 105—106
    muscles 25, 26, 41, 72, 73, 82, 106, 140
        use of to control subglottic pressure
            73, 74, 108, 115
    wall, compression of 73, 82
Abstract thought and speech 2
Abuse
    drug, see Drug abuse
    voice, see Misuse; Trauma
Accents 95
Accessory muscles of breathing 25, 41, 72,
    82
Acting, hints on 123—124
Actor, the, and the use of the voice 91, 95,
    97
Acute laryngitis, see Laryngitis
Adam's apple, locating laryngeal structures
    in the neck 116
Addiction
    to drugs 157
    to tobacco 144
Adenoids 20
Adolescence 126
    avoidance of singing during 126—127
    voice changes in 99
Age 127
    the aging singer 134
    the mature singer 132—134
    and the voice 57
    the young voice 120
Air
    conditioning, respiratory 19

inspiratory, modification of 44—50
leakage and the "breathy" voice, see
    Breathing
modification 20
    and the nose 44—50
pollution 18, 44
relative humidity 48
stream, nasal 19
temperature 48
travel 157
    air of airplanes 48
    airotitis 133
    avoidance of excess talking during
        133
    jet lag and exhaustion 133
volume of breathed during a day 16
waste of in phonation 63
see also Ambient air
Airborne materials and the nose 44
Airflow 34—36, 40, 62, 63, 69, 73, 85, 86,
    92, 105, 106
    resistance to 18, 49
    through nose 45, 46
    see also Breath; Control
Airotitis 133
Airway secretions, see Mucus; Secretions
Airways
    conducting 16
    lower 23
    oropharyngeal 40, 48, 71
    role of 18
    upper 18—23
    see also Mouth; Nasal; Nose; Oral
Akvavit 132
Alcohol consumption and protection of the
    voice 127, 132, 154

Allergic disease and the voice 132, 147 to
    148, 157
Allergy, problems of in detecting source of
    trouble 131
Alveolar
    air 44
    ridge 63
    surface area 16
    see also Pressure
Ambient air 18, 44, 45
Amphetamine, avoidance of 157
Amplification of sound 53, 54
    electronic 85, 99
Anatomy 16—32
Anesthesia and surgery followed by
    hoarseness 149
Anesthesia, general and intubation, hazard
    to larynx, see Endotracheal intubation
Anesthesiologist, importance of in protecting
    larynx 131
Animals, communication in 2
Antibiotics, usefulness of 131, 136, 157
Antihistamines, use of 131, 147, 157
Apes, lack of speech 2
Aphonia, hysterical, see Hysterical
Apnea after talking 68
Apollo, God of music 5
Appearance of effort 41
Apposition of vocal folds 55, 63
Apprehension 133
Arduous schedule 133
Arias 114
Art of singing 103—124
Articulation 92
Artificialty of speech 96
Artist, singer as 120
    and mood 157
Artistic interpretation 116
Aryepiglottic folds, apposition during
    swallowing 27
Arytenoid cartilages 27, 55, 56
Aspirin, use of 131, 137
Asthma
    and breathing in phonation 139
    and music 8, 11
    and smooth muscle 23
    and syncopation 11
Atmosphere pressure 35
Attack of sound, tone, at T.L.C. 81, 82,
    105—108, 146, 154
    see also Initiation
Aubry C. asthma and music 11
Audibility of voice 85, 89, 92, 93
Audience
    captivation of 104
    eye to eye contact with 120
    feedback from during singing or public

speaking 99
    the measure of success in actor, lecturer,
    or singer 97, 120
    winning attention with softest tones 115
Audiologist, role of in study of the singer or
    speaker 98
Auditory perception and voice production 60
    see also Hearing
Awkward appearance, avoidance of 72, 73

Bacteria in air 44
Bacterial infections, see Infection
Balance between elastic forces 24
Balloon-bellows model of the breathing
    mechanism 24
Baritone
    avoidance of temptation to become tenor
    127
    voice 110
Beauty of voice in speech 96
Bel Canto 109
Bell, A. G., speech for the deaf 11
Bellows-balloon model of breathing
    mechanism 24
Belly, position of in singing 74
Belts, avoidance of tight clothing 132
Benzoin inhalations 136
Berlioz, H., comments on the singing voice
    103
Bernoulli effect and vibration of vocal folds
    60
Big voice 115
Biopsy of vocal cord 99
Birds
    imitation of human speech 2
    the voice in 2
Bishop, B., on use of muscles 74
Blood
    gases, see Carbon dioxide; Homeostasis;
    Oxygen
    pressure, effects of music upon 11
    supply of nose 19
Blow, as communication 2
Body build and singing 41
Bouhuys, A.
    physiological research 104
    symposium on sound production 12
Boy soprano 126
    care of voice during adolescence, see
    Adolescence
Braidwood, T., teaching the deaf to speak 11
Brain
    development of and speech 1
    flow of information between and
    larynx 59
Brassieres, avoidance of tight clothing 132

"Break" in the voice 57, 110—111, 115, 146
     see also Exercises
Breath
     conservation of 114
     control of 67, 120
     deep for public speaking 69
     see also Airflow; Control
Breathing
     and clothing, see Belts; Brassieres;
     Collars; Girdles
     mechanics 34—43
          early studies in 12
          elastic forces in 23
          physiological studies of 67—86
     mechanism
          in speech 89—92
          structure of 16—33
     pump 23—26
     work of 16, 19
     see also Elastic; Pressure
Breaths, quick, and phonation 48
"Breathy" quality to voice 63, 69, 110, 145,
     154
Brevity, the value of in public speaking 99
Brodnitz, F. S.
     castrato singer 5
     dramma per musica 5
Bronchitis, chronic, see Chronic bronchitis
Broschi, C., castrato singer 6
Bunch, M. A., on vocal resonance 115
Bunn, J. C., breathing and reading aloud 68
Burton, R., music a remedy for melancholy
     11
Byrd, W., on singing and health 8

Caccini, G., colleague of Peri 5
Calliope, the muse of poetry 5
Calnan, J., and poor speech 97
Cancer
     laryngeal
          cigarette smoking 99, 144
          early diagnosis 99
     lung 144
Capillary bed and exchange of respired air
     16
Carbon dioxide 44, 68
     response to during phonation 68
Care of the voice 126—140
Career and vocal hygiene 44, 127
Caress as communication 2
Carroll, C., advice to singing teacher 103
Carrying of the voice through a large hall
     92, 153
Cartilages of the larynx 26—28, 59
     see also under individual cartilages
Cartilaginous portion of vocal folds 55

Casserius, J. 5
     illustration from 4
Castrato singer 5, 6
Cat, the purr of 2
Cavagna, G., and airflow 69
Chaingang songs and work 68
Chest
     elastic force of 24, 105
     fixation of during work 68
     girth 83, 84
     physician 138
     radiographs of 22
     register 57, 111
     wall 24, 74, 77, 105—106
     see also Ribs; Thorax; Thoracic
Child
     hoarseness in 99
     prodigy 127
Chimpanzee, communication in 2
Chlorpheniramine 157
Chlortrimeton, use of 157
Choking, sign of vocal cord paralysis 145
Chopin, F., soothing effect of music by 10, 11
Choral performance 120
Chronic
     bronchitis 140, 144
     respiratory infection 99
Cigarettes, avoidance and effects of 99, 132,
     144
Cigars, use of 132
Cilia 20, 26, 48
Cinefluorography
     frames from during speech and singing
     51, 64, 70, 71, 90, 91, 112, 113
     physiological studies 76
Cinephotography, high speed 60
Cineradiography, see Cinefluorography
Circumference, see Abdominal; Chest; Girth
Clarinet, effects of compared to other
     instruments 9, 11
Clavicles 26
     action of sternocleidomastoid muscles on
     25, 41, 106
Clearing the throat, avoidance of 133
Climate 18, 45, 48, 137
Clio, muse of history 5
Closure of larynx 27
     see also Larynx
Clothing, avoidance of tight in singing 132
Cocktail parties, unfortunate effect of on the
     voice 133
Cold
     climate 48
     day 45
Collars, avoidance of tight 32
Coloratura soprano, avoidance of conversion
     of lyric to 127

Comfort and lung volume 69
Commissures of the larynx 27
Common cold and the voice 50, 99, 131, 134
Communication
    and audience 99, 120
    means of 1—2
    problems 98
Compliance of the breathing mechanism 139
    see also Elastic
Complications of a common cold 131
Composers, their avoidance of excessive
    demands on the singer 129
Concert singing 123, 154
Concone, vocal exercises 114
Conducting airways, see Airways
Confidence, in the student 110
Configurations of the vocal folds 55, 57, 63
Conservatories of music 146
Consonants
    and airflow 62, 119
    formation of 63, 88, 153
Constrictors of the pharynx 26
Contact ulcer 149
    see also Granuloma
Contraceptives, oral, adverse effects of 158
Control
    of the breath 41, 67, 108—109, 143,
        146, 153
    of abdominal muscles 73
    of airflow 81
    more delicate for singing than speech 60
    of muscles and muscle spindles 32
    of muscles and phonation 72—76, 106
        to 108, 120
    neural 20
    see also Breath; Muscles
Conversation
    breathing in 42, 69, 85
    and the voice 48, 95, 96, 128, 133
Cooling, artificial 18, 136
Cord, vocal, see Vocal
Corinthians, quotation from the book of 5
Cosmetic surgery of the nose 132
Costumes, singing without need for 123
Cough 42, 148
    and laryngeal trauma 139, 148
    and sinusitis 148
    symptom of laryngeal paralysis 145
"coup de glotte" 154
Covering of tone 111, 115
Cracking of the voice in adolescence 99
Crescendo, performance of 58, 73, 80, 108,
    115, 122, 134, 146
Cricoarytenoid
    joints 30
    muscles 27, 29, 55, 95
Cricoid cartilage 27, 55, 57, 116

Cricothyroid muscles 27, 32, 57, 145
Cricothyroid space 76, 116
Critical audience 120
Criticism, need for 120
Cross section of airway, see Nasal
Cycles per second 54
    in orchestra and voice 85

Darkening of tone 111, 115
Darwin, C., expression of emotions 2
Deaf, speech in the 11
Deafness, see Hearing impairment
Decongestants, nasal, use of 157
Deep breathing 25, 34
Delicate control 123
Deterioration of the voice 127
Diaphragm 25, 35, 40, 41, 72, 73, 106, 138
    relaxation of during phonation 73, 74,
        79, 82
Diction 63, 95—96, 99, 117—118, 120, 152,
    154
Digastric muscles 27
Diminuendo 108, 146
Discomfort
    at low lung volumes 110
    with mouth breathing 45
Dogiel, I. M., physiological effects of
    music 11
Dogs, ability to communicate 2
Dolphins, phonation in 2
Drafts 137
Dramma per musica 5
Draper, M. H., pioneer in field of breathing
    and phonation 12
    on relaxation of diaphragm in phon-
    ation 107
Driness of throat 137, 148
Drinking of alcoholic beverages 127
    see also Alcohol
Drops, nose 157
Drowsiness with antihistamines 157
Drug abuse 157—158
Drugs, see Drug abuse; Medications; names
    of drugs
Drugstore, over the counter medications 156
Dry air 46, 48, 137
Dry throat 47, 148
Drying of mucosa 157
Du bist die Ruh', phrase from 118, 119, 121
Duration
    of phrase 73
    of tone 108
Dust
    in air 44
    free bedroom in allergy 148
Dynamic forces in breathing 39—42
Dyspnea 139

E. R. V., see Expiratory reserve volume
Ears, clearing while flying 133
Effort, maximum 41
Effortless
    production of voice 115
    swelling of tone 73
Elastic forces in breathing and phonation
    25, 38, 76, 79, 92, 105, 106—108, 115,
    138
Elastic properties of breathing mechanism 24,
    104—105
    of larynx 57, 58, 60
Elastic tissue 23, 129
Electromyography 55, 76
Electronic amplification, see Amplification
Elecution, singing and 8
Emotional stress 136, 137, 147, 154, 158
    emphasis 119
    and speech impediments 100
Emphasis
    in speech, tempo, and pitch 97
    in use of voice 59, 78, 92, 98
Emphysema, pulmonary 138
    and breathing in phonation 138
    and cigarette smoking 144
Endocrine disorders 158
Endotracheal intubation, a possible hazard
    to vocal cords 131, 149, 155
English language 63
Enunciation 92, 96, 99
Environment 137, 145, 154
    body's internal 18
Epiglottis, motion of in swallowing 27
Epithelium, respiratory 26
    squamous 26
Erato, muse of love 5
Erectile vasculature of nasal mucosa 20
Erythromycin, use of 157
Esophageal pressure as measure of pleural
    pressure, see Pressure
Esophagus 26
Eunuch, the castrato singer 6
Euphonious speech 69, 89, 92
    goal for those with speech impediments
    100
Euphoria, with amphetamines 157
Euridice, early opera 5
Eustachian tubes 20
Euterpe, muse of music 5
Exercise, physical
    and breathing 23, 41
    and phonation 68
Exercises, vocal 108—110, 114, 127, 133,
    135, 143, 146, 152
Exhaustion 157
Expiration
    elastic forces in 24

    quick after speaking 68
    see also Breath; Control
Expiratory reserve volume 34, 35
Exploration of oceans and space and voice
    problems 63
External intercostal muscles, see Intercostals
External oblique muscles 25, 26
Extralaryngeal muscles 26, 30
    and pitch control 57

F.R.C., see Functional residual capacity
Fabricius, H., on health and singing 11
False cords 27
Falsetto voice 56, 129
Farinelli, castrato singer 6
Faults, detection and correction of 142 to
    158
Fear
    in speaking 100
    see also Stage fright
Feedback
    from audience 99
    neural, in voice production 60
Female, vital capacity in 35
Fenn, W. O., contributions to physiology
    of breathing 12
    on speech 88
Fink, B. R., on the larynx 27
Finney, G., on health effects of singing 7, 8
Flow of air in breathing and phonation, see
    Airflow
Flu, see Influenza
Flute, effects of compared to other
    instruments 9, 11
Flying, cautions for the singer and public
    speaker in connection with
    see Air travel; jet lag
Folds, vocal, see Vocal
Folk music, see Chaingang; Sea chantey
Forced expiratory vital capacity 138
Forced expiratory volume, see Lung volumes
Forces in breathing, see Dynamic; Muscles;
    Static
Formants in voice sounds 62
    fourth formant 85, 114—115, 116
Fortissimo 122
Frequency of sound waves 52, 54, 60
Full voice 41
Functional residual capacity 34, 35, 39, 69,
    73, 78, 84, 110
Fundamental frequency of tone 53, 54

Galen on health and phonation 8
Gange, F. 122, 133
Garcia, M. 6, 7
Gas exchange 16

Gastric pressure, measure of in determination of transdiaphragmatic pressure, see Transdiaphragmatic
Geniohyoid muscles 27
Genitalia, similarity of nasal vasculature to that in 20
Gestures
    as communication 2
    meaningless 123
Girdles, avoidance of tight 41, 132
Girth of abdomen and chest, see Abdominal; Chest
Glaucoma, nose drops in, effect of 158
Glottic, glottis, see Larynx; Subglottic; Vocal configurations, see Configurations
Goblet cells and airway secretions 46
God of music, Apollo 5
Gorillas, communication in 2
Gould, W. J., on muscle training 84
Graceful appearance 73, 133
Grammar 95
Granuloma of vocal folds 131, 149, 155
Greek civilization 2
Greek muses 5
Grimaces, avoidance of 123
Group singing 136

Habit of breath control 153
Hamlet, quotation from 89
Handel, G. F. 123, 127
    and oratorio 5, 73
Harless, E. 58
Harmonics of the fundamental frequency and resonant chambers 62
Harrer, G. 10, 11
Harvard University, physiologic studies at 104—106
Hast, M. H., translator of Casserius 5
Hawking and spitting 48
Hay fever 148
Hay-Market, opera at the 6
Head register 111
Headache 145, 158
Health effects of singing 7—11
Healthy air passages 45
Hearing
    impairment of 60, 99
    range of in man 52, 54
    and the voice 60
    see also Auditory
Heart disease and cigarette smoking 144
Heated buildings 45
Heating, artificial 18, 136
Helium, use of in exploration and speech 63
High tones 56, 58, 62, 111—114, 145

Hirose, H., on voicing control 95
Historical background 1—15
Hixon, T. J., and thoracoabdominal movement 75
Hoarseness 99, 130, 131, 134—135, 145, 147, 149, 150, 152, 155, 158
Homeostatic mechanisms in breathing 67, 68
Homer 2
Hormones 158
Hoshiko, M. S., lung volumes for speech 69, 92
Humidifying
    of indoor air 48, 136
    of inspired air 44
Humming, breathing events in 92
Husky voice in actor 95
Hutchinson, J. M., use of rhythm in teaching the stutterer 100
Hygiene
    of the respiratory tract 44
    of the voice 6, 126, 130—132
Hyoglossus muscles 27
Hyoid bone 26, 116
Hyperkeratosis of the vocal folds 153
Hypertension 158
Hyperventilation 68
    with phonation 68
Hypothyroidism 158
Hypoventilation 68
Hysterical aphonia 153

Idea, flow of in speech 69
Immune mechanisms 20
Impaired hearing, see Hearing impairment
Impediments, speech 100
Infancy, beginning of learning for phonation 59
Infection
    infectious microorganisms 18
    transmission of respiratory 130
    see also Sinusitis; Tonsillitis
Influenza 99, 134
Initiation
    of sound and speech impediments 100
    of speech and lung volume 69, 92
    of tone 60
    see also Attack
Injury, permanent, to the voice 136
Inspiration
    elastic forces 24
    interspersed in conversation 69
    quick 43, 49
    during singing 71
Inspired air, modification of 44—50
Intelligibility of speech 69, 89, 92, 95, 117

Intensity of sound 52, 60, 61—62, 63, 67, 69, 79, 92, 108
  and pitch 59
Interarytenoid muscles 27, 29, 55, 95
Intercostal muscles 25, 41, 73, 74, 75, 79, 82, 92, 106, 138
Internal intercostal muscles, see Intercostal
Internal oblique muscles 25, 26
Interpretation of song 110
Intraoral pressure in phonation 63, 92
Intrinsic laryngeal muscles 95
Intubation, tracheal, see Endotracheal
Isshiki, N., on lung volumes 71
Italian language 116
Itching, pruritis of vulva and anus, avoidance of with antibiotic therapy, see Pruritis

Jargon 111
Jaws, see Mandible
"Jet lag" 133
Job, quote from book of 3
Joint, see Cricoarytenoid; Cricothyroid

Kashima, H. 150
Key, transposition of 122
Keyboard, range of in piano 54
Khambata, A. S., on unlimited voice 123
Kirchner, J., and auditory perception 60

Lactinex, use of in antibiotic therapy 157
Ladefoged, P., pioneer in field of breathing and phonation 12
  on muscle use in singing 79, 80
Language differences and speech 63
Laryngitis 99, 133, 154, 155
  acute 134—136
  chronic 143, 147, 153
Laryngologist, role of 98, 130, 134, 142, 144—146, 150
Laryngology, birth of with Garcia's invention 6
Laryngoscopy, direct 99, 149, 150
Larynx 23, 26—32, 54
  anatomy 28—31
  as a valve 16
  cancer, see Cancer
  capacity to produce aerosol 11
  cartilages 28
  glottic aperture 23, 27
  growth of at adolescence 99, 126
  lowering of in neck 85, 103, 114
  muscles of 26—29, 55, 59
  palpation of 115—116
  photograph of 128

phylogenetic development of 1
physiology of 26
  see also Configuration; Vocal
Latissimus dorsi muscles 25
Laziness in the employment of supraglottic organs and diction 63
Lecturing 99
  and the audience 97
  and breathing 48
  and speech 91
Legato 74, 111
Leith, D., on muscle training 84
Length of vocal folds and pitch control 27, 28, 32, 57—59, 129
Leonardo da Vinci on speech 99
Lieder singing 133
Ligaments of the larynx 26, 28
Linear velocity of airflow 45
Lips, use of in phonation 54, 62, 63, 88
London, G., on conservation of voice 114
Loud tone, see Tone
Loudness, see Intensity
Low tones 56
Lower airways, see Airways
Lung volumes 24, 34, 35, 69—72
  for singing 107
  for speech 92—93
  see also under various divisions of volume
Lungs 23
  elastic tissue 23, 104, 138
  see also Pulmonary
Lymphoid tissue 20
  see also Adenoids; Tonsils
Lyric soprano, undesirability of conversion to coloratura 127

McGinnis, C. S., on resonance 117
Mackenzie, M., on the hygiene of the voice 6
Mandible 26
  lowering of in singing 23, 114
Marriage and the castrato 6
Mask, face, use of in physiological studies 37
Mass per unit length of vocal folds and pitch 57—59
Mature voice 126, 132—134
Maximum effort in breathing 34
Mayow, J., early respiration physiologist 12
Mead, J.
  breathing and reading aloud 68
  physiological research 103
  and thoracoabdominal movements 75
  use of muscles 74
Mechanic, M. 155
Mechanics of breathing, see Breathing
Mechanism of breathing, see Breathing

Medications 131, 136, 137, 156—158
    over-the-counter 156
    prescribed 156
    see also under various drug names
Melamet, D. S. 108, 114, 127, 134
Melancholy, music a remedy for 11
Melody in the speech of early man 3
Melpomene, muse of tragedy 5
Membranous portion of vocal folds 55
Messiah, oratorio, phrases in 73
Mezza voce 115, 133, 135, 143, 146
Microscope, operating, use of in laryngoscopy
    150
Mid range of voice, see Middle register
Middle ages and the castrato 5
Middle register 127, 133, 135, 143
Minetti, P. 114
Minute volume and phonation 68, 78
Misuse of voice 126, 147, 148—152
Mnemonic device, olfaction 2
Model to represent breathing mechanism 24,
    37, 77
Moist
    air 48
    surface
        in larynx 42
        in nose 48
Monteverdi, C., and opera 5
Mood modifying drugs 157
Moreschi, last of the castrato singers 6
Motor supply of laryngeal muscles 32
Mouth breathing 23, 45, 49—50
    and conversation 69
Mouth, opening of 23, 40
Mucociliary system 19, 48
Mucous glands 26, 46
Mucous membranes 20, 23, 45, 136—137
Mucus 26, 46, 157
    see also Secretions
Multidisciplinary approach to problems of
    the voice 98
Muscles
    control of 72—76, 106—108
    of larynx, see Larynx
    respiratory 25
    sequence of use in singing 79, 80
    smooth 23, 139
    spindles 32, 81, 107
    strap, in neck 145
    training 84—85
    see also Abdominal; Accessory; names
    of individual muscles
Musical instruments 53
Musical intelligence 124
Musical shows, and talking for the singer
    99, 152
Musicality 85

Mylohyoid muscles 27
Myoelastic theory of pitch control 60

Nasal
    air passages 40
    breathing 49—50
    cavities and voice resonance 6
    cross section of airway 19
    problems 147—148
    septum 19, 45, 132
    turbinates 19, 20, 45
Nasality of speech 95
Nasopharynx 19
Natural frequency of the voice 57
Neck
    palpation of 115—116
    relaxation in 115
    suspension of larynx in 26
Nerves
    recurrent laryngeal 32
    superior laryngeal 32
Nervousness 133, 148
Neural feedback
    control of nasal structures 20
    in voice production 60
Neurochronaxic theory of pitch control 60
Neuromuscular activity 32
Nicolini, castrato singer 6
Night club, singer working in 145
Node, vocal 147, 148—152
Nodule, see Node; Vocal nodule
Noise and speech 95, 133
Nose 18—23, 44—50
    see also Airways; Nasal
Nose drops and sprays 156
Nostrils 19, 45

Occupationally related hazards of singing
    11
Older singer 126, 134
Olfaction 19
    as means of communication 1
Omohyoid muscles 27
Onset of phonation, see Attack; Initiation
Open tone 115
Opera, early development 5
    house, Venice first site 5
Operatic
    performance 120, 128, 133
    singer 156
Optimum thoracoabdominal action 41
Oral airway 23
    see also Mouth
Orator and speech 98
Oratorio 114, 127
    early development of 5
Orchestra, symphony 85

Orfeo, early opera 5
Oropharyngeal airway, see Airway
Otis, A., contributions to physiology of
    breathing 12
Otolaryngologist 99, 132, 133
    see also Laryngologist
Otrivin 156
Overtones 53, 54, 62
Oxygen 44

Pain on vocalization 149, 155
Palate 20, 46, 54, 63, 88, 103, 114
Paralysis of vocal cords 45
Paranasal sinuses, see Sinuses
Pause
    inappropriate 69
    in singing 122
Peabody Conservatory of Music 127
Pectoral muscles 25
Penicillin 157
Pepys' diary and the castrato 6
Performance and pitfalls 118
Performer, accomplished 73
Peri, J. 5
Pharmacological agents, see Medications
Pharyngeal constrictor muscles 27
Pharynx 20, 63, 85, 115
Phenomenal voice 123
Phonation
    and breathing mechanics 67—86
    and excessive subglottic pressure 62
    and exercise 68
    and health 8
    initiation of 60
    movement of laryngeal cartilages 27
    time 146, 153
    and work of breathing 16
    see also Singing; Speech
Phonatory
    mechanism, structure of 16—33
    quality 50
Phoniatrist, role of 142, 144, 145, 152
Photography, early use in studying larynx
    11
Phrasing
    in song 73
    in speech 69, 92
Phylogenetic development of larynx 1
Physiological studies of breathing and
    phonation 75—84, 104—106
Physiology
    of breathing, early history 11, 12
    of nose 44—50
    see also Physiological studies
Pianissamo 122
    attack 146
Piano 53

Piccolo, effect of compared to other
    instruments 9, 11
Pilocarpine 158
Pipe smoking 132
Pitch
    change of in speech 97
    and intensity 61
    sound and 54
    of voice 26, 57—59, 60, 81
Pitfalls in performance 118
Plethysmograph, body 37, 75, 76, 104
Pleural
    pressure 34, 77
    space 24
Pneumograph 83, 84, 105
Pneumotachometer 35, 76
Pneumothorax 38
Poetry 2
Pollution, see Air pollution
Polyhymnia, muse of oratory 5
Polyp of vocal cord 147, 155
"Pop" singers 85, 104, 145
Position of body and lung volumes 35
Postnasal discharge 47, 131, 145, 147
Posture
    and breathing 25
    and singing 132
    as communication 2
Pressure 34—36, 40, 41, 55
    alveolar 37, 105
    esophageal 37, 76
    intraoral 63, 92
    intrapleural 37
    intrathoracic 27
    involved in breathing 24
    measurement of 104—106
    subglottic 37
    tracheal 37
    transdiaphragmatic 37
    see also Subglottic
Pressure-volume diagrams 38, 77, 81, 107
Professional singing 42, 104, 118, 127, 133,
    137, 157
    and muscle use 84
Props, avoidance of dependency on 123
Pruritis 157
Psychiatric problems 157
Psychiatrist and speech problems 98, 100
Psychological problems 133
Puberty, growth of larynx in 57
Public performance 120
Public speaking
    and pulmonary disease 138
    and speech impediments 100
    and the voice 48, 69, 85, 99, 128, 152
Pulmonary disease 137—140
Pulmonary ventilation and phonation 68

Pump, breathing, see Breathing
Purr of the cat 2
Pyribenzamine 157

Quality of voice 49
Quick inspirations 42

R.V., see Residual volume
Rahn, H., contributions to physiology of
     breathing 12
Range of voice 108
     danger of overextending 127
     see also High tones; Low tones;
     Exercises
Rapidity of speech 95
Reading aloud 92, 94, 153
     and speech 97
Recitative 73, 114
Recoil, elastic, see Elastic
Recording of voice and learning 97, 117,
     153
Rectus abdominis muscles 25, 26
Recurrent laryngeal nerve 145
Regional accents 95
Register, see Chest; Head; Middle
Rehearsing soundlessly 133
Relative humidity of air 44
Relaxation of muscles 41, 115
     see also Diaphragm; Strain
Repertoire 120
Residual volume 34, 35, 71, 73, 81, 82, 106,
     107, 110, 119, 138
     R.V./T.L.C. ratio 84
Resistance to airflow, see Airflow
Resonance 49, 53, 57, 62, 73, 85, 114, 115 to
     117, 147, 152, 154
Resonance chambers 20
Respiratory disease 48
     see also Infection; Pulmonary; Sinusitis;
     Tonsillitis
Rest 41
     instead of amphetamines 157
     of the voice 99
     see also Voice rest
Rhinitis 131, 148
Rhinoplasty 132
Rhyme in poetry 3
Rhythm in poetry 3
     song 120, 153
     speech 96, 98, 100
Rib cage, forces affecting 75
Ribs, action of muscles upon 25, 41
Robust individual and singing capacity 41
Rohrer, F., contributions to physiology of
     breathing 12
Roles, selection of 133

Rolling of "Rs" 117
Rough voice in actor 95
Ruhe meine Seele, phrases from 123

Salesman and the use of the voice 91
Salivary secretions 148
Scalenus muscles 25
Scales 110, 114, 146
Schubert, F. 118
Screaming as vocal abuse 97, 115, 134, 149
Sea chanteys and work 68
Sears, T. A., on subglottic pressure 67
Secretions, airway 20, 46, 47—48, 148
Sedation 158
Sensory nerves 32, 59
     see also Superior laryngeal
Septum, nasal, see Nasal
Serratus muscles 25
Sex and singing 41, 57
Shakespeare, W., quote from 89, 118
Shaw, G. B. 95
Sign language in communication 2
Silence, value of in songs 122
Singer
     ability to sing when auditory perception
     is blocked 60
     conversation and 48, 133
     and muscle control 72—76
     and pulmonary disease 138
     and speech in musical shows 99
Singer's node 128
Singing
     breathing mechanics in 34, 41
     control of breathing for effective 69
     lung volumes in 79, 86
     pressures in 79, 86
     and pulmonary disease 138
     right and wrong way 41
     in teaching those with speech
     impediments 100
     use of entire vital capacity in 49
Singing teacher
     advice to 103
     collaboration with others 146
     role of 142, 144, 152
     and song and speech 98, 128
Single tones 79
Sinuses, paranasal 20, 21
     as resonators 20
Sinusitis 50, 131, 145, 147, 155
Sitting position and lung volume 35
Skilled performer 73
Sleep 157
Smoking, avoidance and effects of 99, 127
     see also Cigarettes
Smooth muscle, see Muscle
Sneezing 132

Soft tone, see Tone
Song
    and airflow, pressures 62
    in early man 3
    lack of stammering or stuttering in 100
    singing 74, 110, 119—123
Sonninen, A. A.,
    on pitch control 57
    on vocal nodule 128
Soprano, avoiding conversion of lyric
    to coloratura 127
Sore throat 145
    see also Tonsillitis
Sound
    generation of 34
    production 52—63
Speaker
    and conversation 48, 92, 94
    fast and slow 97
    and lung volume 71
Speaking
    breathing mechanics in 34
    voice 88—101, 152—154
Speech 62—64, 69, 74, 75, 78, 85, 86
    and airflow pressures 62
    after deafness 60
    and different languages 63
    habits 96
    hyperventilation and 68
    impediments 100
    and man's development 1
    problems 98—101
        in exploration of oceans, space 63
        in school children 97
    teacher 99
    therapist 98
Spindles, muscle, see Muscles
Spine, action of muscles on 25
Spirometer 36
Spirometry 36, 146
Spitting 48
Sprays, nasal 156
Squamous epithelium, see Epithelium
Squeeze on chest 73
Stabilizing of larynx in neck 26
Stage fright 47, 139, 148
Stammering 100
Stance, graceful 133
Standing position and lung volumes 35
Static forces in breathing 37—39, 82, 83
Steam inhalation 136
Sternocleidomastoid muscles 25, 41, 106
Sternothyroid muscles 27
Sternum 26, 41
Steroids 157
Stockhausen, effects of music by 10, 11
Stomach, clearance to 46

Strain, stress, vocal, chest, neck 73, 115
Strauss, R. 119, 122
Stringed instrument, the voice likened to 6
Student of voice 110, 117
Stuttering 100
Stylohyoid muscles 27
Subglottic pressure 34, 37, 55, 57, 58, 60,
    61—62, 63, 67, 69, 73, 75, 76, 79, 93,
    97, 105, 106, 108, 111, 115, 119, 138,
    147
Sulfur dioxide 45
Sundberg, J., on resonance 85, 117
Superior laryngeal nerve 145
Supine position and lung volumes 35
Support of the voice 110
Supraglottic airway, spaces 54, 59, 61, 62,
    63, 73, 85, 88, 92, 111
Surface area in nose 19
Surgeon 131
Surgical care 131
Suspension of larynx in neck 26
Sustained tone 63, 79, 105, 146
Swallowing 26, 27, 42, 47, 145
Symbols and abstract thought 2
Symphony orchestra 85, 117
Syncopation in music and asthma 11
Syrinx, as "larynx" in birds 2

T.L.C., see Total lung capacity
T.V., see Tidal volume
Talented singer, temptations of 124
Talking 49, 69, 92, 149
    for the singer 133
Tape recorder, use of, see Recording
Teacher of voice 67, 110, 117, 124, 129
    and voice problems 149, 155
    see also Singing teacher; Voice
Teaching methodology 95—96
Teeth and phonation 63
Temperature of air 44, 46
Tempo, change of 122
    varying in speech 97
Tenor, avoidance of making baritone into
    127
Tension of vocal folds 57—59
Terpsichore, muse of dance 5
Tetracycline 157
Thalia, muse of comedy 5
Theater and speech 91, 99
Thoracic cage 16, 41, 138
Thoracic cavity 25
Thoracoabdominal movements 41, 74, 105
    to 106
Thorax 39
Thornton, W., teaching the deaf to speak 11
Thought, abstract, and speech 2

Throat
    clearing 48
    sense of strain in 115
    sore, see Tonsillitis
    see also Dry
Thyroarytenoid muscles 27, 29, 81
Thyrohyoid muscles 27
Thyroid cartilage 27—32, 57, 116
Thyroid surgery in the singer 145
Tidal volume 34, 35, 92
Timing 122
Tone
    attack, see Attack
    of muscles 75
    quality 49, 115, 117
    soft and loud 107, 115
    sustained 63, 74
    see also Covering; Dark; High; Low;
        Open; Single
Tones
    full, rich 73
    highest 111—112, 116, 127
    see also High; Low
Tongue 20, 23, 54, 62, 63, 72, 88, 103
Tonsillectomy 131
Tonsillitis 131
Tonsils 20
Tosi, P. F., on singing 6
Total lung capacity 34, 35, 71, 72, 106, 107,
    110, 138
Touch as communication 2
Trachea 23
    tracheal cartilage 27
Tracheal intubation 131
    see also Endotracheal
Tracheobronchial tree 16, 23, 26, 57
Training
    ability of trained singer to sing when
        hearing is blocked 60
    and use of muscles 74
    early 130
    progress in 114
    trained singer
        and lung volumes 71, 92, 94
        phonatory airflow, minimizing 62
        resonance 85
        vocal nodule 150
    see also Formants
Tranquilizers 158
Transdiaphragmatic pressure 77, 82
Transglottic pressure, see Subglottic
Transposition of key 122, 133
Transverse abdominis muscles 25, 26
Trapezius muscles 25
Trauma to larynx 92, 129
Travel, air, see Air travel
Trill 114

Trilling of "Ls" 117
Tripelennamine 157
Troches 137, 148
Trouble, sources of 114
Tuberculosis, spread of in group singing 10
Tuning the voice 54
Turbinaire decadron 157
Turbinates, see Nasal

Upper airways 16
    see also Airways; Nasal; Nose
Urania, muse of astronomy 5
Utterance of speech sounds 75, 153
Uvula 63

V.C., see Vital capacity
Vaccai, vocal exercises 114
Vaginal pruritis 157
Valve, larynx as a 1
Vasculature, of nose 19
    see also Blood; Erectile
Vasoconstrictors, see Otrivin
Venice, site of first opera house 5
Ventilation, pulmonary 16
Ventricles of larynx, see Larynx
Verdi, G. 114
Vertebrae 26
Vestibular folds, see Larynx; Vocal
Vibration of vocal folds and sound 54—57
Violin 53
    effects of compared to other instruments
        9, 11
Viral infections 134
Viruses in air 44
Vital capacity 34, 35, 72, 73, 77, 78, 79, 83,
    84, 85, 92, 104, 106, 115, 119, 138, 146
    of castrato singer 6
Vocabulary 95
Vocal abuse, see Misuse
Vocal cords (folds) 23, 26, 27, 42, 56
    action in phonation 55
    generators of sound 54
    injury to 128—129
    in pitch control 57—59
    visualized by Garcia 6
    see also Node; Polyp
Vocal disability, causes of 126
Vocal exercises 108—110
    see also Exercises
Vocal hygiene 126—140
Vocal nodule 128, 156
Vocalis muscles 55, 57, 58, 60, 81
    see also Thyroarytenoid muscles
Voice intensity, detrimental effects upon the
    voice 48

Voice
    big 115
    early theories of vocal mechanism 6
    human 55—57
    loud 115
    physiology 57—60
    quality, modulation of 59
    rest 99, 134, 150, 154
    student, author's experience as 103
    teacher 84, 147
    training 84, 111
    see also Misuse
Volume, see Lung
Vowel sounds 63, 88, 95, 103, 114, 116

Waste of air in phonation 63
Water vapor in air 44, 45
    see also Humidifying; Relative humidity
Weather 18, 45
Welsh language and speech beauty 97, 116
Wet climate 48
Where'er you walk, phrase from 123
Whisper 55, 92, 135

Whistle 62, 92
Whitteridge, D., pioneer in field of
    breathing and phonation 12
Wind instrument playing 53
    occupational hazards of 11
    physiology of 12
Wine 132
Wobble 114
Women
    breathing in 6
    Pepys' preference of voices of to the
    castrato 6
Work, heavy, and talking 68, 91
    see also Breathing
Wyke, B., 1972 conference on phonation 12
Wyndham, C. H., on speech during work 91

Xylometazoline 156

Yelling as vocal abuse 97, 115, 134, 149
Young singer, temptations of 124

Zueignung, phrases from 120, 121